RESEARCH ON SUPPORT FOR PARENTS AND INFANTS IN THE POSTNATAL PERIOD

Research on Support
for Parents and Infants
in the Postnatal Period

edited by
C.F. Zachariah Boukydis
Children's Hospital
and Harvard Medical School, Boston
Bradley Hospital and Women & Infants Hospital
and Brown University Medical School,
Providence

Ablex Publishing Corporation
Norwood, N.J. 07648

Library of Congress Cataloging-in-Publication Data

Research on support for parents and infants in the
  postnatal period.

  Bibliography: p.
  Includes index.
  1. Parents—Social networks.   2. Infants.
I. Boukydis, C. F. Zachariah.
HQ755.8.R45   1987   306.8'74   87-1349
ISBN 0-89391-333-2

Ablex Publishing Corporation
355 Chestnut St.
Norwood, New Jersey 07648

Contents

To my mother,
Margaret Stevenson Boukydis

Acknowledgments

Thanks to my friends in the Parent Care network whose dedication to helping parents deal with the uncertainty of having a premature high-risk infant has been admirable.

Also, thanks to my colleagues at the Child Development Unit, Children's Hospital, Boston, and Department of Psychiatry, Bradley Hospital and Department of Pediatrics, Women and Infants Hospital, Providence, Rhode Island, who supported me and helped the book from its beginning.

I dedicate this book to the memory of my mother, Margaret Stevenson Boukydis.

Introduction

This volume portrays the range of contemporary research on social support for early parenting. The contributors represent several disciplines and theoretical backgrounds, yet there is a common focus in questioning what constitutes social support, and how variations in adequate support contribute to developing familial relationships. Each contributor has a lengthy history of work with families and infants and this experience shows through in the quality of their research and insightful writing.

The book is divided into two sections. The first section contains chapters that provide an analysis of naturally occuring systems of support in different populations of parents and infants. The section contains chapters that deal with issues related to adolescent mothers, parents of premature and high-risk infants, mothers of twins, fathers, and single parents. The second section includes chapters that detail research on strengthening informal support systems for early parenting. This ranges from providing alternative options, or programs, for strengthening supportive resources in parents' and babies' lives to developing strategies to strengthen parents' existing networks. The second section includes chapters on important components of parent-infant support programs, peer support for parents of preterm and high-risk infants, program design for parent- and infant-support systems, and a preventive program for couples becoming parents.

A brief overview of the field of research on social support indicates a movement from exclusive reliance on measures indicative of the structure of a parent's familial and friendship network, to the development of different typologies delimiting what constitutes social support; and finally, parents' perception of the adequacy and cost of social support in their network. Included in the design of more differentiated measures of social support is an effort, evident in several chapters in the first section, to determine conditions in people's lives (i.e., differing levels of stress, or available resources) where social support is operative and potentially, most functional. Several chapters in the first section include data on how social support influences the development of the parent–child relationship, and the growth of parenting capabilities.

The second section presents research on the creation of new programs to meet the needs of parents and infants. The chapters in the second section present research that identifies factors which contribute to effective programs for providing support. This section includes an emphasis in two chapters on the development of volunteer organizations that provide peer, or mutual self-help resources.

It is expected that this volume will be useful in many different arenas, including the area of those studying the complex interrelationship between biological and social factors influencing child development, and those studying the effects of normative events, and stress, on family functioning. This volume will also be useful to people shaping social policy affecting the lives of new families by identifying important factors contributing to social support of early parenting, and critical factors which determine effective programs for parents and infants.

PART I

RESEARCH ON
SOCIAL SUPPORT
IN DIFFERENT POPULATIONS

CHAPTER 1
Support for Adolescent Mothers during the Postnatal Period: Theory and Research

Susan Crockenberg
University of California, Davis

The welfare of teenage mothers and their babies has been a long-standing concern of American society. Figures which indicate a marked increase in the rate of babies born to unmarried teenagers (from 148 per 1,000 births in 1960 to 429 per 1,000 births in 1977, Furstenberg, Lincoln, & Menken, 1981) and a comparable increase in the percentage of unmarried teenagers who keep their babies continue to focus attention on this population, despite an overall decrease in the adolescent birthrate. Research on the latest generation of adolescent mothers and their babies reflects this concern. The research has brought with it, however, the recognition that adolescent mothers are not a homogeneous group. Some do quite well in their role as mothers, which suggests that age alone is not a sufficient predictor of maternal behavior. Rather, recent research indicates that differences in social context may determine how individual adolescent mothers care for their babies. This chapter focuses on social context, particularly on the possible effect of social support on the maternal behavior of adolescent mothers.

SOCIAL SUPPORT AND MATERNAL BEHAVIOR

The expectation that social support will affect maternal behavior in beneficial ways is derived from the social-network theories of sociologists and community psychologists (Cochran & Brassard, 1979). At the heart of those theories is the assumption that participation in a social group, and, in particular, being the recipient of the various types of assistance

This research was funded by the Agricultural Experiment Station, University of California, Davis, and by a Kellogg Public Service Research Grant. The author thanks Mary DeLost, Maureen Davis, and Helen Walka for their central roles and special skills in executing this study; Karen McCluskey, Cheryl Stankiewicz, and Teri Clark for their assistance in data reduction; and Curt Acredolo and Leanne Friedman for their help with data analysis and programming.

provided by the group (social support) will facilitate individual adaptation, possibly by serving as a buffer or mediator of stress (Dean & Lin, 1977; Mitchell & Trickett, 1980). Mothers experience a range of stressful events that may affect the way they fulfill their roles as mothers. In addition, becoming a mother is in itself a potentially stressful role transition (Rossi, 1968). It follows that with social support, mothers, especially those for whom the arrival of a new baby is accompanied by other stresses, should be better able to meet their babies' needs. Bronfenbrenner (1979) expands further on this theory. He suggests that the child's opportunities for development may depend on the extent to which other people present in the setting help or hinder the parents.

Definition and measurement of social support. A social-support network includes those people who engage in activities and exchanges of an affective and/or material nature with the individual (Cochran & Brassard, 1979). The assistance provided by the network, which may be instrumental, informational, or emotional in nature, constitutes the available social support. The distinction between the social network and social support is essential because the two are not necessarily coincidental; there may be people in the network who not only fail to provide support but who may also place additional demands on the mother's time and energy. Although network variables often correlate with adaptive maternal behavior, it is likely that these correlations reflect a high degree of congruence between network size and the support provided by network members. If network size and amount of social support were discrepant, we would expect only the latter to correlate with maternal behavior. Belle's study (1981) of low-income mothers demonstrates the greater power of social support relative to social network in predicting maternal well-being. None of Belle's eight measures of network size or contact correlated with maternal depression or mastery, while all four support variables were significantly related to mastery, and two of the four correlated with maternal depression.

A related issue is whether the mother perceives the assistance rendered as support. If it is not wanted, or if it is too insistently offered, or if it conveys to the "helped" person that she is incompetent, it may be viewed as intrusive and possibly as stressful rather than supportive. The implication here is that the measure of support most likely to show the expected relationship with maternal behavior is one that quantifies the amount and quality of the assistance provided from the perspective of the recipient.

Design issues in social-support research. Research on social support and maternal behavior typically addresses one or two primary questions.

1. Does social support influence some aspect of the mother's behavior with her baby?

2. Is any observed relationship between social support and maternal behavior a function of stress reduction, as the theoretical model would predict?

A critical design issue has to do with the degree of causality in the link between social support and maternal behavior. Theory predicts that social support will reduce stress experienced by the mother and thereby influence the care of her child. However, social support is only one of many variables that may affect how a woman behaves in her role as mother. Her past experiences, her attitudes and beliefs about child-rearing, her level of maturity and readiness for motherhood, and her baby's characteristics are also likely influences. The implication of such a multivariable model for research on social support and maternal behavior is this: any other variables that might account for the observed relationship between social support and maternal behavior must be controlled if we are to have confidence that observed relationships between social support and maternal behavior are causal in nature.

Although the second question is rarely addressed directly, reduced stress is offered as an explanation of support-behavior relationships. In addition, the shape of the expected relationship between support and maternal behavior is affected by the amount of stress in the population under study. If the average stress level of the sample is reasonably high, even mothers with relatively less stress in their lives may need help from others to cope effectively with their children. "Low stress" in such a sample would be moderate to high stress on an absolute scale, and social support should therefore predict maternal behavior. If, on the other hand, the average stress level of the sample is reasonably low, mothers who experience little stress should show appropriate maternal behavior in the absence of social support. Main effects of support on maternal behavior would not be apparent, although interactions between stress and support could be expected. That is, highly stressed mothers who receive social support should engage in more appropriate maternal behavior than stressed mothers without such support. Thus, if an adequate test of social-support theory is to be made, it is essential that the sample either be drawn from a population of mothers likely to be especially stressed, or that it include a distinguishable subsample of such mothers.

RESEARCH STUDIES

Research on mothers and infants confirms the expected relationship between social support and adaptive maternal behavior. When the mothers' life circumstances are stressful by virtue of the babies' characteristics or the families' circumstances, social support significantly predicts maternal behavior and the quality of the mother-child relationship. Crockenberg (1981) looked at the relationship between infant irritability, social support for the mother, and subsequent security of the infant-mother attachment. Social support was associated with secure attachment only in the group of irritable babies. Irritable babies whose mothers received inadequate support showed frequent insecure attachments. Those whose mothers received adequate support typically showed secure attachments to their mothers. Maternal behavior was a likely mediator of this relationship: when the 11 mothers with inadequate support and insecurely attached babies were considered, 10 had been slow to respond when their babies cried. Feiring and Taylor (1982) reported comparable findings with their sample of low-income, primarily black, inner-city mothers and infants. Mothers who were rated as involved and responsive also tended to be rated as perceiving a high amount of positive support from the secondary parent, typically the mother's mother or the baby's father.

The results of a third study are also consistent with the expectation that support effects should be most apparent when stress is high. Crnic, Greenberg, Ragozin, Robinson, and Basham (1983) reported that, for both general life satisfaction and several aspects of maternal behavior, there were significant stress/support interactions. Mothers with high stress and high support showed more sensitivity to cues and more frequently fostered social-emotional growth in their babies than did mothers who experienced high stress and low support.

In the studies just reviewed, mothers were considered stressed by virtue of having an irritable or difficult baby, by living in poverty, or on the basis of the amount of reported stress in their lives. Adolescent mothers often share these stressful life circumstances but they are also assumed to be at risk for maladaptive mothering by virtue of their age-related immaturity. Because of their youth, mothers who bear babies during their teenage years are likely to be engaged in developmental transitions around issues of identity and intimacy that may create their own stresses and compete with the maternal role for the mother's energy and involvement (Erickson, 1950). An adolescent absorbed in her own development as an individual and perhaps also in finding a partner may be unable to differentiate her own needs from those of her baby and to respond to the baby's needs when they are in conflict with her own.

Several studies indicate that adolescent mothers are indeed more likely than older mothers to be unresponsive to their babies' needs or cues. Adolescent mothers were more concerned with spoiling their babies (Williams, 1974; Wise & Grossman, 1980) and indicated more punitive child-rearing attitudes in comparison with older mothers from similar, lower-class backgrounds (Field, Widmayer, Stringer, & Ignatoff, 1980). Oppel and Royston's (1971) teenage mothers spoke little, provided little intellectual encouragement, and were less close emotionally to their babies than were older mothers; Sandler, Vietze and O'Connor's (1981) 14- to 19-year-old mothers looked at and talked with their babies less frequently than did their 20- to 26-year-old mothers; and Roosa, Fitzgerald, and Carlson's (1982) teenagers provided less verbal stimulation and less contingent responsiveness to their infants than did older mothers.

Evidence that adolescent mothers express affection toward their babies despite their lack of talking and playful interaction (Osofsky & Osofsky, 1970) has led some researchers to suggest that adolescent mothers may differ from older mothers primarily in those aspects of behavior related to the child's cognitive development. Such an interpretation must be viewed with caution, however, as displays of affection may be an expression of the mother's emotional needs rather than evidence of her responsiveness to the baby. Mercer, Hackley, and Bostrom's (1984a) data support this distinction. Although adolescent mothers expressed loving feelings about their babies comparable to those of older mothers, they were observed to engage in less appropriate maternal behavior of all kinds throughout their babies' first year. Less appropriate behavior included high use of punishment, low attentiveness, low flexibility with respect to general care-giving routines, and difficulty in coping with their babies' irritating behaviors.

There is increasing recognition, nonetheless, that some adolescent mothers are quite involved with and responsive to their babies. Moreover, it has been suggested that the availability of social support, particularly from extended family members, may account in part for the differences among mothers. If adolescent mothers constitute a highly stressed group, they should be particularly in need of and responsive to the support provided them by significant others. The research is consistent with this prediction. A study by Aug and Bright (1970) found that single mothers (adolescents and young adults) who enjoyed the support of family and relatives had more positive attitudes toward themselves and their babies than comparable mothers without such support. Regardless of marital status, mothers without support from family and relatives showed less positive attitudes.

Furstenberg's (Furstenberg & Crawford, 1978) data from a large, primarily black sample of teenage mothers indicate further that the children of mothers who remained living with their families of origin scored higher on cognitive tests, experienced fewer behavior problems, and showed less antisocial behavior than did the children of teenage mothers who lived alone with their children. Furstenberg infers the availability of support from the mother's residence and assumes also that the mother's family improves her parenting through advice and assistance. However, there were no differences in the behavior of mothers as a function of residence, which suggests that rather than improving maternal behavior, family support may have directly affected the children by providing them with involved adults.

Several additional studies verify the link between social support and maternal feelings and behavior, although they do not rule out the possibility of a direct impact of the support person on the child. Colletta's (1981) questionnaire data on 50 adolescent mothers indicate that with low family support, especially low emotional support, mothers reported more hostility, indifference, and rejection of their 1- to 3-year-old children. Mercer, Hackley, and Bostrom (1984b) reported similar self-report findings. At 1-month postpartum, adolescent mothers with high instrumental support had stronger feelings of love toward their babies and a greater sense of competency in the maternal role. Emotional support was also associated with feelings of love and with the young woman's gratification in the mothering role. These results are supported by Crockenberg's (in press) study of English teenage mothers and Epstein's (1980) research with American adolescents. English mothers who received emotional and instrumental support from family members during the postnatal period reported more responsive attitudes and were independently observed to respond more quickly when their babies cried. American mothers who had part-time help from grandparents and/or the baby's father stimulated their babies appropriately, knew when and how to intervene to change behaviors, and evidenced clear enjoyment of their child. Similarly, Wandersman and Unger (1983) found that in their adolescent sample, social support from the baby's father was associated with a more adequate caretaking environment at 1-month postpartum.

In sum, these studies reveal fairly consistent relationships between the availability of social support and adolescent maternal feelings and behavior during the postnatal period. When adolescent mothers have social support from their families, they appear to be more responsive to and involved with their babies and young children. It is tempting to conclude from these studies that the provision of social support causes, or contributes to, the maternal behavior of interest. Such a conclusion is unwarranted, however, as most of the reviewed studies have failed to control for other potential causal variables that might have accounted for the observed support-behavior relationships. It could be argued, for example, that mothers whose childhoods were characterized by rejection and separation would underestimate the importance of responding to the child's needs and cues (hold unresponsive attitudes) and experience less social support from their families. If this were the case, a correlation between social support could be spurious—a function of prior developmental history and the attitudes associated with that history.

The present study is designed to consider: (1) the relative contributions of several variables considered likely to influence adolescent parenting; and (2) the relationship of social support and maternal behavior controlling for those variables through extensive partialing. Specifically, this study considers whether other risk variables such as early separation from parents, unresponsive attitudes, current life stresses, and ethnicity, combine with, modify, or account for any observed relationships between social support and maternal behavior.

METHOD

Sample

Seventy-seven mothers between the ages of 15 and 19 at the time of their babies' births participated in the study. Thirty-eight mothers were Anglo-white, 18 were Mexican-American, and 7 were Black. Fifty-five of the mothers lived in nonmetropolitan areas; 22 lived in urban areas. Thirty-three mothers were married; 44 were unmarried, but 9 of these lived with the baby's father.[1] Forty-nine mothers received AFDC benefits.

Fifty-nine babies were firstborn, 17 were second born, and I was third born. There were 44 male and 33 female babies. Birth weight ranged from 2 pounds, 12 ounces, to 11 pounds. Six babies were identified as premature births, and two as having severe medical problems at birth.[2] Twenty-nine of the mothers were contacted through the Sacramento Medical Center; 48 were contacted through Woodland Memorial Hospital. Only 63 of the mothers participated in both the interview and observation, and, of those, 2 mothers were not their babies' primary caretakers. Thus, descriptive data are based on the full sample of 77 mothers, while correlational and other analyses are based on a subsample of 61. Of these 61, 27 mothers had been separated from a mother, father, or both parents prior to age 16 for periods of time ranging from several months to an entire lifetime.

Procedures

Mothers were interviewed when the babies were 2½ to 3½ months old. Mothers and babies were observed in their homes at 3 to 3½ months post-40 weeks gestation by a trained assistant unfamiliar with the interview data. At the end of the observation the assistant rated the mother's behavior.

[1] The fathers of the babies ranged in age from 16 to 49. Thirty-one percent were under age 20; 62% were between 20 and 25 years; and 7% were over 25 years.

[2] Neither of these two babies was included in the observational phase of the research.

Maternal interview and questionnaire. Questions adapted from Simms (1981) and others developed by this researcher were used to assess the mother's sources of social and financial support and her satisfaction with that support. Social support was assessed by two methods: (1) By requiring the young mother to place dots bearing the individual's name on a paper target which located the mother and baby in the center and which determined frequency of help (very frequently, frequently, occasionally, rarely, and never) by distance from the center; and (2) By asking specifically how often each individual provided help (more than once a day to less than once a month). These procedures yielded two measures of support: Family support—the number of family members, including the baby's father, who helped frequently or very frequently; and Daily support—the number of individuals, family and nonfamily, who helped the mother on a daily basis. To correct for the quality of that support, individuals were deleted from family and daily support measures if a mother expressed strong dissatisfaction[3] with the support given. Thus, the measures of support employed were based on both the amount and the quality of the assistance provided.

During the interview, mothers were asked to respond to a 10-item questionnaire concerning the degree to which mothers thought they should and the degree to which they would respond to the needs and demands of their infants in the areas of crying, feeding, and sleeping. These items were derived from a larger set of 34 items by subjecting the responses of 95 pregnant or recently delivered women to a principal components factor analysis with a quartimax rotation (Crockenberg & Smith, 1982). This procedure yielded three factors, which included the 10 items related to responsiveness and flexibility. These items were summed to create a general index of maternal responsiveness which has shown good predictive validity to independent measures of maternal behavior and infant cognitive and social-emotional development. High scores on the maternal responsiveness index were associated with: more rapid responses by mothers when their babies cried and more involved contact between mothers and babies (Crockenberg & Smith, 1982); higher scores on the Mental Development Index of the Bayley Scales of Infant Development (BSID) and higher ratings of persistence on the Infant Behavior Record of the BSID (Crockenberg, 1983); and, in a separate sample, more rapid responses to crying and more smiling and eye contact between mothers and babies (Crockenberg, in press).

---

[3] A comment was considered indicative of strong dissatisfaction with a support person if it was so identified by two independent judges using two criteria: (a) the mother felt she was not encouraged, not considered competent, or given advice to the point it angered her or resulted in arguments about the baby; or (b) the baby was mistreated in some way by the helper-e.g., yelled at.

Stress Questionnaire. At the end of the interview mothers filled out a 37-item stress checklist modified from Cochrane and Robertson (1973), on which they indicated whether a potentially stressful event had occurred since the baby's birth and, if so, how upsetting that event was for them on a continuum of 1 (not at all upsetting) to 6 (extremely upsetting). The measure of stress was the sum of the upsetness ratings, a subjective assessment of the mother's reaction to potentially stressful events.

Mother-infant observations. Mother behavior and infant state (alert, fuss/cry, sleep/drowsy) were observed for 3½ hours by a trained observer unfamiliar with the interview data. A 10-second observe, 10-second record time-sampling schedule was used from which two mutually exclusive summary categories of mother behavior were dervied: routine contact and smiling and eye contact. Routine contact was any contact between mother and baby while the baby was awake and not crying that involved holding or caretaking but no additional involvement with or stimulation of the baby. Smiling and eye contact occurred when a mother's and baby's eyes met. The average time it took a mother to respond when the baby cried was also calculated. Low frequencies of routine contact, high frequencies of smiling and eye contact, and rapid responses to crying were considered indicative of "appropriate mothering." Interobserver reliability was based on three pilot families. Frequency of occurrence agreement between two observers ranged from .85 to 1.00 for smiling and eye contact, and from .91 to .98 for routine contact.

Maternal Ratings. Mothers were rated on three 9-point scales, developed by Ainsworth, Bell, and Stayton (1974) along the dimensions of: *sensitivity* to the baby's signals and communications; *acceptance* of the baby and resolution of conflicting feelings; and *accessibility* to the baby when both mother and baby are at home.

RESULTS

Who Helps the Teen Mother

As Figures 1 and 2 illustrate, the mother's mother and the father of the baby were the most frequent sources of social support for these teenage mothers. This pattern is apparent in who helps very frequently, who helps more than once a day, and who helps with the various household and child-care chores. Friends, other relatives (in particular the mother's sisters and sisters-in-law), and professionals were mentioned also, but less frequently than were the mother's mother and the baby's father.

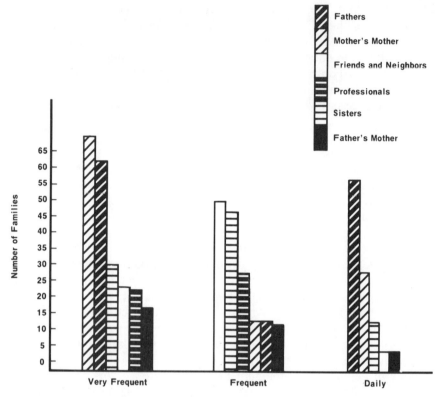

Figure 1 Most Frequent Sources of Social Support Provided Mothers

The only exception to this pattern was the central role played by professionals, particularly doctors, in providing teen mothers with advice and encouragement. The importance of professionals in the lives of these teen mothers is apparent also from the dissatisfaction mothers expressed with their professional contacts. Forty-three percent of the mothers reported dissatisfaction with professionals, most often directed toward doctors and hospital nurses.

Correlates of Appropriate Caregiving

To identify the characteristics and conditions associated with appropriate caregiving in this group of teenage mothers, Pearson product-moment correlations were calculated between a set of selected predictor variables and each of several maternal behaviors. Included in the set of predictors were mother's separation from her own family early in life, maternal attitudes toward responsive caregiving, ethnicity, current life stress, and two measures of social support-family support and daily support.

Both zero order and partial correlations were calculated. In the partial correlations, the influence of all other predictors was controlled (Cohen & Cohen, 1975). In addition, the time the baby was alert was partialed when analyzing the predictability of the observational variables: routine contact and smiling and eye contact. Maternal outcomes included ratings of maternal sensitivity, accessibility, and acceptance, and three measures of mother-baby interaction, amount of routine contact, amount of smiling and eye contact, and responsiveness to crying.

Table 1 summarizes the correlations. In terms of zero order correlations, family support and daily support were positively associated with appropriate caregiving. Teen mothers with good family support were more sensitive toward and more accessible to their babies; those with good daily support responded more quickly when their babies cried. Moreover, teen mothers who believed they should be responsive to their babies' needs and signals engaged in less routine contact and more smiling and eye contact during the 3-month observation. Mothers with high stress in their lives also engaged in more routine contact. Mothers separated from their families early in life were less accepting of their babies. Mexican-American mothers engaged in more smiling and eye contact than Anglo mothers.

Not included in the set of risk predictors was the mother's marital status, which was expected to be unrelated to maternal behavior. Results of correlational analyses were congruent with this expectation: there was no significant relationship between marital status and any maternal

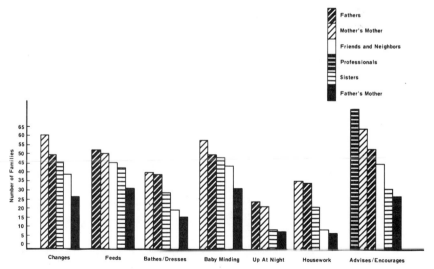

Figure 2   Types of Social Support Provided Mothers

Table 1. Partial^a (and Zero Order) Correlations between Maternal and Contextual Predictors and Adolescent Maternal Behavior

Predictors	Sensitivity	Acceptance	Accessibility	Routine Contact	Smiling and Eye Contact	Responds to Cries
Early Separation	.01 (.07)	.21 (.24)*	−.13 (−.06)	.00 (−.09)	.01 (−.05)	.04 (.00)
Responsive Attitude	−.02 (.05)	.05 (.07)	.00 (.08)	−.21 (−.26)*	.19 (.28)**	−.22 (−.19)
Stress	−.05 (−.13)	.15 (.04)	.01 (−.06)	.35*** (.36)***	−.03 (−.13)	−.13 (−.09)
Family Support	.32** (.30)**	.23 (.21)	.31** (.29)**	(.03)	(.08)	(−.02)
Daily Support	(−.06)	(−.13)	(−.10)	−.15 (−.11)	.16 (.13)	.33** (.37)***
Ethnicity	−.08 (−.08)	−.12 (−.14)	−.08 (−.08)	.25 (.16)	.27* (.33)**	−.17 (−.13)

Note: The time the baby was alert during the observation was partialed from routine contact and smiling and eye contact partial correlations.
^{a}All other single predictors partialed.
*p < .05; **p < .025; ***p < .01.

behavior. Nor were there any significant relationships between parity and maternal behavior.

Partial correlations provide a more conservative test of the relationships just noted by reducing the possibility that unmeasured variables account for the observed relationships. Table 1 indicates that, after partialing of all other predictors, support continued to be associated with responsiveness to crying, sensitivity, and accessibility; ethnicity was associated with smiling and eye contact (Mexican-American mothers exhibited more); and high stress was associated with frequent routine contact.

The moderating effects of support on stress-behavior relationships. To further investigate the possibility that support would show stronger relationships with maternal behavior under conditions of particularly high stress, a support by stress interaction was entered as a predictor of maternal behavior. Again all single variables were partialed from the equation. This interaction showed a significant relationship with smiling and eye contact ($pr = -.28$, $p < .05$), but in a direction opposite of theoretical predictions. Only when stress was low was daily support associated with smiling and eye contact. High stress (one SD above the mean) obviated the expected relationship between support and maternal behavior.

Post-hoc analysis to consider the moderating effect of stress on other predictors revealed that stress modified the relationship between responsive maternal attitudes and maternal behavior. Again, only when stress was low (one SD below the sample mean) did mothers who expressed responsive attitudes engage in more smiling and eye contact ($pr = -.33$, $p < .025$) and receive higher ratings on sensitivity ($pr = -.30$, $p < .05$).

Professional Support and Maternal Caregiving

Although the primary sources of daily support were family members and to some extent friends, professionals were mentioned by nearly half the mothers as frequent or very frequent sources of support, almost exclusively in the area of listening, encouragement, and advice giving. It would be reasonable, therefore, to expect professional support to influence a mother's behavior. This influence might not be apparent from correlational data, however, because frequent professional support tends to occur in the most at-risk families, whose behavior may be more deviant than low-risk families even with professional support (Colletta, 1983). Thus, a more appropriate test of the impact of professional support requires a comparison of high-risk families, with and without professional support.

Risk was assessed on the basis of five variables: mother's age (17 or under); early separation from parents; high stress (above median); low responsive attitudes (below median); and daily help (one or fewer sources). Mothers with risk scores of 4 or 5 were considered high risk, those with scores of 3 or below as low risk. Professional support was considered high if a mother mentioned at least one professional who helped frequently or very frequently, and low if professional help was less frequent. To assess differences in maternal behavior between the high- and low-risk groups associated with professional support, t-tests and analyses of covariance, covarying the amount of time the baby was alert during the observation, were calculated using the three maternal ratings and the three maternal behaviors as outcomes. There was no evidence that high professional support was associated with more appropriate mothering within either high- or low-risk groups.

DISCUSSION

These data demonstrate the central role of family members, particularly the baby's father and the mother's mother, in providing support for the teenage mother. This support is in turn associated with appropriate mothering in this "at-risk" population. Teenage mothers who get more support do better as caretakers than do mothers with less support. Second, stress, either alone or in combination with other risk variables, is a significant correlate and likely determinant of maternal behavior. And third, professional support, as it is experienced by the mothers in this sample, appears to have little effect on mothers' behavior toward their babies.

The Nature and Impact of Social Support

The link between family social support and effective parenting both supports and extends earlier studies. In this study, social support showed the expected relationships with maternal behavior after several possible confounding variables had been partialed from the equation. On the other hand, the results indicate also that maternal attitudes, stress, and ethnicity are independently related to the maternal behavior of these adolescent mothers.

That fathers play such a significant role is noteworthy in view of the fact that fewer than half of the fathers are married to the adolescent mothers. Nonetheless, the father's significant support role cannot be viewed with complete equanimity. There is reason to believe that these young men pose many problems for the teenage mothers. Mothers more frequently express dissatisfaction toward fathers than toward any other single category of helpers. One mother commented, "He has a temper and screams and yells at the baby." Others mention that the fathers get mad when the baby cries, urge the mother to let the baby cry, and are jealous of the time the mother spends with the baby. Several mothers mention that they do not trust the father to care for the baby because "he likes to give her food she's not supposed to have yet" and "won't change his diaper." In addition, more mothers mention serious arguments with a husband or boyfriend as a source of stress than they do any other area tapped by the questionnaire. Some of these arguments undoubtedly center around the baby, as the above comments suggest, but instability in the relationship itself is also a source of stress. Fully 20% of the mothers indicated, for example, that their husbands or boyfriends were seeing someone else. We are reminded here of Colletta's (1983) statement that, "The married (adolescent) mother lives alone with her husband who is often still an adolescent himself," p. 7, and of Belle's (1981) report that, "Husbands and boyfriends were frequently described by respondents as a mixed blessing," p. 8, and Gonsalves's (1980) finding that, "Husbands were most likely to be a primary source of support, but also most often the source of stress," p. 34.

These comments suggest that adolescent mothers may not only experience more stress in their lives, but may also have less adequate support than older mothers regardless of their marital status. The baby's father may be an unsuitable source of support even when he is available. Although it can be dangerous to overinterpret nonsignificant findings in studies with many predictor and outcome variables due to the possibility of Type II error, the extremely low degree of correlation between marital status and outcomes give us some confidence in these results. The results suggest, moreover, that the concern we have for unmarried teenage mothers relative to those who are married may be misplaced. What seems to make a difference in the way mothers care for their babies is the social support they receive. If a married mother receives support then she is likely to be a more responsive mother, but marital status is not a very good predictor of whether that support will be forthcoming.

Under some circumstances the mother's mother may fill in as a secondary parent and source of support. However, conflict between the grandmother and mother, which has its roots in the pregnancy and the events which preceded it, may either prevent the giving or accepting of support or make this a costly source of support for the young mother. It may be, therefore, that inadequate social support accounts not only for differences in the way teenage mothers care for their babies, but also for differences in the maternal behavior of older and younger mothers. Mercer et al.'s (1982) study confirms that teenage mothers receive significantly less emotional support from others than do older mothers, but does not indicate whether differences in support across the age groups account for the age-related differences in maternal behavior. It should come as no surprise that the mother's age, or more accurately her status as an adolescent, should be related to the adequacy of the support she receives. To the extent that the adolescent is engaged in the stage-appropriate task of separating from parents and of forming heterosexual relationships, the conflicts which accompany those tasks can be expected. Those conflicts may not serve simply to distract the mother from her baby, but may also interfere with the process by which support is given and accepted. A further implication of this line of reasoning is that any absolute distinction between age and social context as determinants of behavior is unwarranted. Adolescent status should perhaps be viewed as a marker variable, theoretically and probabilistically linked to a range of personal characteristics and social events, but not coincident with them.

Also noteworthy is that the mother's ethnic background appears not to have its effect on maternal behavior primarily through social support. Hispanic background was associated with smiling and eye contact between the mother and baby after support was partialed, suggesting that the value of the maternal role in that culture may affect the mother independently of any support she might receive from the traditional, extended Hispanic family (Martinez, 1981). There was no relationship between family support or daily support and ethnic status in this sample.

Stress, Social Support, and Maternal Behavior

Variation in the stressfulness of a mother's life circumstances was associated with the quality of the contact she had with her baby. When stress was high, routine contact was frequent; the mother cared for her baby but her care lacked the verbal, visual, and tactile contact that constitutes the mother's contribution to early mother-infant communication. This is reminiscent of Crnic et al.'s (1983) finding that mothers who reported high stress were less sensitive to infant cues. Moreover, only when stress was low did social support predict the frequency of smiling and eye contact between mother and baby; the relationship was negligible under conditions of very high stress. This unexpected finding suggests a modification of the model of stress and support which predicts that support, because it reduces the impact of stress on the individual, should show the strongest beneficial effects on behavior under conditions of high stress.

As suggested earlier, the expected relationship between support and maternal behavior will depend on the overall stress level of the sample studied. In a low-stress sample, we would expect a relationship between support and maternal behavior primarily for mothers experiencing high levels of stress in their lives. When stress is low, most mothers should be able to cope effectively with the requirements of mothering even with little support. In a high-stress sample, we would expect relationships between support and maternal behavior even under relatively low levels of stress (i.e., moderate-high stress on an absolute scale). Main effects of support would be apparent because most mothers would need support to cope with the combined stresses of motherhood and life in general. In addition, however, a highly stressed subgroup of a sample which, as a whole, experiences high stress may be relatively impervious to the effects of what could reasonably be identified as "high support." The support by stress interaction reported in this study may be a case in point. The following description illustrates the extreme life circumstances of one adolescent mother in this sample who reported high support.

She lost her job, and because her live-in boyfriend is a seasonal tractor driver, this loss resulted in a pile-up of debts. Just before the baby's birth, her brother was sent to prison on a murder charge and her father, whom she sees quite a lot of, began drinking heavily again. Since that time her grandfather became very ill, a friend died in childbirth, and she injured her back when the family moved. Although she and her boyfriend plan to marry, they argue constantly and have split up several times since the baby's birth. When the splits occur, the boyfriend gets in the car with the baby and says he is taking him to Los Angeles.

One implication of this analysis may be that the extraordinarily high level of stress in particular populations cannot be ameliorated by the type of support usually provided by families. Another possibility, however, is that when the support is provided by a person who is also a source of much stress, that support may be less functional than support provided by someone else. In the example just cited, the boyfriend was a primary support but, at the same time, a tremendous source of stress. While he helped with the baby considerably, he was also known to run off with him. This may well have been "support" the mother could have done without. Moreover, controlling for dissatification with the help received, as in this study, may not have captured the more general dissatisfaction with the relationship illustrated by this example. As Belle (1981) suggests, future research may need to consider the costs and benefits of social relationships if we are to have a measure of social support which adequately assesses the nuances of certain various life circumstances.

Professional Support and Maternal Behavior

In view of the frequency with which professionals give advice to young mothers, one must consider why that advice appears to have little relationship to the mother's behavior with her baby. The possibilities are numerous. It may be that professionals do influence mothers, but in areas such as the baby's health, which were not assessed in this study. Or, professionals may give advice that contradicts that given by family members who have more influence over the teen mother. Possibly the effect of professional advice may be apparent after a period of time during which the mother may get her own life in order and may be better able to use the advice given her. Alternatively, the dissatisfaction mothers express toward professionals may explain why professional advice is not reflected in a mother's behavior. Mothers were more dissatisfied with professionals as a group than with any other group of helpers and their dissatisfaction with doctors was second only to their dissatisfaction with the babies' fathers.

What does it mean to say a mother is dissatisfied with the help/advice she receives from professionals? The mothers' comments indicate that different mothers are dissatisfied for different reasons. Some of these inexperienced teenagers asked for information they didn't get, but were "yelled at" for asking. This type of experience was mentioned by several mothers who described their hospital stay following delivery. One mother called a nurse when her baby had been crying for quite a long time and was angrily told, "Couldn't you have waited? It wouldn't have hurt him to cry." Others were reluctant to ask for nonhealth advice because doctors or nurses seemed so busy. One young mother was at a loss as to how to change her baby's diaper and how to dress the baby when it was time to leave the hospital. No one volunteered the information or asked if she needed help. Still other mothers indicated that some doctors were "hard to talk to," but they couldn't get to see a preferred doctor because "at the clinic you have to see whoever is available." Some mothers mentioned that it was how the advice was given that upset them. One public health nurse insisted that a mother continue breast-feeding despite her several breast infections and sore, cracked nipples. She implied that the mother would be doing the wrong thing for her baby if she stopped breast-feeding. This complaint repeated that of English teenage mothers who reported strong disapproval from some home health visitors around the issue of bottle-feeding (Crockenberg, in press). Another type of conflict occurred when professional advice conflicted with that of family members or other professionals. One mother was told by her doctor to put her baby on cereal when the baby was two weeks old. This contradicted everything the mother had read about feeding and what she had been told in her school program. Another complaint had to do with the vagueness of doctors' comments. One mom, told by her doctor that her baby was doing "fine," told us, "I can see that, but I want to know more!" These comments parallel those reported by Epstein (1980) whose adolescents commented on unsympathetic hospital staff and the failure of hospital personnel to provide child-development information beyond instruction in basic caregiving.

Implications for Practice and Research

It would appear, then, that a substantial group of teenage mothers— about a third of this sample—want something they aren't getting from professionals. That something seems to be advice on all aspects of baby care from diaper changing and feeding to dealing with crying, *given early in motherhood*, by someone knowledgeable about babies, sympathetic to mothers, and understanding of the larger family contexts in which mothers and babies live. Special programs for adolescent mothers often have this sort of orientation to service delivery and have apparently been successful in shaping the caretaking practices of adolescent mothers (Badger, 1981; Field et al., 1980; Epstein, 1980). What is striking in this sample is how few of the mothers (only 11 of the 77) were involved in such a program.

What kind of research do we need? This question requires a dual answer which focuses both on questions of developmental process and of service delivery. We need to know whether social support affects children as well as mothers, and if so, the extent to which this effect is indirect through the mother or direct between the support person and the child. This will require data on the amount and quality of contact between the support person and the child as well as that between the mother and child. It will also require information on the child's cognitive and social-emotional development over time. We need to know, too, the extent to which the young mother elicits or fails to elicit, or make use of potential sources of support, and what accounts for her behavior in this area. What mothers say about obtaining social support would be useful here as would a model which identified characteristics, behaviors, or experiences of the mother which might influence the amount of social support she receives. We need to know more about the stress/support relationship, the conditions under which support mediates the negative impact of stress and vice versa. And we need to take seriously the cost/benefit aspects of support in operationalizing the concept of social support for research purposes. This means asking mothers about the demands individuals place on her as well as the support they provide and doing so in a way that results in quantifiable data.

Equally important are questions of service delivery, for as Wandersman (1981) suggests, "lack of attention to problems of implementation may be a major factor in the limited success of human service programs". How should professional support be provided to teenage mothers? Who should provide it, when, and where? How can professional support be best used to facilitate informal sources of social support which show the most consistent relationship with maternal behavior? The answers to these questions depend in part on the mothers' preferences and suggest the need to ask them about service delivery. Given a choice, would they rather talk about child-care issues with a medical doctor or with some other professional? How would they feel about someone coming to their home to provide advice and suggestions about child care? What bothers or upsets them about professionals who currently consult with them about their children? Would the baby's father attend a class on parenting, talk with a visiting nurse, watch a TV program on child care? These data could form the basis for designing experimental service-delivery programs with some promise of success. Ultimately, of course, the culture-wide implementation of change in the health-care-delivery system will depend on the cost of providing additional services to a reasonably large group of young mothers. This reality points up the importance of interdisciplinary research, involving psychologists, sociologists, economists, and members of the medical profession, in the areas of health-care delivery and parent education. It indicates also the need for stronger links between scientists who produce the research and policy makers who will draft the legislation and provide the funding for change in the services provided parents and children.

REFERENCES

Ainsworth, M., Bell, S., & Stayton, D. (1974). Infant mother attachment and social development: "Socialization" as a product of reciprocal responsiveness to signals. In M.P.M Richards (Ed.), The integration of a child into a social world. London: Cambridge University Press.

Aug, R., & Bright, T. (1970). A study of wed and unwed motherhood in adolescents and young adults. Journal of the American Academy of Child Psychiatry, 9, 577–594.

Badger, E. (1981). Effects of parent education program on teenage mothers and their offspring. In K. Scott, T. Field, & E. Robertson (Eds.), Teenage parents and their offspring. New York: Grune & Stratton.

Belle, D.E. (1981). The social network as a source of both stress and support to low-income mothers. Paper presented at the biennial meeting of the Society for Research in Child Development, Boston.

Bronfenbrenner, U. (1979). *The ecology of human development.* Cambridge, MA: Harvard University Press.

Cochran, M., & Brassard, J. (1979). Child development and personal social networks. *Child Development, 50,* 601–616.

Cochrane, R., & Robertson, A. (1973). The life events inventory: A measure of the relative severity of psycho-social stressors. *Journal of Psychosomatic Research, 17,* 135–139.

Cohen, J., & Cohen, P. (1975). *Applied multiple regression/correlation analysis for the behavioral sciences.* Hillsdale, NJ: Erlbaum.

Colletta, N. (1981). Social support and the risk of maternal rejection by adolescent mothers. *The Journal of Psychology, 109,* 191–197.

Colletta, N. (1983). At risk for depression: A study of young mothers. *Journal of Genetic Psychology, 142,* 301–310.

Crnic, K.A., Greenberg, M.T., Ragozin, A.S., Robinson, N.M., & Basham, R. (1983). Effects of stress and social support on mothers and premature and full-term infants. *Child Development, 54,* 209–217.

Crockenberg, S. (1981). Infant irritability, mother responsiveness, and social support influences on the security of infant-mother attachment. *Child Development, 52,* 857–865.

Crockenberg, S. (1983). Early mother and infant antecedents of Bayley Scale performance at 21 months. *Developmental Psychology, 19,* 727–730.

Crockenberg, S. (in press). English teenage mothers: Attitudes, behavior and social support. In E. J. Anthony (Ed.), *International Year Book Series of the International Association for Child Psychiatry and Allied Professions.* New York: John Wiley.

Crockenberg, S., & Smith, P. (1982). Antecedents of infant irritability and mother-infant interaction in the first three months of life. *Infant Behavior and Development, 5,* 105–119.

Dean, A., & Lin, N. (1977). The stress-buffering role of social support: Problems and prospects for systematic investigation. *Journal of Nervous and Mental Disease, 165,* 403–417.

Epstein, A. (1980). *Assessing the child development information needed by adolescent parents with very young children.* Final report of Grant OCD-90-C-1341, Office of Child Development, Department of Health, Education and Welfare, Washington, DC (ERIC Document Reproduction Service No. ED 183286)

Erickson, E. H. (1950). *Childhood and society.* New York: Norton.

Feiring, C., & Taylor, J. (1982). *The influence of the infant and secondary parent on maternal behaviors.* Unpublished manuscript, Educational Testing Service.

Field, T., Widmayer, S., Stringer, S., & Ignatoff, E. (1980). Teenage, lower-class black mothers and their preterm infants: An intervention and developmental follow up. *Child Development, 51,* 426–436.

Furstenberg, F. (1980). *Teenage parenthood and family support.* Paper presented at the National Research Forum on Family Issues, Washington, DC.

Furstenberg, F., & Crawford, A. (1978). Family support: Helping teenage mothers to cope. *Family Planning Perspectives, 10,* 322–333.

Furstenberg, F., Lincoln, R., & Menken, J. (1981). *Overview.* In F. Furstenberg, R. Lincoln, & J. Menken (Eds.), *Teenage sexuality, pregnancy and childbearing.* Philadelphia: University of Pennsylvania Press.

Gonsalves, A.M. (1980). *Follow up of teenage mothers at age 25: A longitudinal study on the island of Kauai.* Unpublished Master's thesis, University of California, Davis.

Martinez, A.L. (1981). The impact of adolescent pregnancy on Hispanic adolescents and their families. In T. Ooms (Eds.), *Teenage pregnancy in a family context.* Philadelphia: Temple University Press.

Mercer, R.T., Hackley, K.C., & Bostrom, A. (1982). *Factors having an impact on maternal role attainment the first year of motherhood.* Final Report of Grant MC-R-060435, Maternal and Child Health and Crippled Children's Services Research Grants Programs. Bureau of Community Health Services, H.S.A., PHS, DHHS.

Mercer, R.T., Hackley, K.C., & Bostrom, A. (1984a). Adolescent motherhood: Comparison of outcome with older mothers. *Journal of Adolescent Health Care, 5,* 7–13.

Mercer, R.T., Hackley, K.C., & Bostrom, A. (1984b). Social support of teenage mothers. *Birth Defects: Original Article Series, 20,* 245–290.

Mitchell, R.E., & Trickett, E.J. (1980). Task force report: Social networks as mediators of social support. *Community Mental Health Journal, 16,* 27–44.

Oppel, W., & Royston, A. (1971). Teenage births: Some social, psychological, and physical sequelae. *American Journal of Public Health, 61,* 751–756.

Osofsky, H., & Osofsky, J. (1970). Adolescents as mothers: Results of a program for low income pregnant teenagers with some emphasis upon infant's development. *American Journal of Orthopsychiatry, 40,* 825–834.

Roosa, M.W., Fitzgerald, H.E., & Carlson, N.A. (1982). Teenage and older mothers and their infants: Descriptive results. *Adolescence, 17* (65), 1–17.

Rossi, A. (1968). Transition to parenthood. *Journal of Marriage and the Family, 30,* 26–39.

Sandler, H., Vietze, P., & O'Connor, S. (1981). Obstetric and neonatal outcomes following intervention with pregnant teenagers. In K. Scott, T. Field, & E. Robertson (Eds.), *Teenage parents and their offspring.* New York: Grune & Stratton.

Simms, M. (1981). Teenage mother interview. Institute for Social Studies in Medical Care, London, England.

Wandersman, L.P. (1981). *Supportive parent education programs: What are we learning.* Paper presented at the biennial meeting of the Society for Research in Child Development, Boston.

Wandersman, L.P., & Unger, D.G. (1983). *Interaction of infant difficulty and social support in adolescent mothers.* Paper presented at the biennial meeting of the Society for Research in Child Development, Detroit.

Williams, T. (1974). Childrearing practices of young mothers: What we know, how it matters, why it's so little. *American Journal of Orthopsychiatry, 44,* 70–75.

Wise, S., & Grossman, T. (1980). Adolescent mothers and their infants: Psychological factors in early attachment and interaction. *American Journal of Orthopsychiatry, 50,* 454–467.

CHAPTER 2
Maternal Stress, Social Support, and Coping: Influences on the Early Mother–Infant Relationship

Keith Crnic and Mark Greenberg
University of Washington

The impact of parental social-support systems on familial functioning and child development has become a recent focus of research with children and families. Interestingly, this research has produced a dual orientation; one that has focused on the role of support systems as a coping mechanism under times of stress (Powell, 1979), and another that attempts to delineate the role of social networks to the normal developmental process of childhood (Cochran & Brassard, 1979). Both areas of study are of importance to our continuing understanding of children and families and their psychological well-being under stressful conditions. In this chapter we explore both the theoretical and empirical issues concerning the effect of social support during the beginning stages of parenthood. In doing so we will present longitudinal data from a comparative study of premature and fullterm infants and their families.

THEORETICAL AND METHODOLOGICAL ISSUES

Given the history of the development of social support as a psychological construct, it is not surprising that much of the research done with parental support systems has involved studies that measure support as a buffer during times of stress. Historically, social support has been considered to encompass several dimensions, including instrumental assistance, information provision, and emotional empathy and understanding provided to one individual by another. Such supportive relationships operate on a number of ecological levels, including intimate

This research was supported by a grant from the USPHS, Maternal and Child Health Services, Grant Number MC-R-530431.

relationships, friendship and extended family ties, and both formal and informal neighborhood or community contacts (Henderson, 1981). A well-functioning social support framework usually provides information that one is cared for, valued, and a member of a network of mutual obligation (Cobb, 1976). A number of recent research reviews have substantiated the positive effects of adequate social support for the individual's psychological and physical well-being (Gottlieb, 1981; Haggerty, 1980; Mueller, 1980; Pilisuk, 1982), although the studies reviewed primarily measure social support as a moderator of the adverse effects of life stress. Within the general support literature, only recently has support been viewed as an independent factor related to individual well-being regardless of the presence of significant stress (Mueller, 1980).

Specific interest in parental social-support networks was greatly facilitated by Bronfenbrenner's (1977) ecological model, which organized the variables of importance to familial functioning and child development according to their ecological level. These levels involve both primary and secondary developmental contexts, and include interactions within immediate settings—e.g., home, school, workplace (Microsystem); the interrelations among major settings containing the individual (Mesosystem); the formal and informal social structures that impinge on the individual, e.g., neighborhood, media, government agencies (Ecosystem); and the ideological institutional patterns of the culture and subculture (Macrosystem). Concurrently, both clinical and developmental researchers initiated research on family stress and transitions, including the stresses associated with the transition to parenthood and the early postpartum period (Miller & Sollie, 1980; Sollie & Miller, 1980), child abuse (Garbarino, 1982), and divorce (Hetherington, 1981). Powell (1979) has suggested that social networks and the family–environment relationship can affect a family's ability to cope with normal stress as well as unusual crises, and that parental social support has potential for moderating adverse effects of stress (both normal and unusual). In this regard, social support functions as a coping resource for parents, much in the manner presented within the coping model described by Lazarus and his associates (Folkman, Schaefer, & Lazarus, 1979; Lazarus, Kanner, & Folkman, 1980). This model details five general resources (health/energy/morale; problem-solving skills; social-support networks; utilitarian resources; general and specific beliefs) that individuals may call upon during times or situations appraised as stressful.

Several studies have attempted to assess the impact of social support on parental attitudes and behavior during early stages of parenthood. Wandersman, Wandersman, and Kahn (1980) found that attending postpartum parent-support groups did not have a significant positive impact on parents' postpartum adjustment, although emotional support from the spouse did facilitate positive postpartum adjustment. Similar results had been reported by Shereshefsky & Yarrow (1973). Crnic, Greenberg, Ragozin, Robinson, and Basham (1983) found that intimate support from a spouse or partner moderated the effects of high life stress on maternal life satisfaction during early infancy—such that mothers with high stress and low support reported the lowest life satisfaction while mothers with high stress but also high support reported the greatest life satisfaction. Unger and Powell (1980) noted that mothers of young infants experiencing high levels of stress were more actively involved with their infants when they had more frequent supportive contacts, and Longfellow, Zelkowitz, Saunders, and Belle (1979) found that certain types of social support (instrumental assistance, emotional support) were found to buffer mothers against the effects of stress and depression.

Cochran and Brassard (1979) have specifically suggested that parents' personal social networks influence their attitudes and behavior and, in turn, have both direct and indirect effects on the child's development. The notions of Cochran and Brassard (1979) and Bronfenbrenner (1977) are important as they emphasize the potential influence of support systems to families within a broader developmental context, as opposed to the more traditional context of support as a moderator of stress.

Although few empirical investigations have been conducted, data are beginning to accumulate that suggest that parental social support indeed influences various domains of parenting and child development. Crnic et al. (1983) found that maternal social support from several ecological domains (neighborhood, friendships, intimate relationships) was related to greater parenting satisfaction and more positive behavioral interactions with young infants. Further, they reported that indirect, positive effects on the infants' behavioral interactions were also apparent. Two studies assessed the relationship of infant temperamental status and parental support. Crockenberg (1981) reported that maternal social support was significantly related to the security of the infant–mother attachment at 12 months, and that support had its strongest positive influence with irritable infants and their mothers. Wandersman and Unger (1983) have reported that social support from fathers and nearby relatives was positively related to mothers being able to provide a high-quality environment when infants were judged to be difficult. A similar relationship was not found when infants were judged to be easy.

Together, the few available studies suggest that parental social-support systems can serve as a coping resource under various stressful conditions, as well as influence both parenting and child development independent of the presence of stress. However, there is a need for further clarification as several studies have not found that social-support variables were related to actual parenting behavior with the child (Longfellow et al., 1979; Belsky, 1983). It does appear that there is some specificity of effect within parental-support influences, as has been suggested previously (Crnic et al., 1983; Unger & Powell, 1980; Wandersman et al., 1980). Among variables that may account for the variability in findings are parental and child age, the developmental transitions occurring when support is measured, types of support measured, and the specific dependent variables measured.

Although numerous issues involving the roles of parental support have yet to be investigated, especially within a developmental context (Gottlieb, 1983), several appear to be particularly important during the postpartum period and the transition to parenthood. To what extent do perceived maternal stress and support affect maternal parenting across the first year postpartum? Does social support serve the stress-buffering role for parenting variables seen for individual physical and psychological well-being? Does social support produce differential effects on parenting at different developmental phases? Is parental social support stable over time and can early support relationships predict later parenting factors? The research reported in this chapter addresses these issues.

As noted earlier, social support encompasses several dimensions (information or material assistance and emotional empathy or understanding) and involves several ecological levels. Henderson (1981) has provided both a model and measure of support which details various levels at which social support operates. These levels include intimate support from a spouse or partner (or very close friendships), friendships, extended family, and casual relationships within neighborhoods, organized community groups, or the workplace. Each of these potential support sources may have specific roles or impacts on an individual's functioning, and may operate differentially.

In our longitudinal study of mothers and their premature or fullterm infants, we incorporated a measure of maternal social support adapted from Henderson's (1981) Interview Scale for Social Interaction. Our adaptation shortened the scale to focus on social support from three sources: intimate relationships, friendships, and community contacts. It was our intention to assess the role that maternal social support might play in mediating parenting behavior, and moderating the greater stress predicted to be apparent in families who had premature infants.

Subjects in our study were 52 mother-preterm and 53 mother-fullterm infant pairs. The preterm infants were less than 38 weeks gestation and weighed less than 1,800 grams ($M = 1,378$ gms.), and the fullterm infants were 39 to 42 weeks gestationally and weighed more than 2,500 grams ($M = 3,501$ gms.). Infants were carefully matched on background variables and 52% of the infants were firstborn. Mothers ranged in age from 16 to 38 years ($M = 24.6$ years) and had completed 9 to 16 years of education ($M = 12.6$ years). Families in the study were predominantly white, middle-class, two-parent families in which the mother was currently a homemaker.

PROCEDURE

Data were collected at four measurement intervals during the first year postpartum. Maternal interview and questionnaire data were collected at infant ages 1 and 8 months, mother-infant behavioral interactions were observed at 4, 8, and 12 months, and infant developmental assessments were conducted at 4 and 12 months. All infant ages at the measurement periods were corrected for gestational age so that the effects of premature birth on infant and maternal behavior, as well as infant development, would not be confounded with biological immaturity. The preterm infants were chronologically older than the fullterm infants at each measurement.

Measures

A structured interview was conducted with the mothers at home when the infants had been home from the hosptial 1 month, and again at 8 months during a clinic visit. Four measures were collected as part of this interview: (1) social support, (2) life stress, (3) satisfaction with parenting, and (4) general life satisfaction. The social-support measure involved a series of questions regarding available support sources and maternal satisfaction at three ecological levels: (1) intimate relationships, (2) friendships, and (3) neighborhood or community support. Satisfaction was rated on a 4-point scale (very satisfied to very dissatisfied), and separate scores were obtained for each type of support (Cronbach alphas of .69, .65, and .50 were obtained for these indices, respectively). We used the Life Experiences Survey (LES; Sarason, Johnson, & Siegel, 1978) as a measure of life stress. The LES involves rating a series of 46 life events as having occurred or not occurred, whether the impact was "good" or "bad," and their degree of effect (none, some, moderate, great). The score obtained provided an index of negative life stress over the preceding 8- to 10-month period of time.

Two maternal attitude measures were incorporated into the interview. One was a single-item measure of perceived general life satisfaction (GLS), rated by mothers on a 5-point scale from very good to very poor. The other was a 12-item satisfaction with parenting scale (SWPS) that assessed the mothers' degree of pleasure in their infants and in their parenting role, with a Cronbach alpha = .67 (Crnic et al., 1983).

Behavioral observations were conducted at 4, 8, and 12 months when the mothers and infants visited our clinic. The observation sessions involved both free play (10 minutes) and a structured situation (5 minutes) in which mothers were asked to try to encourage their infants to vocalize (at 4 and 8 months) or look through a picture book with their infants (at 12 months). Each interaction session was observed and videotaped from behind a one-way mirror.

Mother-infant behavioral ratings were made from the videotaped free-play and structured episodes. Three separate 5-point ratings were made from the two episodes for both mother and infant on the following dimensions: (1) gratification from interaction, (2) affective tone/quality, and (3) responsiveness. The interactions were rated by two trained observers and reliability was calculated as the percentage of exact agreements (76%) and agreements within one scale point (97%). These three dimensions for both mother and infant were combined into a single score for the mother and a single score for the infant (both called AFFECT). The AFFECT ratings for mothers' behavior across the two behavioral episodes were highly correlated ($r = .61$) and were combined to provide a single summary score for analyses. In contrast, the infants' AFFECT ratings were not highly correlated ($r = .30$) and were analyzed separately.

RELEVANT FINDINGS

In our analyses of the social support data, we combined the preterm and fullterm groups, as there were no differences on the measures of support or life stress between the groups. The failure to find group differences was surprising, as we anticipated that mothers of preterms would at least report greater perceived stress. The lack of group differences, however, may have been a function of the generally healthy status of the preterms, and the fact that the groups were carefully matched on variables other than infant birth status. It may also have been related to the times at which the measures were collected, as infant health status was no longer in jeopardy, and the initial month at home may have allowed sufficient time for the initial neonatal crisis to stabilize and for the mother and infant to subsequently establish comfortable routines.

Due to a skewed distribution, scores for each type of social support were dichotomized into high and low support, with a 75% (high support)–25% (low support) split. Scores on the negative life-stress measure were similarly dichotomized with a 25% (high stress)–75% (low stress) split. A 75%–25% split was employed as most of the subjects reported having supportive relationships and few stressful life events, and therefore the 75%–25% split provided a more meaningful categorization. To examine the effects of the support variables and life stress on the dependent measures of maternal attitudes, maternal behavior, and infant behavior, both two-way ANOVA and hierarchical multiple-regression analyses were employed. Five demographic co-variates were entered first in each analysis (maternal age, education, parity, receipt of public assistance, and preterm or fullterm birth status).

STRESS AND SUPPORT INFLUENCES

Table 1 provides a list of the dependent measures that were significantly related to the stress and/or social-support variables. It is apparent that both perceived negative life stress and various types of support influence maternal attitudes, satisfaction, and behavior toward infants when measured concurrently. To a lesser degree, maternal perceived stress and support also influenced infant interactive behavior with mother. In each case, the direction of the relationship was in the predicted direction. Mothers with high support are more satisfied with their babies, their parental roles, their lives in general, and are more positive in their behavioral interactions with their infants. Conversely, mothers who report high stress are less satisfied and less positive in their behavioral interactions than are mothers with low stress.

Mothers' subjective perceptions of their child-care roles and pleasure in their infants, as well as their perceived life satisfaction, were more

Table 1. Significant Stress and Support Predictors of Mother and Infant Measures across the First Year Postpartum

| | Mother and Infant Dependent Measures | | | |
Predictors	One Month	Four Months	Eight Months	Twelve Months
One month				
Stress	GLS***	Maternal sensitivity*	—	—
	SWPS**	Infant responsiveness*		
Intimate support	GLS***	Maternal AFFECT*	GLS**	—
	SWPS**	Infant responsiveness*		
		Infant AFFECT*		
Friendship support	GLS**	—	—	—
Community support	GLS***	—	SWPS*	—
	SWPS*		Maternal AFFECT*	
Eight months				
Stress			GLS**	—
Intimate support			GLS**	Maternal AFFECT*
			SWPS*	
Community support			SWPS*	Maternal AFFECT*

*p < .05; **p < .01; ***p < .001.
GLS = General life satisfaction.
SWPS = Satisfaction with parenting.

consistently influenced by both the stress and support factors than were their global behavioral styles. Also, the magnitude of the effects were greater for these maternal-attitude measures than for the measures of mothers' behavior with their infants. Regression analyses indicated that stress and the various types of support accounted for 8% to 12% of the variance in the SWPS and GLS measures, while accounting for 5% to 6% of the variance in the behavior AFFECT measures.

SUPPORT AS A MODERATOR OF PARENTAL STRESS

Of great interest in our study were the anticipated interactions between the stress and social support variables which would indicate the presence of the classic "buffer" effects. Surprisingly, however, such interaction effects were nearly nonexistent in our results. In all, only one significant interaction was found. Mothers with high stress and high intimate support at one month reported greater general life satisfaction than did mothers with high stress and low support $(F = 11.9, p < .001)$. Thus, this moderator effect was not even specifically related to a parenting variable. Interestingly, several significant stress-by-support interactions were present on measures of infant behavior at 4 months (AFFECT, responsiveness to parent), but such effects are difficult to interpret in a meaningful way. Bronfenbrenner (personal communication), however, has suggested that such moderator effects are demonstrated by children because they are more vulnerable to environmental variation than adults, and particularly variations with the significant people in their lives, of whom parents are the most important. It may be that in this case children reap some specific yet indirect benefit from the moderating impact of parental social support on perceived stress. This is an empirical question worthy of greater attention.

DEVELOPMENTAL PERIODS AND SOCIAL
SUPPORT FUNCTIONS

Suggestions have been made that the effects of social support on parenting and child development may vary depending upon the developmental period in which it is measured (Belsky, 1983; McCall, 1979). Of particular interest has been the early postpartum period, which represents the transition to parenthood, as numerous normative changes occur at this time (Miller & Sollie, 1980; Belsky, 1983). Analyses of our data suggest that social support effects on maternal functioning are greatest during this transition period and up to infant age 4 months (see Table 1). Both the breadth and the magnitude of social-support effects on mothers' attitudes and behavior are greater at 1 and 4 months postpartum than at 8 and 12 months. Further, each type of support produced significant effects for mothers at 1 and 4 months, while the majority of significant effects during the later postpartum period were produced only by the intimate support variable. Infant behavior at 4 months was likewise influenced by the measures of maternal social support at 1 month, but similar effects were not found for the 8 month maternal-support measure on infant behavior at 8 and 12 months.

These findings support the notion that supportive relationships may be most productive during times which represent major life transitions, or when stresses are greater. During early infancy, mothers are adapting to their infants, their role-changes, and perhaps greater responsibilities. While these processes may not be perceived as stressful, independent effects of support may be greater during this transition. Later, once mother and infant routines have become established, support functions are somewhat less critical although still meaningful. Whether similar findings will emerge in relation to child developmental transitions is yet another issue to be resolved in future research.

ISSUES IN MEASURING PARENTAL SOCIAL SUPPORT

Analyses of our data across the first year postpartum substantiated the notion that maternal social support is a multidimensional concept (Wandersman et al., 1980) in that different levels or types of support appeared to affect maternal parenting differentially. Although both community and friendship support produced significant effects on maternal attitudes, and in some cases maternal behavior (see Table 1), neither of these factors produced the consistently strong effects that maternal intimate support did across the first year postpartum. Further, intimate support was the only support variable to moderate the effects of high life stress on one maternal measure. The power of intimate support likely reflects its proximity and immediate availability to mothers, as well as the probability that families with young infants spend less time in outside social activities with friends and community groups, and more time together as a family unit. Fathers too may increase their own involvement and focus on the family, producing more positive perceptions of their supportiveness by mothers and more positive evaluations of the marital relationship.

Another measurement issue of importance involved the delineation of those aspects of the support measure which produced significant effects during early infancy. Two-way ANOVAs were employed to analyze separately the items on the intimate support factor, two of which described the availability of such support and two which measured mothers' perceived satisfaction with the available support. Results for the SWPS measure indicated that the items describing the availability of support were not significant, while both satisfaction with the presence or absence of an intimate relationship and mother's satisfaction with the presence or absence of someone with whom to share private feelings were significant ($F = 8.6$, $p < .01$, $F = 12.8$, $p < .001$, respectively). These results clearly suggest that measures of social support must consider both the amount and availability of support and the individual's satisfaction with the support available, further denoting the multidimensional nature of social support as a variable.

Our social support, stress, and outcome measures were collected longitudinally across the first year postpartum, which allowed for analyses of the long-term predictability of the stress and support variables to maternal outcome as well as analysis of the stability of the stress and support factors over time. Results of regression analyses indicated that there was little predictability for the 1-month stress and support indices to maternal attitudes at 8 months or mother-infant behavior at 8 or 12 months. Only intimate support at 1 month significantly predicted maternal GLS at 8 months, accounting for 9% of the variance. No other long-term predictive relationships were apparent for any of the specific parenting factors. The failure to find long-term predictions was most likely related to the fact that the support and stress factors were only moderately stable over this period. Stability coefficients from 1 to 8 months were .54 ($p < .001$) for stress; .40 ($p < .001$) for intimate support, and .29 ($p < .01$) for community support (friendship support was omitted from this analysis). In our sample, relationships or mothers' satisfaction with them were somewhat ephemeral. This may again suggest that the changes involved in this transition period are many, and are at times costly for supportive relationships.

DISCUSSION

Our results, along with those described by others (Crockenberg, 1981; Unger & Powell, 1980; Wandersman et al., 1980, Wandersman & Unger, 1983) clearly suggest that parental social support is a meaningful ecological variable affecting parenting and the early mother-infant relationship. Mothers' perceived satisfaction with their intimate, friendship, and community supports showed generally positive relationships to their reported life satisfaction, satisfaction with parenting, and the quality of their behavioral interactions with their infants.

Although community and friendship support were both related to various aspects of maternal parenting, the intimate support factor produced the strongest, most consistent, and predictive relationships to maternal functioning. The differences between these support sources and their effects underscores the importance of considering social support as a multidimensional concept which operates on several ecological levels. From our findings, it appears that both support from a spouse and satisfaction with that support are the most influential support factors during the early postpartum period for the development of positive maternal parenting. Both Belsky (1981) and Cowan and Cowan (1983) have previously suggested that a satisfactory marital relationship is a major support to competent parenting and more positive parent-child relationships, and our data across the first year postpartum validate that notion.

One aspect of the role that social support may play in regard to parenting that has received little attention involves the developmental nature of support functions and the notion of developmental periods or transitions. It may be that social-support networks are most influential at particular times in both parents' and children's development. The transition to parenthood has produced some recent interest in this regard. Our data suggest that both stress and social support have a greater impact during this transition and early postpartum period than in later infancy. It seems likely that support plays a major role at this time because the addition of a child to the family promotes considerable change in routines, expectations, and individual behavioral patterns which require numerous adjustments, both physically and emotionally. Subsequent major developmental transitions for both parents and children during preschool, school age, and adolescence may be equally amenable to social-support influences.

The assumption that social support would play a more crucial role during various transitions or developmental periods involves the notion that parents are more vulnerable or under more stress during these times. It was interesting in our results that few relationships were found in which social support moderated the adverse effects of high life stress, even during the early postpartum period. The failure of our data to substantiate such moderator effects may reflect a measurement problem, in that our stress measure only involved major life stresses rather than focusing on the particular stresses associated with parenting (Pearlin & Schooler, 1978), or more daily annoyances (Lazarus & Delongis, 1983). Certainly, both the experience of major life stress and social support independently affect maternal attitudes and behavior, but more relevant measures of parental stressors may be necessary to explicate the moderator effects of parental-support systems. Nevertheless, the potential of social support to act as a moderator of stress should not overshadow the potential contribution of parental social networks as an independent variable influencing family and child development.

Another issue of importance involves the measurement of social support itself. Previous studies have focused primarily on the availability or amount of support available to parents, as well as the sources of support. While the amount of support available from various sources is important, our data suggest that mothers' perceived satisfaction with their support sources may be more influential than the amount or availability per se. In short, having a greater support network may not always be better, and perhaps having too much creates other novel stressors such as increased time demands and expectation to be a support (Belle, 1981). This suggests that measuring some index of the perceived appropriateness or satisfaction with the social support available to parents is critical in determining its specific influences. Yet, there is also the need to go beyond this present status and assess also those factors which underlie the perception of satisfaction, including various psychosocial factors as well as individual difference or personality variables. One variable of particular interest might be parental attributions as to why various events occurred and why they turned out as they did. How such events are conceptualized may well be related to perceived parental satisfaction.

While we have demonstrated that a mother's perceived satisfaction with her relationships is related to both her current attitudes and subsequent behavior (between 1 and 4 months), we believe that it would be unwise to consider these findings causal in nature. This project as well as others (Belsky, 1983; Crockenberg, 1981; Longfellow et al., 1979; Cowan & Cowan, 1983) raise three critical questions about both the meaning and importance of the construct of social support.

The first issue concerns the relationship between perceived satisfaction and the dynamic of relationships. If one considers that something about one's social relationships may be causal in later parenting (as we do), surely one's global perceptions are not an adequate assessment of those factors operating within the relationship which influence one's satisfaction. Thus, we believe that there is a need to gain greater clarity and detail regarding the factors (trust, communication, role arrangements, etc.) that affect relationships and their dynamic interrelationships across time, as these factors may account for both one's satisfaction and subsequent parenting attitudes and behavior (Cowan & Cowan, 1983). For example, one might hypothesize that the different provisions of social support (Henderson, 1981; Weiss, 1974; Mitchell & Trickett, 1980) such as emotional support, information/advice, and sense of identity may operate differently in different types of relationships (spouse, friends, neighbors, etc.). Furthermore, there is a need to investigate how cultural or subcultural values regarding the importance of such factors as marital communication and role arrangements may differentially affect satisfaction and its correlates.

The second concern involves the way in which one's perceptions of social support may be related to and/or confounded with one's physical health, mental health, and personality and ego functioning. This question has recently received attention from a variety of researchers (Heller, 1979; Hammer, 1981; Henderson, 1982), and it seriously clouds the theoretical and methodological value of measuring social support per se. For example, one might explain the finding that depression and lack of satisfaction with one's relationships are correlated as (1) poor relationships lead to depression, (2) feelings of depression lead to deterioration in relationships, or (3) people who are depressed are currently unhappy with life in general as well as their relationships. In a similar manner, adaptive ego functioning (Heinecke, Diskin, Ramsey-Klee, & Given, 1983; Grossman, Eichler, & Winnickoff, 1980) prior to parenthood or good coping skills may lead one to report higher satisfaction as well as lead to better adaptation to parenthood. Furthermore, social support may function as a "proxy" for a myriad of social competencies and personality characteristics. That is, skills such as open communication, friendly affect, and the ability to give and receive assistance, or feelings such as high self-esteem and an internal locus of control may lead one to both choose and maintain healthy relationships as well as good parenting behaviors. Thus, we believe that it is critical to note that while social support itself may carry some direct causal effect, it may also serve as a proxy variable (Pedazur, 1982) which would include within it a variety of factors that require further exploration.

The third and related issue is how to usefully conceptualize the relationship of social support to adaptation. We believe that two models are useful (Crnic, Friedrich, & Greenberg, 1983). First, social support can be viewed as one of a variety of coping resources utilized in adapting to stress and transition, much as outlined in the coping model of Lazarus and his colleagues (Folkman et al., 1979; Lazarus, Kanner, & Folkman, 1980). Within the Lazarus model, utilization of social support is one of five specific coping resources. The other resources include health/energy/morale, problem-solving skills, utilitarian resources, and general and specific beliefs. It would appear that these coping resources themselves affect and are affected by one another. For example, a satisfactory support system may affect general beliefs about the world, such as locus of control or attributional style and vice versa. Further, the information and assistance one gains from a spouse, friend, etc., may improve one's problem-solving skills, alter one's health, and create access to utilitarian resources such as contact with service agencies, parenting classes, etc. While the complexities of the interrelationships (1) among coping resources, (2) between coping resources and outcomes, (3) between coping resources and one's appraisal of stress, and (4) between coping resources and one's developmental history appear overwhelming, we believe that such factors must be included to fully understand the process of coping. Future studies should adopt more prospective, longitudinal designs which address issues of parent functional status and coping resource use under low-stress conditions and follow family process through higher-stress conditions and subsequent adaptations.

Various high-risk populations would provide good tests of such relationships. Families with no "risk" status, however, should also be studied to understand coping processes through more normative stresses (e.g., daily hassles; beginning school; birth of a sibling, etc.). Such a model appears clearly applicable to the issue of adaptation to parenthood as well as other transitions in the individual and family life cycle.

The second useful model involves the concept that different sources of social support can be categorized to examine the influence of specific ecological domains on parenting attitudes and behavior. Within this context, we believe that Bronfenbrenner's model (1977) and its elaboration by others (Cochran & Brassard, 1979; Garbarino, 1982) can be usefully integrated with that of Lazarus in order to understand how different sources of support affect adaptation. The coping resources available or utilized at any specific time are likely to be influenced by the ecological settings relevant to the situation (home, school, work, community group, etc.) and the interactions both within and between these contexts. The behavior and attitudes of others in these various settings are likely to influence such factors as supportive social contacts, as well as beliefs, problem-solving, morale and other resources. At the outset of this project our incomplete conceptualization of social support led us to only assess three domains. With hindsight we would now assess both the mother's and father's perceptions of support as well as add the domains of each spouse's extended family and co-workers to begin to address these issues.

A final point is worthy of discussion. Results from our ongoing longitudinal investigation and those from other studies indicate that parental social-support influences are not uniform in promoting or influencing positive parental behaviors. In fact, it is apparent that differing levels of social support (and varying appraisals of satisfaction) have differing effects on parents. These findings imply that careful assessment of parental-support systems on an individual basis is necessary to delineate the specific needs of an individual parent in a difficult or demanding situation. Friendships, extended family contacts, or community-group support may affect certain functional domains at particular times, whereas intimate support may affect others. So, while it is appropriate to encourage social contacts with supportive individuals to facilitate more adaptive and positive parenting, it is incumbent upon future research to explore the conditions under which various levels of support operate most effectively. Such research could subsequently guide more appropriate interventions and planning for families under difficult circumstances.

REFERENCES

Belle, D.E. (1981). *The social network as a source of both stress and support to low income mothers.* Paper presented at the biennial meeting of the Society for Research in Child Development. Boston.

Belsky, J. (1981). Early human experience: A family perspective. *Developmental Psychology, 17*, 3–23.

Belsky, J. (1983). *Social network contact and the transition to parenthood.* Paper presented at the biennial meeting of the Society for Research in Child Development, Detroit.

Bronfenbrenner, U. (1977). Toward an experimental ecology of human development. *American Psychologist, 32*, 513–531.

Cobb, S. (1976). Social support as a moderator of life stress. *Psychosomatic Medicine, 38*, 300–314.

Cochran, M.M., & Brassard, J.A. (1979). Child development and personal social networks. *Child Development, 50*, 601–616.

Cowan, P.A., & Cowan, C.P. (1983). *Quality of couple relationships and parenting stress in beginning families.* Paper presented at the biennial meeting of the Society for Research in Child Development, Detroit.

Crnic, K.A., Greenberg, M.T., Ragozin, A.S., Robinson, N.M., & Basham, R.B. (1983). Effects of stress and social support on mothers and premature and full-term infants. *Child Development, 54*, 209–217.

Crnic, K.A., Friedrich, W.N., & Greenberg, M.T. (1983). Adaptation of families with mentally retarded children: A model of stress, coping, and family ecology. *American Journal of Mental Retardation, 88*, 125–138.

Crockenberg, S.B. (1981). Infant irritability, mother responsiveness, and social influences on the security of infant-mother attachment. *Child Development, 52*, 857–865.

Folkman, S., Schaefer, C., & Lazarus, R.S. (1979). Cognitive processes as mediators of stress and coping. In V. Hamilton & D. Warburton (Eds.), *Human Stress and Cognition.* New York: Wiley.

Garbarino, J. (1982). *Children and families in the social environment.* New York: Aldine.

Gottlieb, B.H. (Ed.). (1981). *Social networks and social support.* Beverly Hills, CA: Sage.

Grossman, F.K., Eichler, L.S., & Winnickoff, S.A. (1980). *Pregnancy, birth, and parenthood.* San Francisco: Jossey-Bass.

Haggerty, R.M. (1980). Life stress, illness, and social supports. *Developmental Medicine and Child Neurology, 22*, 391–400.

Heinecke, C.M., Diskin, S.D., Ramsey-Klee, D.M., & Given, K. (1983). Prebirth parent characteristics and family development in the first year of life. *Child Development, 54*, 194–208.

Heller, K. (1979). The effect of social support: Prevention and treatment implications. In A.P. Goldstein & F.H. Kanfer (Eds.), *Maximizing treatment gains.* New York: Academic Press.

Henderson, S., Byrne, D.G., & Duncan-Jones, P. (1981). *Neuroses in the social environment,* New York: Academic Press.

Hetherington, E.M. (1981). Children and divorce. In R.W. Henderson (Ed.), *Parent-child interaction.* New York: Academic Press.

Lazarus, R.S., Kanner, A., & Folkman, S. (1980). Emotions: A cognitive phenomenological analysis. In R. Plutchik & H. Kellerman (Eds.), *Theories of emotion.* New York: Academic Press.

Lazarus, R.S., & Delongis, A. (1983). Psychological stress and coping in aging. *American Psychologist, 38,* 245–254.

Longfellow, C., Zelkowitz, P., Saunders, E., & Belle, D. (1979, March). *The role of support in moderating the effects of stress and depression.* Paper presented at the biennial meeting of the Society for Research in Child Development, San Francisco.

McCall, R.B. (1979). The development of intellectual functioning in infancy and the prediction of later IQ. In J. Osofksy (Ed.), *Handbook of Infant Development,* New York: Wiley.

Miller, B.C., & Sollie, D.L. (1980). Normal stresses during the transition to parenthood. *Family Relations, 29,* 459–465.

Mitchell, R.E., & Trickett, E.J. (1980). Task force report: Social networks as mediators of social support. *Community Mental Health Journal, 18,* 27–44.

Mueller, D.P. (1980). Social networks: A promising direction for research on the relationships of the social environment to psychiatric disorder. *Social Science and Medicine, 40,* 147–161.

Pearlin, L.I., & Schooler, C. (1978). The structure of coping. *Journal of Health and Social Behavior, 19,* 2–21.

Pedazur, E.J. (1982). *Multiple regression in behavioral research (2d ed.).* New York: Holt, Rinehart & Winston.

Pilisuk, M. (1982). Delivery of social support: The social inoculation. *American Journal of Orthopsychiatry, 52,* 20–31.

Powell, D.R. (1979). Family environment relations and early child rearing: The role of social networks and neighborhoods. *Journal of Research on Development in Education, 13,* 1–11.

Sarason, I.G., Johnson, J.H., & Siegel, J.M. (1978). Assessing the impact of life changes: Development of the Life Experiences Survey. *Journal of Consulting and Clinical Psychology, 46,* 932–946.

Shereshefsky, P.M., & Yarrow, L.J. (1973). *Psychological aspects of a first pregnancy and early post natal adaptation.* New York: Raven.

Sollie, D.L., & Miller, B.C. (1980). The transition as a critical time for building family strengths. In N. Stinnet & P. Knaub (Eds.), *Family strengths: Positive models of family life.* Lincoln: University of Nebraska Press.

Unger, D.G., & Powell, D.R. (1980). Supporting families under stress: The role of social networks. *Family Relations, 29,* 566–574.

Wandersman, L., Wandersman, A., & Kahn, S. (1980). Social support in the transition to parenthood. *Journal of Community Psychology, 8,* 332–342.

Wandersman, L., & Unger, D. (1983, April). *Interaction of infant difficulty and social support in adolescent mothers.* Paper presented at the biennial meeting of the Society for Research in Child Development, Detroit.

Weiss, R. (1974). The provision of social relationships. In S. Rubin (Ed.), *Doing unto others,* Englewood Cliffs, NJ: Prentice-Hall.

CHAPTER 3
A Comparative Study of Social Support for New Mothers of Twins

Kristin Glaser
Montpelier, Vermont

CONCEPTUAL BACKGROUND

In survey studies, there have been two traditional approaches to social support. Most frequently examined are intimate relationships (spouse, partner, or confidant) and extensivity of, and amount of contact with, social network. An emotionally supportive spouse or partner has been found to protect against poor mental health in both general populations (Henderson et al., 1978; Lieberman, 1982) and among those experiencing stress (Burke & Weir, 1977; Gore, 1978).

Some researchers operate with a belief that "more is better." Extensivity of, and amount of contact with, social network are expected to equate with support (Lin, Ensel, Simeone, & Kuo, 1979). Others (Liem & Liem, 1979; Gottlieb, 1981) have argued that the larger social context that envelopes individuals, the overall cost of maintaining relationships, and flux in both need for support and quality of relationships cannot be ignored. They argue that there is no hypothetical level of general support that is beneficial to all people at all times.

In fact, relationships with a range of friends, family, and neighbors have been found to correlate with adjustment in some studies (Berkman & Syme, 1979; Finlayson, 1976; Henderson et al., 1978; Hill, 1958; Lin et al., 1979; Miller & Ingham, 1976). Other studies have found that relationships other than spouse have no effect (Brown & Harris, 1978; House, 1981) or that extensive contact with social network members is correlated to negative mental health measures (Belle, 1979; Cohler & Lieberman, 1980; Stack, 1974).

The material for this chapter was taken from the author's dissertation, *Social Support and Mothers' Adjustment to the Birth of Twins*, University of Chicago, 1983. The study was part of a larger NIMH-funded research project, "Self-Help and Urban Problems: Alternative Help Systems": (PHS#3, R18-CA1640-0151), an investigation of six different self-help systems. The principal investigators were Morton A. Lieberman of the University of California, San Francisco, dissertation advisor; and Leonard Borman of The Self-Help Center, 1600 Dodge, Chicago, IL. Author's address: 25 Court Street, Montpelier, Vt. 05602.

An alternative approach suggests that need for support is situation specific. Parkes (1971), Silverman (1976), Weiss (1976) and others have theorized that specific needs arise during major life changes. These needs are "to contain distress within limits that are personally tolerable; to maintain self-esteem; to preserve interpersonal relationships and a sense of belonging to a valued group; to meet the conditions and demands of the new situation and to prepare for the future" (D. Hamburg, Adams, & Brodie [1976] as cited in B. Hamburg and Killilea, [1979]).

B. Hamburg and Killilea go on to suggest that emotional support is needed in all difficult situations to alleviate distress. Depending on the demands of a particular event, different informational, appraisal, and instrumental support may also be needed.

This study examines one specific stressful situation, women's adjustment period following birth of twins. The question is raised whether general support such as an emotionally supportive spouse and broad network contact or specific help for specific problems are better able to predict women's adjustment. New mothers were questioned about their needs and the help they received. The role of the husband both as a specific helper and in giving emotional support was examined. Number of people in, and contact with, social network was compared to actual providers of help. The effect of all these supports on women's emotional and role adjustment were considered.

THE STRESS OF TWINS

Assessing the "demands of the situation" of having twins allows prediction of what specific types of support might be helpful. While the amount of stress new parents of singletons face has been the subject of disagreement (Jacoby, 1969), there is evidence that many parents find the experience stressful. New mothers of singletons have been reported to suffer from role conflict, lack of preparation, unrealistic expectations, lack of role models, isolation, overwork, and physical exhaustion (Brandt, 1968; Dyer, 1963; LeMasters, 1957; Liefer, 1977; Rapoport & Rapoport, 1977; Rossi, 1968). The last three problems have also been reported with subsequent children (Richman, 1976; Rossi, 1968). New mothers and veterans also show a high level of depression and other psychiatric symptoms which are attributed to the stress of mothering if evidenced after the first few months of birth (Ballinger, Buckley, Naylor, & Stansfield, 1979; Boesky, Cross, & Morley, 1960; Cohler, 1984; Larsen, 1966; Weissman & Klerman, 1977).

There are additional stresses to having twins. Medical complications may increase physical, emotional, and financial stress. Chances of prematurity and delivery-room complications are significantly higher than with a single child (Neubauer, 1972; Illingworth, 1975).

Gosher-Gottstein (1979) reports that mothers of twins spend considerably more time in infant care-taking than mothers of one infant. Reports from fieldwork and the popular twin literature[1] suggest that many new mothers complain about exhaustion and find it hard to balance caring for the babies and other work in the home.

Adjusting to the role of mother of special children can be difficult. Twins are quite unusual: one birth out of 100 produces twins (Novitski, 1977). A mother may be at sea as to how to manage the situation. She may wonder about developmental issues specific to twins. She may not know what can be done simultaneously with both babies and what needs to be done separately for each. Not knowing whether she is "doing it right" is a frequently expressed concern of new mothers.

The new mother may also encounter difficulty managing people's reactions to twins. Anthropological studies reported by Hagerdern and Kizziar (1974), Plank (1958), and Scheinfeld (1967) suggest that twins have been historically regarded as taboo. Reactions to twins in present society are varied. Stein and Wolner (1978) document the almost morbid interest that people can have. The most extreme reaction is to regard identical twins as true freaks, as if they were really one person in two bodies. A more conservative reaction is to regard twins as unusual and entertaining.

Based on informal testimony from mothers of twins and from the popular literature, a mother and her babies in public seem to be a magnet for attention. All standards of personal distance are broken down as strangers express amazement and ask highly personal questions. The universal comment on seeing twins is "My, you must have your hands full." "I don't know how you do it," runs a close second; a muttered "God spare me," a not so distant third. These remarks frequently come from mothers who are themselves burdened by an infant or infant-toddler combination.

While mothers of twins report pleasure in having their babies admired, the constant attention is wearisome. The preceding comments contain a mixed message, and mothers report feeling set aside from other mothers as well as pitied and/or admired for doing a superhuman task. This

---

[1] The assertions about mothers of twins are made on the basis of nine months of participant observation in the Mothers of Twins Clubs, a self-help system, by the author who herself was a mother of infant twins. Corroboration of these observations appears in a small, popular literature written to assist new parents in understanding the biology, psychology, and care of twins. See Cassill (1982), Collier (1974), Gehman (1965), Hagedern and Kizziar (1974), Massachusetts Mothers of Twins Association (1967), Scheinfeld (1967), Theroux and Tingley (1978).

attributed differentness is stressful for some women and a source of pride and enjoyment for others.

Finally, lack of adequate resources is noted as a secondary stressor for some mothers of twins. Reliable knowledge about and direct experience with twins is limited to a small segment of the population. As a result, it may be difficult to get accurate information and validation of role, leading to exacerbation of distress.

From this assessment, it can be expected that mothers of twins may need help with the physical parameters such as child care and housework, the material dimension such as equipment, clothing, and money; they may need advice and information about twins, and emotional support and reassurance about their roles as mothers.

SAMPLE AND MEASURES

The sample for the study was generated with the assistance of numerous local chapters and the National Organization of Mothers of Twins Clubs. A self-administered, one-time questionnaire was mailed to 470 women in 1979 with a resulting sample of 250. Thirty-one percent were members of a Mothers of Twins Club (MOTC), another 28% reported intentions of joining; the rest were not members.

Almost half the sample were first-time mothers, slightly over a third had another child, and the rest had two or more other children. The twins were between 7 and 9 months old, on average. Fifty-six percent were fraternal and 44% were identical or "uncertain." The mothers were white, 28 years old on the average, had been married about six years, and had some postsecondary education.

Kind of support was measured by a series of questions designed for this study. Women were asked whether they needed instrumental help (child care, housework, gifts of equipment and clothing, or money), informational support (advice and information about twins), and appraisal-emotional support (support and reassurance as a mother). They were asked to rate the amount of help received (right amount, almost enough, not enough). Women then checked as many categories of *providers* as assisted in each area. Listed were husband, members of Mothers of Twins Clubs, other mothers of twins, parents, other relatives, friends with single babies, friends without babies, neighbors, and no one.

Husbands' emotional support was measured by a subscale of the Marital Strain Scale (Menaghan, 1981). The items on the scale are Likert-type choices for rating whether a woman feels appreciated by her spouse in several ways, whether she can confide in him, and whether she feels he is affectionate. *Husbands' general helpfulness* was measured by asking women to write in who had been their single most important helper in the last four weeks.

Extensivity of *social network relationships* was measured by asking women to circle number of close friends, confidants, friends with babies, and mothers of twins the respondent can call on. Amount of contact was measured by asking women to rate the frequency of contact with the same list of network members used for measuring providers. Frequency of playgroup attendance was also determined.

Adjustment was measured in two ways. Comfort with mothering, a Likert-type scale was designed to measure role adjustment or comfort. Women were asked to react to a series of positive and negative statements about twin care, feelings about twins, and feelings about themselves as mothers.

Weiss (1976) suggests that a deficit response to a stressful life event is manifested by depression and other symptoms of mental and/or physical illness. To measure the rate of depression, a subscale of the Hopkins Symptoms Checklist (Derogatis, Lipman, Covi, & Rickles, 1971) was used. Respondents were asked to rate on a Likert-type scale how frequently they had experienced each of 10 symptoms in the previous week.

PRIMARY RESULTS

Needs

Choosing from six areas of need, mothers of twins claimed an average of 3.99 needs (*SD* 1.29), with 52 women needing help in all areas. Examination of the frequencies of needs demonstrated that while all women had needs, some were more universal. Ninety percent of the women cited need for child care. Need for help with equipment and help with housework were also frequently checked (80% and 72%). Fewer women cited need for information and advice about twins (66%) and support and reassurance as a mother (55%). (The sixth area, financial need, was dropped from further analysis due to the small number needing help [37%].)

Kind of Support

It was predicted that getting the right amount of instrumental, informational, and appraisal-emotional support would be correlated to adjustment. For the women who had these needs, receiving the right amount of help was positively correlated to both measures of adjustment (see Table 1).

Table 1.   Correlations between Amount of Help Received
and Adjustment for Women Who Needed Help in Each Area

	Adjustment Indicators	
Amount of Help with:	Comfort with Mothering (N)	Depression (N)
Instrumental help		
Child care	.29*	.32*
	(222)	(224)
Housework	.26*	.34*
	(170)	(170)
Equipment	.28*	.20*
	(193)	(194)
Information	.23*	.23*
	(152)	(154)
Appraisal–emotional	.36*	.25*
support (reassurance)	(132)	(134)

*All correlations significant at .005 level or better.

Since such a small group (N = 52) claimed needs in all areas, a method was sought which would allow a larger sample to be considered to be able to use regression analyses to look at combined effects of help. By reasoning that people who checked that they did not need help (with child care, for example) were indicating that their need was already met, a redefinition of the amount of help scale was devised. Women with no need, who presumably had already received help with child care, or were coping adequately themselves, were added to the top of the amount of help scales. The previous 3-point scale was converted to a 4-point scale, thus increasing the regression sample to 182.[2]

It was posited that specific kinds of support meet distinct needs. This implies that metness of each kind of need should have an independent effect on adjustment.

A regression model was used to examine what portion of the variance of adjustment metness of needs variables in combination could predict. First, a univariate regression found that each metness of need variable independently explained between 3 and 13% of the variance of both measures of adjustment, with instrumental support and reassurance being the strongest predictors. For comfort with mothering, childcare (R^2 = .13), reassurance (R^2 = .12) and information (R^2 = .08) were the strongest predictors. For lack of depression, housework (R^2 = .13), child care (R^2 = .11), and reassurance (R^2 = .10) were the main predictors.

[2] To assure that this maneuver did not distort the meaning of the original scale, an analysis of variance was done to compare the mean adjustment scores between women with "no need" and those who had "the right amount of help." These differences proved insignificant using a Duncan Multiple Range test, with one exception. The new metness of need scales were deemed acceptable to stand in for the amount of help scales.

To examine the metness of need variables in combination, a stepwise regression was used. The combined effect of metness of five needs accounts for twice as much of the variance as any single variable. The overall R^2 was 25% for comfort with mothering and 24% for depression. For comfort with mothering, help with child care, reassurance and information make significant contributions to the overall variance. For lack of depression, all the variables except equipment make significant contributions.

The data thus suggest that while there is some overlap of effect, mothers' needs are specific and that the meeting of the individual needs is relevant to how women adjust to the experience of having twins. The combination of adequate physical help, information about twins, and reassurance about role predict adjustment more strongly than any single type of support.

Providers

The people who provide help for each area of need were also examined. The emphasis on the spouse in the general support literature and the finding that his emotional and practical support is influential to adjustment of mothers (Belle, 1979; Brown & Harris, 1978; and Paykel, Emms, Fletcher, & Rassaby, 1980) suggested that the husband would be a pivotal helper to the new mother of twins.

Weiss (1974) states that people seek guidance from trustworthy authorities. Borkman (1979) has argued that veterans of a problem with "experiential knowledge" are more accepted authorities than friends or family. The mothers of twins were expected to be the primary providers of advice and information about twins.

People in other relationships to the mothers were expected to offer help more generally. For mothers of twins, was having a wide range of assistance helpful ("more is better"), irrelevant, or harmful? The present study argued that multiple helpers would improve the chance of getting sufficient child care, help with housework, and clothing and equipment.

The twin-care literature (for example, Gehman, 1965; Massachusetts Mothers of Twins Association, 1967) suggests that having twins is an event where a women can unabashedly ask for and expect help from her social network. Women are encouraged to allow themselves to be the focus of attention without expectation of immediate or complete reciprocity. The present study speculated that this is made possible by the combined circumstances of acknowledged large-scale physical demands, positive ambiance (twins are "doubly blessed"), and unusualness. This suggested that helpers would be available and not likely to represent a drain to the new mother.

Turning to the results, the husband was the most frequent helper (see Table 2). For example, 90% of the mothers checked husbands for child care, while 57% checked parents, and 44% checked other relatives. The spouse was 1.5 times more likely to help with child care, three times more likely to help with housework, and 1.5 times more likely to offer support and reassurance than parents, the next-most-frequent contributors. Other relatives were the next-most-frequent helpers. The expectation that the family would be generally helpful was thus confirmed. Friends and neighbors were less likely to be seen as providing help while mothers of twins were the most frequent providers of information.

Examining the consequences of having multiple helpers, the expected positive link between number of helpers and amount of help was found (see Table 3). Correlations ranged from .20 for reassurance to .38 for information. The present study also suggested that having multiple helpers would not be stressful. In fact, number of helpers (see Table 3) had no relationship to comfort with mothering. Number of providers for child care, housework, and information had low positive correlations with lack of depression. Thus, having many helpers was linked to receiving help, and seemed to show no evident cost to mental health.

The significance of the husband as a helper was also examined. The adjustment scores of women who claimed their husband or some other person (parent, friend, neighbor, or paid help) as their best helper over the last 4 weeks were compared. An analysis of variance found that

Table 2. Frequencies of Providers Checked for Areas of Need

	Areas of Need									
	Child Care		Instrumental Help Housework		Equipment		Information		Reassurance	
Helpers	N	%	N	%	N	%	N	%	N	%
Husband	215	(86.0)	127	(50.8)			24	(9.6)	182	(72.8)
MOTC	0		0		16	(6.4)	59	(23.6)	17	(6.8)
Other MOT	2	(0.8)	1	(0.4)	33	(13.2)	64	(25.6)	20	(8.0)
Parents	142	(56.8)	40	(16.0)	147	(58.8)	37	(14.8)	123	(49.2)
Other relatives	110	(44.0)	26	(10.4)	163	(65.2)	25	(10.0)	86	(34.4)
Friends with baby	35	(14.0)	3	(1.2)	139	(55.6)	24	(9.6)	81	(32.4)
Friends no baby	45	(18.0)	7	(2.8)	88	(35.2)	8	(3.2)	50	(20.0)
Neighbors	50	(20.0)	4	(1.6)	54	(25.6)	10	(4.0)	39	(15.6)
No one	8	(3.2)	85	(34.0)	26	(10.4)	84	(33.6)	26	(10.4)
Missing	5		17		14		20		21	

Table 3. Correlation of Extensivity of Providers to Adjustment
and Amount of Help Received, for Women Who Need Help

| Number of Helpers in Each Area | Adjustment Indicators | | Amount of Help Received (N) |
	Comfort with Mothering (N)	Depression (N)	
Instrumental help:			
Child care	.01 NS	.23***	.22***
	(225)	(227)	(224)
Housework	.04 NS	.26***	.23***
	(179)	(180)	(170)
Equipment	.12 NS	.10 NS	.25***
	(200)	(201)	(194)
Information	.00 NS	.17*	.38***
	(165)	(168)	(154)
Emotional–appraisal			
support (reassurance)	−.08 NS	−.12 NS	.20***
	(137)	(139)	(134)

$*p < .05; **p < .01; ***p < .001.$

both comfort with mother and depression scores were better for women
whose husbands were their best helpers.

On the other hand, no differences were found when the amount of
help received, in each area of need, was compared for women whose
husbands were their best helpers with women who claimed another
person for best help. Having a husband as their best helper was not
related to getting better help, although it did relate to feeling less depressed. Thus, while the husband was the most frequently cited helper,
and having him as the main helper was linked to adjustment, other
people were very much involved in helping. The more people who
helped, the better the help was rated.

The data examined so far indicate that mothers of twins had needs
specific to having new babies and that when they felt that these needs
were being adequately met, they felt less depressed and more comfortable
about themselves as mothers. The husband was the most frequent helper,
but having other people involved made women rate their help as more
adequate. More support seemed better and having a helpful husband
correlated to women feeling better.

COMPARATIVE INQUIRY: EMOTIONALLY SUPPORTIVE
SPOUSE AND SOCIAL NETWORK

Given the importance of the spouse and number of helpers, it can be
asked, "Can one get the same grasp on adjustment by examining spouse

emotional support and social network characteristics?" Perhaps the emotionally supportive spouse is also the helpful one and size of social network is similar to number of helpers. If traditional and therefore more common measures predict adjustment adequately, why use new measures?

Emotionally Supportive Spouse

Examining husband emotional support, most mothers of twins experienced their husbands as fairly emotionally supportive. Level of husband emotional support was also linked to other measures of support. Women were more likely to name their spouse as their best helper if he was emotionally supportive. Husband emotional support was linked to amount of help received (see Table 4). The highest correlation was with housework (.28); the lowest with information (.13), where the husband was not a frequent helper. Thus, while there was a relationship between an emotionally supportive spouse and amount of help received, it was not one-to-one.

Looking at the correlation between husband emotional support and comfort with mothering (.21, see Table 4), it was evident that spouse support was not as strong a predictor as instrumental support or reassurance. Similarly, a univariate regression showed that the independent effect of husband emotional support was not as strong a predictor as

Table 4.   Correlations between Husband Emotional Support, Adjustment, Amount of Help Received

	Husband Emotional Support (N)
Adjustment	
Comfort with mothering	.21***
	(240)
Depression	.37***
	(240)
Amount received of instrumental help:	
Child care	.23***
	(221)
Housework	.28***
	(166)
Equipment	.16**
	(189)
Information	.13*
	(150)
Appraisal—emotional support	
(reassurance)	.23***
	(134)

*p < .05; **p < .01; ***p < .001.

most of the metness of need variables individually or as a group. It would seem, then, that the emotionally supportive husband, while playing a part in a woman's adjustment to her role as a mother, was not as strong a predictor of role adjustment as having her needs met.

On the other hand, the correlation between husband emotional support and level of depression (.37, see Table 4) was as high as any single metness of need variable. A univariate regression showed that the independent effect of husband emotional support (R^2 = .11) was equal to several single metness of need variables.

Can husband emotional support "stand in" for at least part of the effect of metness of need on depression? A hierarchical regression was computed with husband emotional support forced into the equation before metness of need variables. When husband emotional support was added, the overall amount of variance of adjustment explained only increased by three percent above what metness of need variables predicted by themselves (from .24 to .27 of the variance). There was some overlap, but a remaining 16% of the variance still was only explained by metness of needs. Instrumental, informational, and reassurance support still accounted for independently significant portions of the variance of depression.

Of particular note is that housework, for which the husband was the most frequent sole helper, still had an independent effect. From the same person, emotional support and helping with the house met separate needs and had separate effects on a woman's adjustment. Also, the independent effect of reassurance, for which there were many helpers, demonstrates that a loving spousal relationship did not necessarily provide the specific emotional support a woman needed about herself as a mother.

In summary, while the emotionally supportive spouse clearly contributes to meeting a woman's needs, this measure cannot be substituted to explain adjustment. Situation-specific needs were partially distinct from need for loving spousal relationship and multiple providers were necessary to meet many of these needs.

Social Network

Turning to the social network, it was asked whether availability of relationship could stand in for support received. It can be argued that extensivity of relationships reflects potential for support. Actual contact with network members creates the opportunity for help to be given. It was assumed that both extensivity of relationships and amount of contact might be related to amount of help received and adjustment.

In fact, the social network analysis indicated that simply examining amount of contact with network members gave no information (with one exception) about adjustment or amount of help received. Being in touch with others did not equate with support. The more friendly relationships a woman claimed, however, the less depressed she was (while number of relationships had no correlation with comfort with mothering). Amount of contact with mothers of twins, number of close friends, and number of friends with babies each had a low positive correlation with level of depression at the .05 level or better. Frequency of playgroup attendance and number of confidants were more highly correlated (.24, .20). Most social network characteristics thus were not as closely linked to adjustment as amount of help received.

Number of friendly relationships claimed also had no general relationship to amount of help received. Number of relationships claimed was not the same as actual providers of help. However, number of close friends was modestly related to amount of child care, and number of confidants was linked to amount of housework received (see Table 5). Most interestingly, number of mothers of twins known was positively correlated to amount of information (.29), but number of friends with single babies was negatively correlated (−.15). This could mean that women with singleton mothers as friends don't bother to seek out other mothers of twins.

Given the moderately high correlation between play-group attendance and number of confidants and level of depression, an inquiry was launched to determine whether these measures overlapped with metness of need variables. A stepwise regression which considered all the support and network variables showed that frequency of play-group attendance was the third-strongest predictor of depression, while number of con-

Table 5.   Correlations of Social Network Characteristics to Amount of Help Received

| | Amount of Help With: | | | | |
| | Instrumental Help | | | | |
Number of:	Child Care (N = 223)	Housework (N = 169)	Equipment (N = 191)	Information (N = 153)	Reassurance (N = 132)
Close friends	.12*	.04 NS	.00 NS	.05 NS	.11 NS
Confidants	.10 NS	.20**	.04 NS	−.05 NS	.05 NS
Friends with babies	.05 NS	−.05 NS	−.05 NS	−.15*	.00 NS
Mothers with twins	.07 NS	−.05 NS	.00 NS	.29***	.08 NS
Frequency playground attendance	.14*	.02 NS	.06 NS	.00 NS	.12 NS

*p < .05; **p < .01; ***p < .001.

fidants had no significant effect. The overall variance explained, however, was only raised by one point by adding the network items. Play-group attendance did overlap, then, with the metness of need variables. It would seem that the frequency with which a mother met with other mothers and their children did help explain level of depression in the face of other supports and perhaps also explains where some of her needs were being met.

In summary, the "more is better" social network approach (Lin et al., 1979) to social support did not prove very powerful in this study. Contact with social network members had no relationship to either adjustment or amount of help received. Extensivity of several kinds of relationships had a modest correlation to amount of help in a few areas and to level of depression, but none to comfort with mothering. In comparison, when actual providers of help were considered, "more" was related positively to amount of help received. Thus, with the exception of amount of play-group attendance, traditional social network characteristics provided little leverage to the understanding of adjustment, particularly when metness of needs and husband emotional support had already been considered.

DISCUSSION

In this discussion, a closer consideration of adjustment, needs, and helpers will be given. These mothers of twins felt fairly secure in their role as mother. Eighty-two percent strongly agreed that they felt good about themselves as mothers of twins, 17% somewhat agreed, while only 1.6% disagreed. The author's own difficult experience with infant twins had led her to expect other mothers to be more distressed. In fact, the field experience basically corroborated the survey data: many mothers were not evidencing any difficulty. They were coping well, enjoying their social acclaim. Yet the author did meet other mothers who experienced problems and wonders about the mothers who did not respond to the questionnaire or contact Mother of Twins Clubs.

For mothers of twins, the mean depression score was 3.27 (SD .45) on a 4-point scale in which 4 is least depressed. The depression scores of mothers of twins were compared to a subsample[3] of women from the "Life Events and Adult Adaptation" study, an investigation of 2,000 randomly chosen adults from the Chicago area. The subsample were married women, in roughly the same age bracket, with and without

[3] Unpublished data from the NIA-sponsored study PHS#5-P01-HC00123, Morton A. Lieberman and Leonard L. Pearlin, researchers.

children. Sixty-four percent of the "normal" sample fell in the least-depressed ranking, whereas only 21% of the mothers of twins were least depressed. Similarly, 37% of the mothers of twins were in the most-depressed ranking compared with 8% of the normal sample.

While on the surface it would seem that mothers of twins were considerably more depressed than a normal sample, it can be asked how much these women were depressed in any clinical sense or whether they were exhibiting a typical group of postpartum characteristics. Few women checked the more serious symptoms of depression such as hopelessness about the future or thoughts of ending their lives. The most frequently checked items were disinterest in sex, feeling lonely, and loss of energy[4] (at least 20% of the sample checked these symptoms as occurring fairly or very often). All of these are fairly reasonable reactions to being at home as the primary caretaker of infant twins.

Turning to the needs claimed, the overall picture was of women who, in large measure, were getting their needs met in a fairly satisfactory manner. Yet there are some interesting contrasts. The two instrumental needs, housework and child care, were highly claimed and were powerful predictors of adjustment. Child care, however, was a highly met need, with many helpers available; while need for help with housework went largely unmet. Thirty-four percent of the mothers had no help with housework, and 33% had only husbands as helpers. Forty-six percent of the women who needed help said they did not receive enough help. Thus, help with housework was the least-met need in the study. In contrast, only 18% did not get enough child care.

What is the meaning of this difference? It seems as if there were helpers in the home but they did not engage in housework. Does this imply that there is a taboo against friends and family doing the "dirty work"? Is there too much work for two people or is the husband not pulling his weight? Are women's standards too high for this period? The author's feeling is that there genuinely is too much work, that women need outside help, and that there are financial and social restrictions preventing this. The matter bears further investigation.

A similar contrast can be noted between the need for reassurance as a mother and need for information about twins. Neither of these needs were as frequently claimed as the instrumental needs, but need for information was unmet for 28% of the sample, with 18% saying that no one gave them information, while need for reassurance was only unmet by 9% of the sample, and many supporters were claimed.

[4] Examining checklist items also helps explain the relationship between play-group attendance and lack of depression. Obviously, women who attend play groups are likely to feel less lonely and have more energy.

What does this difference mean? The obvious answer is that while reassurance about mothering is available and acceptable from a number of people, these same people cannot adequately give information about twins. Mothers of twins are the most logical source of information and some mothers may not have access to other mothers of twins. The data from the study, however, do not completely support this conclusion.

The number of mothers of twins known did correlate to amount of information received. However, total number of helpers also correlated with amount of information. Given the few number of helpers cited (mean of 1 helper per mother compared with 2.39 for reassurance), the higher number of information givers claimed might only mean that both mothers of twins club members and nonmember mothers of twins had been available, and so they were used, rather than other types of people. However, an analysis of variance found no difference in rating of amount of information received by whether the helpers were mothers of twins or not. Not having any helpers was the only link to getting inadequate information. This puzzle must be left to further sorting out in the future.

The author's personal experience and observation of the Mothers of Twins Clubs, however, led her to believe it does matter who gives information.

All the help the author received during the first months postpartum was from mothers of singletons who were offering "earth mother" advice. Correct mothering was to feed the twins on demand, rock them to sleep, wear them if they were fussy, and generally let the babies' needs rule the day. This led to a frazzled exhaustion and a sense of being out of control on the author's part. Only later, when influenced by other mothers of twins, did the author gain support for a managed care-giving schedule that offered relief.

Borkman (1979) has discussed the ways in which network members may in fact have a negative influence on someone with a specific problem. They may present stereotyped views of the situation, offer inappropriate solutions to the problem, and may not be able to comprehend the emotional texture of the experience. Friends and family, at some level, may be offering "foreign aid."

In contrast, association with other mothers of twins offers access to both specific skills and alternative definitions of the situation. The Mothers of Twins Clubs (MOTC), for example, is a source of easy access to other mothers of twins. MOTC is a mutual-help group or "association of people who band together as individuals, who share the same problem, predicament, or life situation for the purpose of mutual aid" (B. Hamburg & Killilea, 1979, p. 1). MOTC is a highly structured group with about 8,000 members and local, state, and national levels of organization. In existence for over 25 years, there are clubs in almost every state. These clubs hold formal monthly meetings and may, or may not, have informal living room "cope" group meetings for new mothers at other times.

In MOTC, the new mother has access to written materials about twins and professionals who have experience in the area, and exposure to "experiential knowledge." Experiential knowledge is developed in self-help groups "through a process of individuals reflecting upon and trusting as valid his/her lived experience with a focal problem in a shared context of other persons with similar experience" (Borkman, 1979, p. 4).

In MOTC this knowledge recommends a careful balance between acknowledging the problems twins represent, but asserting there is usually an acceptable solution. For example, while members would agree that the first three months are difficult, they point out it is quickly over. Every mother is deemed competent, although she may need a little help. MOTC also stresses that understanding twins and not treating them as freaks is a process to which society must be educated. Thus the new mother of twins is offered a superior understanding with which to deal with social ignorance, allowing her to be less at the mercy of casual feedback.

While very low-keyed and folksy, the MOTC teachings counter the wider social stereotypes of the situation and offer the mother of twins positive personal meaning. Through the group she can pick from a variety of solutions, she can gain a perspective on the situation, and develop a sense of normality by being a group member.

The MOTC experience will not suit all new mothers of twins. There is a wide variation in local groups. An individual mother of twins may not feel comfortable with the mix of women in her area group. She also might have difficulty with a particular group's resolution to the ongoing tension between meeting older members' social needs versus new members' support needs.

A more general problem is that both the teachings of the club and the literature they offer are heavily based on experience with identicals and their social and developmental problems. Thus, new mothers are simultaneously receiving a normalizing group experience and some discomforting information about their children. New mothers, particularly of physically normal, non—look alike fraternal twins, might be led to worry about a series of problems which may not occur.

After considering the role of other mothers of twins, a few final reflections on the role of friends and family and the husband are appropriate. While friends and family may not be the best sources of information about twins, they clearly offer a variety of other services. Offers of baby clothes and equipment, companionship, and help remembering other dimensions of her life are important to the new mother. Only a woman who is dealing with two crying infants knows the relief and gratitude toward the other concerned adult who picks up the second child.

The study shows that the husbands were generally emotionally supportive; were central to housework, child care, and reassurance; and were most frequently considered the best helpers. Only 14% of the mothers were either somewhat or very dissatisfied with assistance from their spouses.

What do all these positive ratings mean? The mother of twins club mythology suggests that having twins is a situation that can either make or break a marriage. The husband who leaves all the work to the wife and manages to put the marriage on the rocks was occasionally discussed. The favorite stories, however, were of husbands who had never helped with previous children, were forced into helping when the twins arrived, and then were glad to have been "hands-on" fathers.

There was also talk about adjusting to the mild stigma of birthing twins. The fathers were reported to have heard jokes about virility; the mothers discussed feeling animal-like, particularly if they were nursing. Thus, the author speculates that if the parents acknowledge each other as the co-conspirators of this cosmic joke, accept being the center of a circus, and can manage the work cooperatively, they may become tightly bonded and appreciative of each other in a new way. The husbands reported in this study seem to have entered into the spirit of the occasion.

CONCLUSIONS AND IMPLICATIONS

The questions raised and answered in this study may seem silly to mothers of twins. Mothers could have probably predicted that the meeting of needs is crucial but that having an emotionally supportive spouse is also central. Similarly, it must be obvious that knowing people and getting help are not the same thing, that a larger number of helpers makes for better help, and that those who give one kind of help don't necessarily give another.

Yet, given the brief history of the study of social support, the questions raised are important. The present study demonstrates that in the case of new mothers of twins, "general support" is not sufficient. Mothers of twins have specific needs, the meeting of which is related to a sense of well-being and comfort with mothering. Emotional support is insufficient. Instrumental and informational needs must also be met. Similarly there are not necessarily general helpers. Those who give child care do not clean house; those who reassure do not give information about twins.

One could criticize these findings on the basis that the ratings of both need and support received were phenomenological. It could be argued that subjects' ratings simply reflected a general sense of well-being or deficit and thus there were no true differences between need, support, and adjustment. While the study cannot offer proof to the contrary, the internal logic of the study suggests there were true differences. First, the measures for need, support, and adjustment were constructed quite differently. There is little possibility that subjects were in a structurally imposed response set. Second, since number of needs was negatively correlated to adjustment, if general deficit was all that was being measured by the study, one would expect at least some relationship between neediness and measures of support. In fact, there was no relationship between number of needs and husband emotional support. Having an emotionally supportive spouse did not protect a woman from experiencing concrete needs.

One implication for further research is that measures and methodology which have "leached over" from the study of social network and general epidemiology may not be the most appropriate for the study of situation-specific stressors. Examination of situational needs, how these needs are met, and who the helpers are, would seem fruitful. Better measures of what helps and who helps are needed.

The practical implications of this study for those involved with new mothers seem clear. For years there have been programs designed to educate pregnant women about prenatal care, birth preparedness, and infant care. This study recommends extending the concept of self-care to the postbirth period, and to include consideration of emotional, informational, practical as well as physical needs. Mothers and the general public should be educated that it is acceptable to actively organize on one's own behalf to get help.

REFERENCES

Ballinger, B., Buckley, D.E., Naylor, G.J., & Stansfield, D.A. (1979). Emotional disturbance following childbirth. *Psychological Medicine, 9,* 293–300.

Belle, D. (1979). *Social links and social support.* Working paper, Harvard University.

Berkman, L.F., & Syme, S.L. (1979). Social networks, host resistance, and mortality: a nine-year follow-up study of Alameda County residents. *American Journal of Epidemiology, 109* (2), 186–204.

Boesky, D., Cross, T.N., & Morley, G.W. (1960). Postpartum psychosis. *American Journal of Obstetrics and Gynecology, 80,* 1209–1217.

Borkman, T. (1979). *Mutual self-help groups: Strengthening the selectively unsupportive personal and community networks of their members.* Presented at American Public Health Association convention, Mental Health Section, New York.

Brandt, K.Y. (1968). What doctors now know about depressed young mothers. *Redbook.* 68–69.

Brown, G.W., & Harris, T. (1978). *Social origins of depression: A study of psychiatric disorder in women.* New York: Free Press.

Burke, R.J., & Weir, T. (1977). Marital helping relationships: The moderators between stress and well-being. *Journal of Psychology, 95,* 120–130.

Cassill, K. (1982). *Twins: Nature's amazing mystery.* New York: Atheneum.

Cohler, B.J. (1984). Personality, social context and adaptation to early motherhood. In R. Cohen, B.J. Cohler, & S. Weissman (Eds.), *Parenthood: A psychodynamic perspective.* New York: Guilford.

Cohler, B.J., & Lieberman, M.A. (1980). *Social relations and mental health among middle aged and older men and women from European ethnic groups.* Unpublished manuscript. The Committee on Human Development, University of Chicago.

Collier, H.L. (1974). *The psychology of twins.* Phoenix, AZ: Herbert Collier, Ph.D., Limited.

Derogatis, L.R., Lipman, R.S., Covi, L., & Rickles, K. (1971). Neurotic symptom dimensions. *Archives of General Psychiatry, 24,* 453–464.

Dyer, E.D. (1963). Parenthood as a crisis: A re-study. *Journal of Marriage and Family Living, 25,* 196–201.

Finlayson, A. (1976). Social networks as coping resources: Lay help and consultation patterns used by women in husbands' post-infarction career. *Social Science and Medicine, 10,* 97–108.

Gehman, B.X. (1965). *Twins: Twice the trouble, twice the fun.* New York: Lippincott.

Gore, S. (1978). The effect of social support in moderating the health consequences of unemployment. *Journal of Health and Social Behavior, 19,* 157–165.

Gosher-Gottstein, E.R. (1979). Family of twins: A longitudinal study of coping. *Twins: Newsletter of the International Society for Twin Studies, 2,* 4–5.

Gottlieb, B. (Ed.). (1981). *Social network and social support.* Beverly Hills, CA: Sage.

Hagedern, J., & Kizziar, J. (1974). *Gemini: The psychology and phenomena of twins.* Anderson, SC: Droke House/Hallux.

Hamburg, B., & Killilea, M. (1979). Relation of social support, stress, illness, and use of health services. In *Healthy people, The Surgeon General's report on health promotion and disease prevention background papers.* Washington, DC: Government Printing Office.

Hamburg, D., Adams, J., & Brodie, H.K.H. (1976). Coping behavior in stressful circumstances: Some implications for social psychiatry. In B.H. Kaplan, A.H. Leighton, & R.N. Wilson (Eds.), *Further explorations in social psychiatry.* New York: Basic Books.

Henderson, S., Byren, D.G., Duncan-Jones, P., Adcock, S., Scott, R., & Steele, G.P. (1977). Social bonds in the epidemiology of neurosis: A preliminary communication. *British Journal of Psychiatry, 132,* 463–466.

Hill, R. (1958). Social stresses on the family: Generic features of families under stress. *Social Casework, 39* (23), 139–150.

House, J.S. (1981). *Work, stress, and social support.* Reading, MA: Addison Wesley.

Illingworth, R. (1975). *The normal child: Some problems of early years and their treatment.* Edinburgh, Scotland: Churchill Livingstone.

Jacoby, A. (1969). Transition to parenthood: A reassessment. *Journal of Marriage and the Family, 31* (4), 720–727.

Larsen, V.L. (1966). Stresses of the child bearing year. *American Journal of Public Health, 56* (1), 32–36.

LeMasters, E.G. (1957). Parenthood as a crisis. *Journal of Marriage and Family Living, 19,* 352–355.

Lieberman, M.A. (1982). The effects of social support on responses to stress. In L. Goldberger, & S. Bernitz (Eds.), *Handbook of stress*. New York: Free Press.

Liefer, M. (1977). Psychological changes accompanying motherhood. *Genetic Psychology Monographs, 95,* 55–96.

Liem, R., & Liem, J.H. (1979). *Some general issues and their application to the problem of unemployment.* University of Massachusetts, Boston, working paper.

Lin, N., Ensel, W.M., Simeone, R.S., & Kuo, W. (1979). Social support, stressful life events and illness: A model and empirical test. *Journal of Health and Social Behavior, 20,* 108–119.

Massachusetts Mothers of Twins Association, Inc. (1967). *Twin care . . . in a nutshell.* Boston.

Menaghan, B. (1981). *Effects of family transitions on marital experience.* Unpublished doctoral dissertation, University of Chicago.

Miller, P.M., & Ingham, J.G. (1976). Friends, confidants, and symptoms. *Social Psychiatry, 11,* 51.

Neubauer, P.B. (1972). Twins. In A.M. Freedman, & H. Kaplan (Eds.), *The child: His psychology and cultural development* (Vol. 1). New York: Atheneum.

Novitski, E. (1977). *Human genetics.* New York: Macmillan.

Parkes, C.M. (1971). Psychosocial transitions: A field for study. *Social Sciences and Medicine, 5,* 101.

Plank, E. (1958). Reactions of mothers of twins in a child study group. *American Journal of Orthopsychiatry, 28,* 196–204.

Rapoport, R., & Rapoport, R. (1977). *Fathers, mothers, and society.* New York: Basic Books.

Richman, N. (1976). Depression in mothers of preschool children. *Journal of Child Psychology and Psychiatry, 17,* 75–78.

Rossi, A. Transition to parenthood. (1968). *Journal of Marriage and the Family, 30,* 26–39.

Scheinfeld, A. (1967). *Twins and supertwins.* New York: Lippincott.

Silverman, P.R., & Murrow, H.G. (1976). Mutual help during critical role transitions. *Journal of Applied Behavioral Sciences, 12* (3), 410–418.

Stack, C.B. (1974). *All our kin: Strategies for survival in a black community.* New York: Harper and Row.

Stein, H., & Wolner, T. (1978). *Parallels: A look at twins.* New York: Dutton.

Theroux, R.T., & Tingley, J.F. (1978). *The care of twin children.* Chicago: Center for Multiple Gestation.

Weiss, R.S. (1974). The provisions of social relationships. In *Doing unto others*, Rubin, Z. (Ed.) Cambridge: Harvard University Press.

Weiss, R.S. (1976). Transition states and other stressful situations: Their nature and programs for their management. In G. Caplan, & M. Killilea (Eds.), *Support systems and mutual help: Multidisciplinary explorations.* New York: Grune and Stratton.

Weissman, M.M., & Klerman, G.L. (1977). Sex differences and the epidemiology of depression. *Archives of General Psychiatry, 34,* 98–111.

CHAPTER 4
Parenting and Social Support Networks in Families of Term and Preterm Infants

C. F. Zachariah Boukydis
Children's Hospital and Harvard Medical School, Boston
Bradley Hospital and Women & Infants Hospital
and Brown University Medical School, Providence

Barry M. Lester
Bradley Hospital and Women & Infants Hospital
and Brown University Medical School, Providence

Joel Hoffman
Children's Hospital and Harvard Medical School, Boston

INTRODUCTION

Social support has been known to play an important role in the early adaptation between parent and infant. Following the stressful event of premature birth, there is a complex relationship between infant status, parent–infant interaction, and levels of social support. Our earlier research indicated that early infant attentional behavior, high levels of parent–infant interaction, and positive social support in the parents' immediate network of family and friends was correlated with amount of visiting to the neonatal intensive-care unit (NICU) (Minde et al., 1978; Boukydis, 1982; 1984). A group of mothers who scored higher on interactive behavior with their infants during visits, compared with a group who scored lower on interactive behavior, had infants who showed more attentional behavior during visits, had more contacts with family and friends during the hospitalization of their baby, had less disruption of the marital relationship, and visited their baby more frequently. This research served to delineate important factors connected with parental visiting to the NICU.

Generally, studies have shown that the increased availability of social support has positive influence on: (1) maternal outcome factors such as health status and psychiatric symptoms (Carveth & Gottlieb, 1979), and life satisfaction (Crnic, Greenberg, Ragozin, Robinson, & Basham, 1983); (2) factors indicative of optimal infant development (Parks, Jenkins, Lenz, Jarrett, & Neal, 1984) including more secure exploration of the environment in toddlers (Howes & Olenick, 1984) and higher Stanford–Binet scores in 3- to 5-year-olds (Burchinal, Bryant, & Sparling, 1984); and (3) mother–infant interactive behavior such as increased affectional and growth-promoting efforts by adolescent mothers (Colletta, 1981) and mothers of term and preterm babies (Crnic et al., 1983). One important area of research on social support and early parenting involves the examination of the relationship between variations in infant status and the composition and functioning of the parents' social network (Crockenberg, 1981; Crnic, et al., 1983; Wandersman & Unger, 1983; Feiring, 1985; Parke & Tinsley, 1985).

1. Relationship between Temperament and Social Support

Differences in early infant temperament place different demands on parental adaption and potentially create different parental needs for social support. Work by Crockenberg (1981) highlighted the relationship between early infant temperament, maternal responsiveness, and social support for parents in the developing parent–child relationship. Crockenberg's work was an integration of different levels of data collection from the fields of child development and family sociology (behavioral observations of mother–infant interaction, temperament ratings, and questionnaires) which provided new information as to different life situations in which social support was most necessary, and potentially effective. Basically, Crockenberg's work showed that adequate social support in the early months was the best predictor of secure attachment at one year of age, and that the effects of social support were most important for mothers with irritable babies. The situation of having low levels of social support and an irritable baby in the early months was most likely to predict insecure attachment and stress in the maternal-child relationship at 1 year of age.

Wandersman and Unger (1983) examined the role of social support for adolescent mothers and found, similar to Crockenberg (1981), that social support from fathers and relatives was crucial in helping those mothers who had difficult temperament infants. Again, this relationship did not appear for mothers of easy-temperament infants.

2. Relationship between Infant Risk Status and Social Support

A few studies have examined the differential effects of social support on the parent–infant relationship in populations of infants varying in risk status. Crnic et al. (1983) were able to assess the relationship between social support and stress on early maternal attitudes and mother–infant interactive behavior in mothers of healthy preterm and fullterm infants. Overall, they found few differences between mothers of term and preterm infants on social support, maternal stress, or parent–infant interaction measures. The lack of differences may have been due to the health status of the preterm infants, and adequate hospital-based support for early parenting. In their analysis, there were several instances where social support had a main effect, predicting satisfaction with parenting or clarity of interactive cues from babies. In relation to predicting general life satisfaction from early stress, social support had a moderator effect. When there was high stress, with low social support, this led to lower levels of later life satisfaction.

The work of Feiring (1985) gives some indication of the influence of infant risk status and health on the response of the social network. Feiring examined the relationship between social support (material goods, services, money, or advice from family and friends) and parent–infant interaction with mothers of either healthy or sick, term and preterm infants. In general, mothers of sick infants reported receiving the least services (baby-sitting, household care), while mothers of sick preterm infants specifically, reported receiving the least material goods. Mothers of sick premature infants reported fewer friends, and fewer total number of people giving material help, than mothers in the other groups. There were relationships between provision of goods and services and mother–infant interactive behavior at three months. Mothers of healthy infants, who received more services, appeared more playful during observed interaction, while mothers of sick infants who received more services were more "proximal" to their infants during interactions. One implication from this research is that mothers of sick preterm infants reported social networks of decreased size. Also, caring for the needs of parents by providing goods and services indirectly affected the parent–infant relationship—probably by giving parents more time with their baby by having other household responsibilities taken care of.

Bronfenbrenner (1979) has portrayed an ecological model which points to the role of different configurations in the child's familial and community networks which affect the child's expanding exchanges or transactions (Sameroff & Chandler, 1975) with the social environment. Research of the type reported in this chapter which compares and contrasts different populations of babies, and network factors which evolve around caring for these babies, is one attempt to examine how individual differences in infants affect demands on the parental, familial, and social network. Concurrently, this research examines how the given networks at a child's birth respond differentially to varying early care-taking patterns necessitated by the infant's status.

3. Neonatal Behavior and Parental Networks

Two decades of research using the Brazelton Neonatal Behavioral Assessment Scale (NBAS; Brazelton, 1984) has examined: (1) differences in early functioning in different population of infants; (2) the relationship between early infant status, as indicated by the scale, and parent–infant interaction; (3) and the relationship between early functioning and later child development (Lester, 1984). Little work has been done which examines the relationship between dimensions of infant behavioral functioning as tapped by the scale, and parents' informal and formal networks. The research presented in this chapter allowed us to begin the examination of some of these relationships.

CURRENT RESEARCH ON NETWORKS OF PARENTS
OF TERM AND PRETERM INFANTS

1. Two Anecdotes

Anecdotal evidence from our work indicated that the range of social support available to parents was quite broad. One of our smallest premies was born to a couple who lived in Gloucester, a coastal fishing town some 45 miles from the intensive care unit in Boston. The baby was confined in hospital for almost 7 weeks, and there were no serious medical complications during this period of time. On the day of the baby's premature birth, the baby's paternal grandmother called a meeting of the extended family in her house. Fifty-four people attended this meeting. A schedule was organized during this meeting whereby someone drove the parents to Boston each day. Child care was arranged for the other four children in the family. All meals and household chores during the infant's hospitalization were taken care of by relatives. A 24-hour schedule was developed so that someone in the family would be available to the parents in case of emergency. A modified form of this plan was carried on after the infant was brought home from hospital. The organization of extended family resources combined the available resources we might expect from a naturally occurring network with the planning of family resources in crisis evident in the strategies employed by family-systems-oriented community workers (Speck & Attneave, 1973). Interviews with the parents indicated another dimension of their response to this organized family network. The mother said that she felt she and her husband appreciated and needed the help, but also that things were set up so that people allowed them all the time they needed to themselves. They knew people were concerned and available. Again, part of this psychological distance was served by the grandmother who acted as a daily nexus for calls of concern about the infant's condition from members of the family and friendship network.

On the other extreme from this organized extended family was a mother who had a 32-week gestational age premie. The baby had a relatively stable course during hospitalization, but was extremely irritable after arriving home. The baby's father was an artist who left, after a week of the infant's unconsolable crying at night, to live in his studio. The mother held on for two weeks waiting for her mother to arrive from far away. Most of the mother's close friends were in another city. She reported having telephone contact, but no backup except a neighbor who watched the baby while the mother went shopping. When the grandmother finally arrived, she stayed one night and left the next day to visit relatives in another town. It was at this point that the mother asked for the help of the hospital follow-up staff in finding resources to help back her up in caring for her irritable baby. She felt too isolated and was not getting enough help from family and friends.

The two anecdotes are in some respects extremes, but they also present some of the complexities involved in studying social support (Gottlieb, 1983; Cochran & Brassard, 1979). Over the years, we have seen that having more network members is not necessarily an adequate index of social support (Belle, 1981). The "organized" extended family situation was adequate in the mother's terms because it was organized in such a way as to ensure that she and her husband had enough private time and a measure of control over their separate lives. The mother with an irritable infant was able to cope for three weeks with few resources as long as she had the expectation that her mother would be coming to help her. Recent writing on the study of social support has called for measures which take into account personal estimates of the adequacy of support, and expectations or violations of expectations, about what constitutes adequate support. Our interviews with parents provided support for the development of this kind of empirical effort, extending from not only personal estimates of the adequacy of support, but personal attributions for what constituted support, and personal weightings of "positive" and "negative" factors.

2. Current Research

In the research reported in this chapter, we had the opportunity to compare and contrast network factors indicative of social support in families of term and healthy preterm infants. We were able to inquire about the role of informal support (spouse, family, and friends) and formal support (ongoing contacts with health care providers, community service agencies). Further, in response to the growing body of literature on the importance of peer support in certain populations of parents, we attempted to question the role of contact with other parents, and participation in some form of parenting network, in the transition to parenthood. Finally, we were able to examine the importance of some factors associated with early infant behavior and status (along with individual differences in temperamental characteristics in both populations of term and preterm infants) on parents' social networks. In the next section, we present preliminary analyses on a limited sample of families from our ongoing work.

METHODS

Sample

As part of an ongoing study on the behavioral and physiological development of preterm and term infants[1], we interviewed parents about issues related to social support, infant temperament, and the transition to parenthood. Information reported in this section arises from a sample of 13 families of healthy preterm babies, and 14 families of term babies. The preterm infants were less than 34 weeks gestational age (average gestational age at birth $M = 32.4$ weeks); were appropriate weight for gestational age (average weight at birth; $M = 1,813$ grams); and were hospitalized for an average of 27.2 days following birth. Preterm infants were healthy, and did not require ventilatory assistance following birth, or have intracranial bleeds. Apgar scores averaged 4.9 at 1 minute after birth, and 6.9 at 5 minutes after birth.

The average gestational age at birth for fullterm babies was 40.2 weeks. Fullterm babies were appropriate weight for gestational age (average weight at birth; $M = 3,351$ grams); and were in hospital for an average of 2.8 days following birth. Apgar scores averaged 8.3 at 1 minute after birth, and 9.0 at 5 minutes after birth. In the families of

[1] March of Dimes Birth Defects Foundation: Social and behavioral sciences research grant. #12-31—awarded to Barry M. Lester, Principal Investigator; "Physiological correlates of the organization of behavior in preterm and fullterm infants."

preterm infants, 6 were primiparas, and 7 were multiparas. In families of term infants, 10 were primiparas, and 4 were multiparas. All families ranged from lower- to upper-middle class (on the Hollingshead 4-factor index). Families of fullterm infants did not differ significantly from families of preterm infants on the social class index. All families were English-speaking, and parents lived together at the time of the study.

The study allowed us to question the situation for parents of relatively healthy preterm infants, all of whom had a stable hospital course, but who by virtue of their prematurity were an ongoing cause for concern to the parents. Inclusion of families of healthy fullterm babies allowed us to compare factors involved with neonatal behavior, social support, early temperament, and the transition to parenthood in the two sets of families.

Procedures

All infants were assessed on the Brazelton Neonatal Assessment Scale (Brazelton, 1984), while heart rate, respiratory activity, and cry acoustics were recorded (Lester, 1985). Preterm infants were assessed at discharge, 40, 42, and 44 weeks gestational age. Fullterm infants were assessed at 40, 42, and 44 weeks gestational age. Mothers, and most fathers, attended the examinations. Following the 44-week exam, parents were interviewed and completed the following questionnaire material: the Infant Characteristics Questionnaire (Bates, Bennett-Freeland, & Lounsbury, 1979); the Transition to Parenthood Questionnaire (Wente & Crockenberg, 1976); network size (the number of people—family and friends—seen in the previous month); number of contacts with friends and relatives, types of instrumental and emotional help from relatives and friends; number of day units helped by friends and relatives, number of visits and calls to health professionals; spousal help with child care and household chores; self-generated rating of factors which were: helpful with parenting, information about child care, what would have been helpful; self-rating of experience, and contact with parents with children similar to yours (preterm/term).

RESULTS

1. Families with Term versus Preterm Infants

Initially, we wanted to examine overall differences in patterns of support between families of preterm and term infants. As might be expected, parents of preterm infants (P), compared with parents of term infants (T), made significantly more visits to health-care professionals $(Mp = 6.0; Mt = 1.7; p = .01)$, and made use of significantly more kinds of services ($Mp = 2.85$; $Mt = 1.57$; $p = .01$) in the first month following discharge from hospital. There were no differences between families of term and preterm infants in the average number of *calls* to health care professionals. As we will see, the number of calls was strongly related to variables tapping behavioral responsiveness and early temperament of the babies, regardless of whether the infants were term or preterm.

Parents of preterm infants reported receiving significantly more emotional support from friends *in general* ($Mp = 1.5$; $Mt = .64$; $p = .05$) during the first month post discharge of their baby from the hospital. Both sets of parents reported receiving equivalent amounts of emotional support and help with household chores or child care from their relatives. It was in the area of emotional support from friends in general, not necessarily friends with children, where the parents of preterm infants reported more overall help. Families with preterm and term infants had networks of equivalent sizes and on the average reported a comparable number of contacts and visits with family and friends during the first month that their baby was home.

When parents were asked whether they had any contact with parents of a baby similar to theirs in the first month (post hospital discharge), more parents of term infants reported having had some contact with other parents who had had babies similar to theirs. Parents of preterm infants, however, who *had* come to know someone with a preterm infant, had a significantly higher number of actual contacts with these parents.

Parents were asked to rate for themselves: (1) what kinds of people or services were most helpful; (2) where they obtained child-care information about their baby; and (3) what kinds of people or services would have been helpful. The responses that were given most frequently for parents of term versus preterm infants were ranked and are indicated on Table 1. From the rankings it is possible to get an indication of the subjective weighting that parents gave to different sources of support and information.

One main theme is the importance that parents of preterm infants place on medical staff as sources of support, extending beyond hospitalization, during the first month post discharge of their baby. Parents of term infants listed their friends with children, their pediatrician, and their own mother respectively as the most helpful during the first month; and books, friends with children, and parenting classes, respectively, as the most important sources of information about child care. Parents of preterm infants listed their pediatrician, pediatric nurse, and spouse as most helpful; and the intensive care nursery staff, other parents of premature babies, and their child's pediatrician as the most important sources of information about child care. When asked what kinds of

Table 1.

	Term	Preterm
What kinds of people and services have been most helpful?		
1st	Friends with kids	Pediatrician
2nd	Pediatrician	Pediatric nurse
3rd	Own mother	Spouse
4th	Parenting class	Parents of prematures
5th	Pediatric nurse	Own mother
6th	Relative	Friends (general)* VNA*
7th	Spouse	
8th	Books* In-laws*	Relatives
9th		In-laws
10th	Friends (general)	Friends with kids, sister, breastfeeding class, own experience, research team*
Where did you get information about child care?		
1st	Books	ICU staff
2nd	Friends with kids	Parent of prematures
3rd	Parenting class	Pediatrician
4th	Own mother	Previous experience
5th	Previous experience	Books
6th	Relatives	Own mother
7th	Nurse	Nurse* Friends (general)*
8th	Friends (general)* Pediatrician*	
9th		Relatives
10th	Breastfeeding class	Parenting class
What kinds of people/services would have been helpful?		
1st	Hired help	Other parents of prematures
2nd	Other parents	Hired help
3rd	Health professionals	Health professionals* Own mother*
4th	Parenting class* Nutritionist*	
5th		VNA after baby is born
6th	Own mother* Pediatrician* VNA after baby is born*	More books on prematurity

* = Tied.

people or services *would* have been helpful, both groups of parents indicated the need for more hired help, more contact with other parents of babies like theirs, and more contact with knowledgeable health professionals.

Major variables in the study had different relationships for families with term versus preterm infants. For families with term infants, parental perception of infant fussy/difficultness (ICQ) was significantly related to total adjustment difficulty. Having a fussy/difficult infant was related to having more adjustment difficulty (r/t = .49; p = .05). For families with preterm infants, network size was significantly related to total adjustment difficulty. Having a smaller network was related to having more adjustment difficulty in the transition to parenthood. Also, parents with smaller networks received more instrumental help from relatives (r = −.62; p = .02). Average network size, average rating of temperamental difficulties, and total adjustment difficulty did not differ significantly between families with term versus preterm infants.

For parents of term infants, the number of services contacted in the first month was negatively correlated with network size (r = .53; p = .04), such that parents with smaller networks tended to contact more services. This relationship was not true for parents of preterm infants, where there was less variability in the number of services contacted, and as indicated, a greater average (per family) number of services contacted. Further, in families with term infants, total adjustment difficulty was inversely related to the number of calls to health professionals (r = −.51; p = .05). Those parents who reported less overall adjustment difficulty in becoming parents were making more calls in the first month.

For parents of preterm infants, having contact with parents of babies similar to theirs was negatively correlated with the number of calls to health professionals (r = −.92; p = .002), indicating that those parents who had contact with other parents of preterm babies made fewer calls to health professionals during the first month after their babies' discharge from hospital.

Parents of fullterm infants who were making a higher number of visits to their pediatrician or pediatric nurse practitioner were also receiving more help from their friends in child care and household care tasks (r = .54; p = .04). Further, parents who were having more adjustment difficulty were also receiving more instrumental and emotional support from relatives (r^{i} = .52, p = .05; r^{e} = .67; p = .008). With the strong relationship between adjustment difficulty and the temperamental status of the infant, we might question whether these parents were drawing more on the resources of their family to cope with the situation of having a temperamentally difficult infant.

2. Total Adjustment Difficulty

Overall comparisons did not show any difference between parents of term and preterm infants in the absolute level of adjustment difficulty. With separate questions on the total adjustment difficulty questionnaire, parents of preterm infants had significantly more concerns about friends

Table 2.   Intercorrelations of Separate Items with Overall TAD Score

Item	Term	Preterm	Overall
Baby's crying	.54*	.31	.42*
Missing sleep	.72**	.86**	.80**
Less time for job	.44	.69**	.56**
Less time for other children	.30	.11	.001
Spouse has less time with me	.64**	.85**	.76**
Being tied down to home	.65**	.71**	.65**
Having to change long-range plans	.23	.68**	.45*
Additional expenses	.60*	.89**	.74**
Spouse and I have less time together	.69**	.71**	.69**
Need more knowledge about parenting	.55*	.37	.45*
Less income/spouse working less	.28	.75**	.52**
Changing diapers	.46	.35	.38*
Feeding the baby	.27	.65**	.49**
Visits from friends and relatives	.28	.32	.24
Change in relationship with spouse	.81**	.45	.63**
More cooking/housework	.12	.55*	.27

*p = .05; **p = .01.

and relatives visiting (Xp = 3.6; Xt = 2.28; p = .04). Table 2 indicates the correlations between the total adjustment difficulty score for all parents, and for parents of term and preterm infants taken separately. This strategy was used by Wente and Crockenberg (1976) and Boukydis (1985b) to examine the contribution that different areas of concern may have in influencing the overall transition to parenthood.

Concerns represented by separate items on the total adjustment difficulty questionnaire were significantly related to network factors and infant temperament. For families with preterm infants, Table 3 indicates significant relationships between network size, temperament, and separate adjustment-difficulty items.

As expected, those parents who reported less experience with babies had more concerns about needing more knowledge about parenting (r = .59; p = .03) and they also had more concerns about how to manage having less time with other children (r = .75; p = .004). Those parents who made higher numbers of calls to professionals were also more concerned about changes in their relationship with their spouses after their infant came home from hospital (r = .55; p = .05).

For families with term infants, Table 3 indicates significant relationships between calls to health professionals, infant temperament, and individual adjustment-difficulty items. Those parents with smaller networks reported more concerns about changes in their relationship after their child was born (r = .52; p = .05).

3. Neonatal Behavioral Assessment Scale
and Network Factors

Our examination of factors connected with neonatal assessment and features of parents' networks at 1 month indicated several important relationships. We report data from the discharge exam, because this marked an equivalent phase for families of term and preterm babies where the baby was about to leave hospital for home, and where we could examine relationships in network factors an equivalent time period from the time of discharge. For term infants, quality of alert responsivity, examiner persistence during the exam, range of states, and a summary score indicative of temperament (Lester, Emory, & Hoffman, 1976) were highly correlated with both the number of contacts with family and friends and the number of visits to health professionals. It appeared to be the robust and energetic infant, with a wide range of states, who demanded more examiner effort during the exam, who was taken more to health professionals, and who was in families who reported receiving more instrumental help from families and friends.

Table 3.   Relations between Adjustment Difficulty Items
and Major Variables

Group	Relation between Variables	Correlation Coefficient
Preterm	Smaller network size with more concern about:	
	Infant sleeping patterns	.54*
	Tied down to home	.54*
	Change long-range plans	.64*
	Additional expenses	.77**
	Knowledge about parenting	.53*
	Less income/spouse not working	.76**
	Changing diapers	.58*
Preterm	More difficult temperament with more concern about:	
	Getting enough sleep	.59*
	Less time for job	.53*
	Less time for other children	.76**
	Worries about extra expense	.58*
	Tied down to home	.55*
	Change long-range plans	.54*
Term	More frequent calls with more concern about:	
	Concerns about crying	.67**
	Less time with spouse	.67**
	Less time for other children	.57*
	Worries about visits	.58*
Term	More difficult temperament with more concern about:	
	Getting enough sleep	.62**
	Worries about extra expense	.59*

*p = .05; **p = .01.

Looking at number of services, visits to services, and calls to health-care professionals, Table 4 indicates the NBAS scale clusters, or supplementary items, which were significantly correlated. The pattern was considerably different for families with preterm infants. Our impression was that it was the infant who scored lower on the state, and attentional, system clusters, with a wider range of scores on reflexes, and who also had higher scores on quality of alert responsivity, orientation (especially inanimate visual and auditory orientation), who was taken to more services, and more visits to health professionals during the first month. It was families with these infants who reported more instrumental and emotional help from friends in general during the first month.

Table 4. Relations between NBAS Items and Types of Contact with Services

NBAS Cluster or Supplementary Item	Type of Contact	Correlation Coefficient
Term		
Quality of response	# of services	.51*
	# of visits	.66**
Range of reflexes	# of calls	.61*
Need for facilitation	# of visits	.62*
Quality of alert response	# of calls	.54*
Examiner persistence	# of visits	.65**
	# of calls	.53*
Range of state	# of visits	.57*
Regulation of state	# of visits	.59*
Temperamental cluster	# of visits	.70**
Preterm		
State system	# of services	.56*
Attentional system	# of services	.55*
	# of visits	−.60*
Range of reflexes	# of services	.70**
	# of visits	.62*
Quality of response	# of services	.63**
	# of visits	.65**
Inanimate visual & auditory	# of services	.68**
	# of visits	.64**
Quality of alert response	# of services	.54*
Orientation	# of services	.62*
Motor	# of services	.64**
Autonomic regulation	# of calls	.58*

*p = .05; **p = .01.

Looking at the number of services, visits and calls to health professionals alone, Table 4 indicates the NBAS scale cluster or qualifiers which were significantly correlated.

4. Infant Temperament

Overall comparisons indicated that average temperamental-difficultness ratings did not differ between term and preterm infants. At 42 weeks, preterm infants were more likely to be seen on the *extremes* as either easy or difficult, while term infants were more likely to be seen as either average or difficult. At 44 weeks, preterm infants were almost equally likely to be seen as easy, average, or difficult; while ratings of term infants remained the same: term infants were more likely to be seen as either average or difficult.

There were important relationships between parents' perception of their baby's temperament, adjustment difficulty, and network factors. As indicated previously, infant temperamental difficultness was significantly correlated with total adjustment difficulty, for parents of term infants; and with more concerns about getting enough sleep, and family financial worries. Parents of fullterm infants, who reported a higher number of contacts with parents of babies similar to theirs, tended to see their own infant as less temperamentally difficult ($r/t = .69$; $p = .006$). Similarly, parents of preterm infants, who also had contact with parents of babies similar to their own, tended to see their own infants as less temperamentally difficult ($r/p = .60$; $p = .009$). Parents of preterm infants who reported less instrumental and emotional help from their relatives tended to see their infants as more temperamentally difficult ($r/p = -.53$; $p = .05$). Parents, in this population, who saw their baby as more difficult reported more overall contacts with friends and family ($r/p = .76$; $p = .02$). Those parents of preterm infants who reported more experience with child care saw their babies as less temperamentally difficult ($r/p = -.60$; $p = .02$).

For both parents of term and preterm infants, ratings of temperamental difficultness at 42 weeks gestational age were significantly correlated with temperament ratings at 44 weeks ($r/p = .60$; $p = .03$, $r/t = .69$; $p = .006$).

5. Paternal Involvement

Initially, we created a summary variable that took into account relative frequencies of paternal involvement in household and child-care activities during typical weekdays and weekends. No family had the father as a primary caretaker. In terms of the summary variable, the average levels of paternal involvement were equivalent for fathers of term and preterm infants. Table 5 indicates percentages of paternal involvement in different kinds of activities and compares fathers of term and preterm infants.

In families with preterm infants, those people who reported higher levels of total adjustment difficulty also tended to have more overall paternal involvement (r = .54; p = .05). In families with term infants, high levels of paternal involvement were correlated with families who had: (1) lower numbers of contacts with family and friends during the first months (r = −.54; p = .04); (2) less contact with health services (r = −.54; p = .04); (3) less contact with relatives (r = −.57; p = .03), and less instrumental help from relatives (r = −.52; p = .05); and (4) less maternal experience with infant care (r = −.67; p = .007).

Generally, patterns of paternal involvement were similar in the two populations, with fathers increasing their level of involvement in both child care and household tasks on weekends. In families with preterm infants, overall paternal involvement was highly correlated with doing household chores during the week; while in families with term infants, overall paternal involvement was significantly correlated with doing both household and child-care tasks during the week. Further, in families with term infants paternal involvement was significantly related to fathers who were more likely to get up and soothe their crying infant when both parents were together in the household.

Table 5.   Percentage Paternal Involvement in Child Care/Household Tasks

Task	Term Percentage	Preterm Percentage
Child care during week	21	15
Child care during weekend	35	37
Housework during week	29	18
Housework during weekend	35	38
Responds to crying	37	29
Changes diapers	34	29
Puts baby to bed	33	28

DISCUSSION

As indicated in the results, parents of preterm babies made more visits to health professionals and were involved with more services than parents of fullterm babies. However, calls to health professionals related more strongly to factors connected with the infants' state organization and behavioral responsiveness than risk status per se, and were correlated with different features of the parents' social network. Parents of term babies, who made more calls to health professionals, had less overall adjustment difficulty. Parents of preterms, who had contact with other parents who had preterm babies, made fewer calls to health professionals. Calling (depending on the availability of resources) may have a different function than scheduled visits to health professionals, and may serve in part, to relieve immediate concern or stress, when something happens in the daily care of an infant. The advent of call hours in pediatricians' offices, and of parenting "warmlines" is one form of response to the concern. Parents of fullterms, whom we would expect to have ups and downs in their worries, but less "chronic" underlying worry compared with a parent of a preterm baby, may have some concerns alleviated by being able to call somebody—in this case a health professional. So potentially, parents of fullterms who called more had less overall adjustment difficulty. Some parents of preterms reported saving their more "serious" concerns for health professionals and making use of other parents who had had premies to discuss day-to-day matters about infant care, their immediate feelings, and their babies' development. Those parents who didn't know anyone who had a premie were the ones who made more frequent calls to health professionals about daily concerns.

Telephone calling is one way in which people attempt to reduce social isolation, and calling deserves attention in the literature as an alternative form of negotiating social support. Many parenting networks serving geographically diverse populations match parents in local areas, and these people may have a high proportion of their contact over the telephone; because, especially when their infant is young, it is difficult to visit or attend meetings.

In our work we have begun to develop a profile of the infant in terms of the assessment of neonatal behavior which may eventually predict early extended use of health professionals, and demand different kinds of response from the familial and friendship network. The profile we tentatively suggest in the results differs noticeably for term and preterm infants. It was the energetic, "all over the place" (in terms of changes of states), temperamentally demanding term infant who required more examiner management, and who was taken more frequently to health professionals. These babies were also in families who reported receiving more help from family and friends in the first month. For preterm infants, it was the infant who had lower scores in the state and attentional systems, yet who also scored higher on some orientation items, who was taken to more services. This may be an indication of greater variability, and less predictability, in behavioral functioning. If this was the case, parents may have felt that they required extra help in understanding and managing these babies during the first months at home.

One important source of support for preterm parents was friends in general, potentially more so than for the fullterm parents in our study. Many parents of preterm babies have discussed the problems, including violations of expectations (baby showers are postponed, birth announcements are not sent out), associated with giving birth to a preterm baby. In this instance, with particular people in the preterm parents' family and friendship networks, receiving support is not simply unconditional and positive. The rise of the popular literature on prematurity, including several books written by parents for parents (Nance, 1982; Harrison, 1983) gives credence to the difficulties parents face dealing with their feelings and in contacts with their families and friends. Parents quite often have to deal with the feelings of other people they are close to about the premature baby and worry about whether, and how, to disclose their own feelings. This doesn't mean we can say that kin relations are somehow less important for parents of premies, or even that because of the difficulties mentioned that parents of preterm babies get less support from kin. Both groups of parents reported similar levels of instrumental and emotional support from relatives. However, coming to terms with the birth of the baby and the reality of ongoing worries requires more effort in long-term intimate relationships. For some parents, it may be easier to initially receive different kinds of support from people, friends in general, who are somewhat less involved than kin with the parents and with issues around accepting the premature baby.

The attempt to explicate this finding forces our empirical understanding of social support from a benign or positive orientation to a dialectical or transactional mode which accounts for both positive and negative factors, and the complex trade-offs which sometimes appear in receiving or giving support. For instance, single mothers' perceptions of their children were most strongly affected by the number of "difficult" kin (Campbell & Cochran, 1983). Research differentiating positive and negative network characteristics has indicated that the strength of negative factors predict outcomes, such as general well-being, more strongly than do positive factors (Rook, 1984; Fiore, Becker, & Coppel, 1983).

Parents of preterm and term infants reported similar-size networks in the first month post discharge from the hospital. In other literature, some researchers have found smaller networks for parents of disabled children (Friedrich & Friedrich, 1981; Dunst, Trivette, & Cross, 1985). One assumption from this work is that parents of disabled children must put more effort into caring for their child and have less time and energy for broader social contact. With our sample of parents, it could be that from the point of actual birth, the overall contacts with family and friends had expanded for parents of preterm babies to end up looking similar in size to those of parents of fullterm babies in the first month after birth. However, the parents of fullterms' networks may expand beyond this point as their babies get older, and the parents of preterms' networks may have stabilized, or condensed over time. A longitudinal study may have highlighted factors connected with expansion or contraction in parents' networks.

One main finding from our work was the relationship between network size and total adjustment difficulty for parents of preterms. Previously, we discussed the complex trade-offs possible for parents of premies in receiving support. Parents with smaller networks had more adjustment difficulty and were receiving more instrumental help—but not necessarily more perceived emotional help—from relatives. Also, parents with smaller networks reported more worries about having relatives and friends visit. Generally, parents of preterm babies have ongoing worries about having their child contract respiratory infection from people visiting especially in the first month post hospital discharge (Minde et al., 1978; Goldberg & Divitto, 1979). The worries about visiting may have been a compound of health factors and dealing with people's complicated feelings and worries for their baby at a time when parents were invested in adjusting to life at home with a baby who, up until several weeks previously, had required specialized 24-hour care in a hospital.

Future work in this area should take into account how much parents over time self-select their regular supportive contacts to include people, family or friends, whom they find maximally supportive. This includes the need for a developmental perspective where different transition periods in the infant's development, and in the infant-parent relationship, will affect different relations, or exchanges with the parents' informal and formal networks over time. One interpretation of Crockenberg's (1981) work is that infants at 2 to 3 months are going through a period of behavioral and physiological reorganization—what Emde calls a biobehavioral shift (Emde, Gaensbauer, & Harmon, 1976). This period is when colic is most commonly diagnosed. During this period, those parents with irritable babies who made adequate accommodations with their informal networks (who got support they found helpful), moved through this period to establish what appeared to be secure attachment relations between parents and infants at 1 year of age. In addition, the conflict about visiting for parents of premies where they are concerned about their baby's exposure to infections requires a look at accommodations to this problem (phone calls, etc.) and even seasonal variations (more difficulty during winter "flu" season) in types of contacts with family and friends.

There were several findings which indicated the value of peer support, particularly for parents of preterm infants. While more parents of fullterm babies indicated having had contact with the parent of "a baby like ours" in the previous month, those parents of preterm infants who knew someone with a baby like theirs had a higher number of contacts with these parents. The self-ratings (see Table 1) of *people or services most helpful* and *information about child care* indicated the relative importance of peer contact and participation in parent groups or networks for all parents in our sample—especially the parents of preterm infants. As indicated, those parents of premies who had contact with another parent of a premie also made fewer calls to health professionals. Our data did not specify whether peer contact meant parents currently with a baby, or "veteran" parents, who had previously had a baby similar to one's own. However, interviews with parents of preterms indicated that, of those parents having contact, half had contact with both current parents and veteran parents in a volunteer network for parents of premature infants; and the other half of the sample had contact with either a current parent or a veteran parent. The benefits of peer support as an extension of sources supporting early parenting has been discussed at length elsewhere (Boukydis, 1982, 1984, 1985a, 1986) and forms the basis for several chapters in this book which discuss interventions aimed at strengthening parents' informal social networks (see chapters in this book by Glaser, Wandersman, Cherniss, Parke, & Tinsley, Cowan, & Cowan).

The information in Table 1 involving the self-rating of information about child care and people or services most helpful gives some indication of the relative importance of relatives, friends, and resources such as books, films, and parenting classes, as sources of support. Formal instruction about parenting and written material teaching parenting skills (books, pamphlets) have actually been in existance for several centuries (Hardyment, 1983). However, with the increasing distance of parents from their family of origin, there has been discussion of these resources as additions to, not replacements for, the spectrum of support for early parenting. One grandmother in our study attempted to accommodate for overwhelming distance between herself and her daughter by mailing helpful material about parenting. Upon hearing of the preterm birth and the stable condition of daughter and granddaughter, the grandmother rushed to a local bookstore in her town in California, found one of the new books on parenting preterm babies, and express mailed the book to her daughter who was still in hospital in Boston.

For parents of fullterm infants, infant temperamental difficultness was significantly correlated with total adjustment difficulty; such that having a fussy-difficult infant was related to having more adjustment difficulty. This relationship was similar to the results from another study (Boukydis, 1985) where parents of 2- to 3-month-old fullterm infants rated the temperament of their baby during research on cry perception. In this study, parental perception of infant difficultness on the fussy/difficult dimension of the ICQ was significantly correlated with overall adjustment difficulty for primiparous and multiparous mothers, and for multiparous fathers. Further, factors such as concerns about baby's crying, and getting enough sleep, were significantly related to total adjustment difficulty in both samples. We expected that parental perception of infant temperament might also be significantly related to overall adjustment difficulty with parents of preterms. There is evidence in the literature that preterm infants become less predictable and more fussy on transferring from hospital to home (Goldberg & Divitto, 1979). In the present sample, even though the average fussy/difficult rating was similar for parents of preterm and term infants, the variability of ratings was less in the preterm group. Preliminary analyses of sleep/wake/feed/fuss daily records indicate that preterm babies were more variable and less predictable in daily cycles during the first months at home. The fussy/difficult dimension focused on crying and consolability. It might be the unpredictability in daily patterning in premies that taxed parents and related more strongly to perceptions of overall adjustment difficulty.

Involvement of the father was important for mothers of term and preterm infants. For parents of preterm infants, the cumulative index of father participation was significantly related to overall adjustment difficulty—such that in families where father participated more, mothers reported less overall adjustment difficulty. Also, the subjective weightings of sources of support indicated the relative importance of the father, especially in families with preterm babies. The data in the study were not extensive enough to provide an empirical test of the relative importance of fathers, compared with other significant people, as sources of support. However, following on the discussion of special issues in the negotiation of supportive relations with kin and close friends in families with preterm infants, it might be the case that the role of the father was more concentrated and important in the transition from the period of hospitalization to the achieving of a successful balance with the preterm baby at home.

Other literature (Parke, Hymel, Power, & Tinsley, 1980) has discussed the role of the father, especially during the early period after preterm birth, when the mother may be confined in a local hospital and separated from her transported baby. The father may act to transmit emotionally charged information on the baby's condition to the mother, and this early crisis involvement may effect different patterns in father participation later on, potentially during the transition period from hospital to home. Our data suggest a slightly different pattern of overall involvement for fathers of term and preterm babies. The highly involved father of a preterm was more likely to do household chores (during weekdays), while the highly involved father of a term infant took up both household and child-care responsibilities. The pattern for fathers of preterm babies reflects a possible back-up pattern where the mother was able to, or required to, concentrate on the needs of the preterm baby. Other data suggest that the preterm babies were more unpredictable in daily patterns of sleeping, feeding, and crying, and couples may have taken on a strategy of the mother becoming a "baby-cue-reading specialist" during the first month at home.

CONCLUSION

The interpretation we have given to research on social support and early parenting points to the need for a developmental perspective on the parent–infant relationship, including an examination of how individual differences in infant behavior necessitate different types of exchanges with parents' informal and formal networks. This calls for more repeated measures designs, and longitudinal work interrelating child development and patterns of social support. It is necessary to tap the existing networks around the time a child is born and examine the complex exchanges that take place around providing for the caretaking needs in the family. Our review of the work on individual differences in infants, based on neonatal behavior, risk status, and temperamental characteristics, accentuates the fact that different babies (during particular phases of development) make unique demands on parents and their accessible networks.

Future work should also take into consideration different members' views of the same network. We have begun to analyze data on mothers' and fathers' views of their formal and informal networks with a view to how much they either overlap or differ in highlighting certain characteristics, and how their views of social support are related to their participation in child care.

The emphasis that we have found on the value of peer support in parenting should be taken into consideration in the design of discriminative studies that consider the varying factors that contribute to the balance of support in parents' networks.

REFERENCES

Belle, D. (1981). The social network as a source of both stress and support to low income mothers. Paper presented at the biennial meeting of the Society for Research in Child Development, Boston.

Bates, J., Bennett-Freeland, C., & Lounsbury, M. (1979). Measurement of infant difficultness. Child Development, 50, 704–713.

Boukydis, C.F.Z. (1982). Support groups for parents with premature infants in N.I.C.U.'s.

In R. Marshall, C. Kasman, & L. Cape (Eds.), *Coping with caring for sick newborns.* Philadelphia: Saunders.

Boukydis. C.F.Z. (1984). N.I.C.U. support groups form in 1970's. *Support Lines,* 2 (1), 1–4.

Boukydis, C.F.Z. (1985a). A theory of empathic relations between parents and infants; Insights from a client-centered/experiential perspective. *Focusing Folio,* 4 (1), 3–28.

Boukydis, C. F. Z. (1985b). Perception of infant crying as an interpersonal event. In B. M. Lester & C. F. Z. Boukydis (Eds.) *Infant Crying: Research and theorectical perspectives.* New York: Plenum.

Boukydis, C.F.Z. (1986). Support for early parenting: Research and theoretical perspectives. In C.F.Z. Boukydis (Ed.), *Support for parents and infants: A manual for parent organizations and professionals.* Boston: Routledge & Kegan Paul.

Brazelton, T.B. (1984). *Neonatal Behavioral Assessment Scale* (2d ed.). Philadelphia: Lippincott.

Bronfenbrenner, U. (1979). *The ecology of human development.* Cambridge, MA: Harvard University Press.

Burchinal, M., Bryant, J., & Sparling, J. (1984, April). *Predicting poverty children's I.Q. from mother's social support networks.* Paper presented at the International Conference on Infant Studies, New York.

Campbell, M., & Cochran, M. (1983). *Perceptions of the child: The personal networks of married and single parents.* Paper presented at the biennial meeting of the Society for Research in Child Development, Detroit.

Carveth, W., & Gottlieb, B. (1979). The measurement of social support and its relation to stress. *Canadian Journal of Behavioral Science,* 11, 179–186.

Cochran, M., & Brassard, J. (1979). Child development and personal social networks. *Child Development,* 50, 601–616.

Colletta, N. (1981). *The influence of support systems on the maternal behavior of young mothers.* Paper presented at the biennial meeting of the Society for Research in Child Development, Boston.

Crnic, K., Greenberg, M., Ragozin, A., Robinson, M., & Basham, R. (1983). Effects of stress and social support on mothers of premature and full-term infants. *Child Development,* 54, 209–217.

Crockenberg, S. (1981). Infant irritability, mother responsiveness, and social support influences on the security of infant–mother attachment. *Child Development,* 52, 857–865.

Dunst, C., Trivette, C., & Cross, A. (1985). Roles and support networks of mothers of handicapped children. In R. Fewell & P. Vadasy (Eds.), *Families of handicapped children: Needs and supports across the life-span.* Austin, TX: Pro-Ed.

Emde, R., Gaensbauer, T, & Harman, J. (1976). Emotional expression in infancy: A bio-behavioral study. *Psychological Issues,* 10 (37).

Feiring, C. (1985, April). *The relationship between social support, infant risk status and mother–infant interaction.* Paper presented at the biennial meeting of the Society for Research in Child Development, Toronto.

Fiore, J., Becker, J., & Coppel, D. (1983). Social network interactions: A buffer or a stress? *American Journal of Community Psychology,* 11, 423–440.

Friedrich, W.W., & Friedrich, W.L. (1981). Psychosocial assets of parents of handicapped and non-handicapped children. *American Journal of Mental Deficiency,* 5, 551–553.

Goldberg, S., & Divitto, B. (1979). The effects of newborn medical status on early parent–infant interaction. In T. Field, A. Sostek, S. Goldberg, & H. Shuman (Eds.), Infants born at risk: Behavior and development. New York: S.P. Medical and Scientific Books.

Gottlieb, B. (1983). Social support as a focus for integrative research in psychology. American Psychologist, 38 (3), 278–287.

Hardyment, C. (1983). Dream babies: Three centuries of good advice on child care. New York: Harper & Row.

Harrison, H. (1983). The premature baby book: A parent's guide to coping and caring in the first years. New York: St. Martin's.

Howes, C., & Olenick, M. (1984, April). Family and child care influences on toddler compliance. Paper presented at the International Conference on Infant Studies, New York.

Lester, B.M. (1984). Data analysis and prediction. In T.B. Brazelton, Neonatal Behavioral Assessment Scale (2nd ed.). Philadelphia: Lippincott.

Lester, B.M. (1985). Introduction: There's more to crying than meets the ear. In B.M. Lester & C.F.Z. Boukydis (Eds.), Infant crying: Theoretical and research perspectives. New York: Plenum.

Lester, B.M., Emory, E., & Hoffman, S. (1976). A multivariate study of the effects of high-risk factors on performance on the Brazelton Neonatal Assessment Scale. Child Development, 47, 515–517.

Minde, K., Trehub, S., Corter, C., Boukydis, C., Celfoffer, L, & Marton, P. (1978). Mother–child relationships in the premature nursery: An observational study. Pediatrics, 61, 373–381.

Nance, S. (1982). Premature babies: A handbook for parents. New York: Arbor House.

Parke, R., Hymel, S., Power, T., & Tinsley, B. (1980). Fathers and risk: A hospital based model of intervention. In D. Sawin, R. Hawkins, L. Walker, & J. Penticuff (Eds.), Psychosocial risks in infant–environment transactions. New York: Brunner/ Mazel.

Parke, R, & Tinsley, B. (1985). The early environment of the at-risk infant: Expanding the social context. In D. Bricker (Ed.), Intervention with at risk and handicapped infants: From research to application. Baltimore: University Park Press.

Parks, P., Jenkins, L., Lenz, E., Jarrett, G., & Neal, M. (1984, April). Correlates of development in six-month olds. Paper presented at the International Conference on Infant Studies, New York.

Rook, K. (1984). The negative side of social interaction: Impact on psychological well-being. Journal of Personality and Social Psychology, 46, 1097–1108.

Sameroff, A., & Chandler, M. (1975). Reproductive risk and the continuum of caretaking casualty. In F. Horowitz, E. Hetherington, S. Scarr-Salapatek, & G. Siegel (Eds.), Review of Child Development Research (Vol. 4). Chicago: University of Chicago Press.

Speck, R, & Attneave, C. (1973). Family networks. London: Pantheon.

Wandersman, L., & Unger, D. (1983). Interaction of infant difficulty and social support in adolescent mothers. Paper presented at the biennial meeting of the Society for Research in Child Development, Detroit.

Wente, A., & Crockenberg, S. (1976). Transition to fatherhood: Lamaze preparation, adjustment difficulty and the husband–wife relationship. Family Coordinator, 24, 351–357.

CHAPTER 5
Fathers as Agents and Recipients of Support in the Postnatal Period

Ross D. Parke and Barbara J. Tinsley
University of Illinois

INTRODUCTION

The father's role in the family is most usefully conceptualized within a family systems framework, in which complementary roles and behaviors of all family members must be considered in order to understand the role and behavior of any one member. Consistent with this view is the recognition of the bidirectionality of influence between fathers and mothers. A common orientation of the research and theory on fathering is to primarily characterize fathers as support agents for mothers, as facilitators of the mother–infant relationship and maternal-parenting performance, without parallel consideration of the role of mothers as support resources for fathers' parenting role. To correct this unidirectional view, the focus of this chapter highlights fathers as recipients of support from mothers as well as providers of support. To complement a family systems view, fathers and families will be considered from an ecological perspective as well. Specifically, the embededness of fathers and families within a variety of other social systems, including both formal and informal social-support systems, will be recognized, and the role of these systems in modifying fathers' role in the family will be examined (Bronfenbrenner, 1979; Cochran & Brassard, 1979; Parke & Tinsley, 1982). Other assumptions which guide our discussion include the acknowledgement that family members play multiple roles; in the case of men, these include participation as a husband and as a father. Thus, it is important to assess the marital relationship as both an important source of support for fathers and as a modifier of fathers' and mothers' behavior.

Finally, as a family systems perspective implies, it is important to distinguish direct and indirect forms of paternal influence within the family. Fathers directly influence their wives and infants through direct face-to-face interaction. In addition, fathers indirectly influence other family members. By sharing care-giving and household tasks with their wives, fathers may indirectly influence their infants by improving the quality of the mother–infant relationship. Mothers, in turn, exhibit similar types of direct and indirect influence within the family.

In this chapter, we consider first the role of the father as a support agent within the family. The impact on the mother is reviewed as well as the factors that may modify the father's role as a support figure. Next we examine the father as a recipient of support from both his spouse and from informal and formal support agencies.

FATHER AS PROVIDER OF SUPPORT

Fathers provide support both directly and indirectly to their spouses in a variety of contexts. In this section, evidence regarding father as a support agent is reviewed. Two main contexts in which father provides support will be noted: childbirth and care-giving. Next, the factors affecting the level of father support will be outlined.

Childbirth: There is a growing body of research that suggests that the presence of the husband during labor and delivery has a variety of positive outcomes for both mother and infant. Some evidence indicates that women whose husbands participated in both labor and delivery reported less pain, received less medication, and felt more positive about the birth experience than women whose husbands were present only during the first stage of labor (Henneborn & Cogan, 1975). Fathers may be indirectly affected themselves by the reduction in maternal medication in light of earlier research (Parke, O'Leary, & West, 1972), which found that fathers interact less with heavily medicated infants and more with an active, alert infant. Other evidence indicates that the presence of a supportive companion—though not necessarily a father—results in a significantly lower incidence of problems of labor and birth—cesarean birth, meconium staining, fetal distress (Sosa, Kennel, Klaus, Robertson, & Urrutia, 1980).

Moreover, the father's presence during the second stage of labor and delivery increased the mother's emotional experience at the birth; mothers reported the birth as a "peak" experience more often if the father was present. Similarly, father's emotional reaction to the birth was heightened by being present at the delivery (Entwisle & Doering, 1980). In another study, Peterson, Mehl, and Leiderman (1979) using both observations and interviews of father, found that a more positive birth experience for the father was associated with enhanced attachment to the infant.

These investigators also found that longer labors at home, in contrast to hospital delivery, were associated with greater paternal attachment. Finally, they note that birth-related events were stronger predictors of attachment than were data from the pregnancy period, thus, arguing that self-selection factors were not as important as the birth experience itself on subsequent involvement with the baby. Together the evidence tentatively suggests that the presence of the father has positive benefits for both mothers and fathers. Finally, in light of the data demonstrating that maternal medication during labor and delivery can have a depressive and disorganizing effect on infants (Conway & Brackbill, 1970; Murray et al., 1981), the father's presence may indirectly benefit the infant as well.

Feeding: In their roles as support figures, fathers contribute to feeding activities both directly as feeding agent and indirectly by supporting the mother in her role as feeding agent. In studies of traditional families, it has been consistently found that mothers feed and care-take more than fathers; the pattern is evident in both studies of parents and infants in structured interaction contexts (Parke & O'Leary, 1976; Parke & Sawin, 1980) as well as unstructured naturalistic situations (Lamb, 1977; Pedersen, 1975). Time distribution surveys of parents in both the United States (Kotelchuck, 1976; Rendina & Dickerscheid, 1976) and in other countries such as Great Britain (Richards, Dunn, & Antonis, 1977), Australia (Russell, 1982), and France and Belgium (Szalai, 1972) show similar patterns. As we discuss later, there are wide degrees of variation across families in the level of father participation, and some of the factors which modify the father's contribution to care-giving will be considered. However, it should be noted that even though fathers participate less in feeding and care-giving activities than mothers, fathers are competent in these activities. Fathers are as sensitive to infant cues in the feeding context as mothers; moreover infant milk consumption is similar for mothers and fathers (Parke & Sawin, 1975, 1980).

Although research on the father's influence in infancy has centered primarily on the direct impact of the father's behavior (e.g., as a feeding or stimulatory agent), his influence, in some cases, may be indirectly mediated through the mother or other members of the family as well (see Lewis & Feiring, 1981; Parke, Power, & Gottman, 1979, for detailed discussion of this issue). Even when they are not directly participating in feeding, fathers can indirectly affect this activity by modifying the behavior of the feeding agent. The father's indirect role in feeding is illustrated by Pedersen's (1975) investigation of the influence of the husband–wife relationship on mother–infant interaction in a feeding context. Ratings were made of the quality of the mother–infant relationship in connection with two time-sampling home observations when the infants were 4 weeks old. Of particular interest was "feeding competence," which refers to the appropriateness of the mother in managing feeding. "Mothers rated high [in feeding competence] are able to pace the feeding well, intersperse feeding and burping without disrupting the baby, and seem sensitive to the baby's needs for either stimulation of feeding or brief rest periods during the course of feedings" (Pedersen, 1975, p. 4). In addition, the husband–wife relationship was assessed through an interview.

Pedersen summarized his results as follows:

The husband–wife relationship was linked to the mother-infant unit. When the father was more supportive of the mother, that is, evaluated her maternal skills more positively, she was more effective in feeding the baby. Then again, maybe competent mothers elicit more positive evaluations from their husbands. The reverse holds for marital discord. High tension and conflict in the marriage was associated with more inept feeding on the part of the mother. (Pedersen, 1975, p. 6)

In short, even if fathers do not directly feed the infant, they may still influence the process by their relationship with their wives.

Nor is the impact of the father on mother's feeding behavior limited to bottle-feeding contexts. The success of breast-feeding has been found to be directly related to the support and encouragement provided by the father (Switzky, Vietze, & Switzky, 1979). Even when the mother breast-feeds the infant, the father can be involved in a number of ways. In addition to being supportive to the mother in her efforts to breast-feed, he can also participate in feeding by providing supplemental bottle-feeding and sharing in nonfeeding related aspects of care-taking such as bathing and diapering. Although recent evidence by Entwisle & Doering (1980) suggests that supplemented bottle-feeding by the father may be associated with the early cessation of breast-feeding, their results must be interpreted carefully. These researchers found that the husbands of the breast-feeding women who stopped breast-feeding by 6 months, compared with those that continued, were bottle-feeding about once a day; husbands of those mothers who continued to breast-feed were giving a bottle only once in 4 days. As the researchers note, "frequent bottle-feeding at this early stage could interfere with breast-feeding because establishing a good milk supply depends on frequent stimulation. Women who give supplementary formula because they "don't have enough milk" are exacerbating their problem rather than curing it, and fathers who feed babies formula may contribute to early cessation of breast-feeding" (Entwisle & Doering, 1980). Thus, the father who feeds his infant supplemental bottles of formula may be problematic, but the father who gives supplemental bottles of breast milk may be providing constructive support for the mother as well as enhancing his own relationship with the infant.

Other evidence is consistent with this view of the father as an indirect support agent for the mother. In a recent study of 4- to 8-month-old infants and their parents, Dickie & Matheson (1984) examined the relationship between parental competence and spousal support. Parental competence was based on home observations and involved a variety of components such as emotional consistency, contingent responding, and warmth and pleasure in parenting. Emotional support—a measure of affection, respect, and satisfaction in the husband–wife relationship as well as cognitive support—an index of husband–wife agreement in child care—were positively related to maternal competence.

The importance of these findings is clear: In order to fully appreciate the father's role in early care-giving, both direct and indirect ways in which he contributes must be considered. Finally, these studies underline the necessity of viewing fathers in a family context and suggest the importance of assessing the total set of relationships among the members of the family.

FACTORS ALTERING FATHERS' LEVEL OF SUPPORT

A variety of factors may affect the extent to which fathers function as a support figure. These include (1) shifts in ideology; (2) recent trends in medical practices; (3) modifications in the timing of the onset of parenthood; and (4) changes in the economic sphere. These factors do not yield uniform effects, either in terms of the amount or the duration of the effects.

Shifts in Sex Role Conceptualizations

In the last decade, our concepts concerning male and female sex-role behaviors have undergone change. Our conceptualization of masculinity and femininity has shifted. Instead of viewing males and females as possessing nonoverlapping sets of psychological traits, current conceptualizations of androgyny stress the extent to which males and females share sex-typed characteristics. According to this view, men can exhibit many traits that were traditionally viewed as feminine such as nurturance, warmth, and affection, while women can be assertive, forceful, and instrumental—a set of characteristics often viewed as masculine. In turn, this suggests that both males and females can assume parenting functions. In support of this expectation, Bem and her colleagues (Bem

& Lenney, 1976; Bem, Martyna, & Watson, 1976) found that androgynous men were as likely to be nurturant toward a 5-month-old infant as androgynous and feminine women. Other evidence suggests that our definitions of our masculinity and femininity may affect the degree to which fathers participate in care-giving. Russell's (1978) recent finding that androgynous men in Australia participate more heavily in care-giving illustrates the impact of self-defined sex-related attributes on the distribution of care-giving responsibilities. Similarly, Entwisle and Doering (1980) found that men who adhered to rigid stereotypes (e.g., nurturing an infant is unmasculine) did show less interest in their new babies or less "fatherly" behavior. However, some more-recent work in the United States (Radin, 1982) and Sweden (Lamb, Frodi, Hwang, Frodi, & Steinberg, 1982) have failed to confirm this relationship between care-giving levels of fathers and androgyny. For example, Radin (1982) found no significant differences on the Bem Scales of sex-role orientation between primary care-giving fathers, who assumed major responsibility for child care, and traditional fathers, who were less actively involved in child care. Similarly, in a study of highly participant Swedish fathers (Lamb, et al., 1982), no relationship was found between sex-role-orientation scores and level of participation. In summary, the relationship between fathers' sex-role orientation and their level of child-care participation remains an intriguing hypothesis rather than an established fact. (See Russell & Radin, 1983, for a detailed review of this issue.)

The Impact of Changes in Medical Practices on Fathers' Role as Support Figures

Recent research suggests that certain changes in the medical sphere can alter fathers' level of participation in infant care-giving activities. Two trends will serve to illustrate not only the modifiability of paternal roles but the importance of viewing the father from a family systems perspective. First, the examination of c-section deliveries permits evaluation of the impact of reduced maternal availability on father's role. Second, through an examination of preterm infants, the effects of modifying the demandingness or burden of the infant on mother and father roles can be examined. These examples of the impact of shifts in the capacity of either mother or infant on fathers illustrate the alternative paths through which changes in fathers' support level are mediated.

For a variety of reasons, there has been a dramatic increase in the percentage of c-section deliveries over the past decade. In 1970, only 5.5% of infants were delivered by c-section; in 1980, this figure was 18% (Bottoms, Rosen, & Sokol, 1980). Recent research suggests that cesarean childbirth can alter the fathers' level of participation in routine care-taking activities. In a recent study, Pedersen, Cain, Zaslow, and Anderson (1980) found that fathers of cesarean-delivered infants engaged in significantly more care-giving at 5 months than fathers in a comparison group whose infants were vaginally delivered. While the fathers of the cesarean-delivered infants were more likely to share care-giving responsibilities in several different areas on an equal basis with the mother, fathers in the comparison sample tended to "help out," with the mothers still meeting the major proportion of care-giving needs. Other investigators have found similar patterns. In an interview study of 84 couples and nine additional women through pregnancy, birth, and their child's infancy, Grossman, Eichler, and Winickoff (1980) found that in families in which the infant was cesarean-delivered, fathers seemed more involved with their infants at 2 months of age than fathers of vaginally delivered infants.

Vietze, MacTurk, McCarthy, Klein, and Yarrow (1980) also report that cesarean delivery results in more active paternal care-taking. Seventy-five families with a first child were observed through the first year of life. Fathers of cesarean-delivered infants demonstrated more soothing behavior toward their infants than fathers of vaginally delivered infants at 6 months, although this was not observed at 12 months. The most probable explanation for these findings suggests that mothers, as a result of the surgery, are unable to assume a fully active role in care-giving during the early postpartum weeks. Fathers, in turn, as a result of their increased involvement in early care, continue this care-giving activity even after the time that mother is able to resume a more active role. Support for this analysis comes from a recent study by Doering and Entwisle (1980), who found that women who underwent cesarean delivery were less positive about caring for their baby than vaginally delivered mothers.

The Pedersen et al. study, as well as other studies of the effects of cesarean birth on paternal involvement, underline the importance of the early postpartum period for establishing role definitions. However, this should not imply that these early established patterns are not modifiable, as evidence by Vietze et al. (1980) suggests that by the end of the first year these differences in father participation between the two types of deliveries have disappeared. The research, however, does alert us to another type of second-order effect, namely, the mother's behavior and needs—as a result of the cesarean birth—may influence the father–infant interaction (Pedersen et al., 1980).

The birth of a premature infant may also modify the father's role in a similar fashion, by creating a situation in which it is more important than usual for the father to provide nurturance for the mother as well as increasing the need for paternal involvement in care-taking.

A number of factors associated with the birth of a preterm infant may increase father involvement. First, the context of care for preterms may elicit greater father involvement. Part of the reason for the lower rates of mortality for preterm infants is the change toward centralized hospital units that specialize in the care of high-risk infants. Since one facility usually covers a large geographic region, infants are often transported from the delivery hospital to a central high-risk nursery. Because the mother is usually not transported with the baby and is still unable to travel to visit her infant, the father often has the major amount of contact with the high-risk transported infant. There is some evidence (Leiderman & Seashore, 1975) to suggest that this situation may be stressful and be a contributor to family disharmony—in part due to the fact that mothers, in this case, are being supplanted by fathers as the primary parent. Alternatively, the opportunity for fathers to have contact and to be involved early in the infant's care may, in part, account for the finding that fathers continue to show a high level of interest in the infant even after the mother is able to participate more fully, as indexed by rates of hospital visitation by fathers to see their preterm infants. Moreover, fathers contribute in this situation, not only by their direct participation, but indirectly as well. Research by Minde et al. (1978) has shown that mothers who have supportive husbands tend to visit their premature babies in the hospital more often, and that mothers who visit more have fewer parenting problems later than mothers who visit less frequently. Again, we see that fathers can influence their infants indirectly by affecting the mother–infant relationship. Father support in families with preterm infants continues beyond the hospital period. In an interview study of more than 100 families with premature infants, Herzog (1979) found that the most important function of fathers of premature infants was to provide support for the mother to facilitate her care-taking role and her positive feelings toward the infant. Further support for this position comes from a study of parental visiting patterns in an English high-risk nursery (Hawthorne, Richards, & Callon, 1978). These investigators found that mothers of premature infants were helped by fathers who became highly involved in care-taking the infant. Similar evidence comes from a recent Canadian study by Marton, Minde, and Perrotta (1981) who reported that fathers of preterm infants are more involved in care-taking than fathers of fullterm infants. Finally, in a U.S. sample, Yogman (1981) found that fathers of premature infants exhibit higher levels of care-taking involvement (e.g., bathing, diapering) than fathers of fullterm infants.

      These patterns of heightened father involvement may be due, in part, to the difficulties associated with the care of the preterm infant. A number of investigators have suggested that premature infants place greater interactional demands on their parents than fullterm infants because of their irritability, unpredictable alertness, and limited responsivity (Goldberg, 1983; Field, 1979). Brown and Bakeman (1980) report that parents find preterm infants less enjoyable and less satisfying to feed. Moreover, because of their low weight, these infants often are fed more often than fullterm infants. In a series of observational studies comparing parent–infant interaction with fullterm and preterm infants, Goldberg (1979) finds that in the newborn period, mothers of preterm infants are less actively involved with their babies than mothers of fullterm infants. Preterm infants were held farther from the mother's body, touched less, talked to less, and placed in a face-to-face position less often than fullterm infants. Other studies of mother–premature infant interaction have found that, in the feeding context, mothers are more likely to stimulate their infant's feeding and in a less contingent manner than mothers of fullterm infants (Brown & Bakeman, 1980; Goldberg, 1979). This has been hypothesized to be a reaction to the premature infant's lower responsivity and alertness. Thus, prematurity may elicit greater father involvement in care-taking at least partially because of the father's desire to relieve the mother of full responsibility for the extra time and skill required for caring for these infants. In turn, the father may indirectly influence the premature infant by positively affecting the mother-infant relationship. Finally, fathers probably play an important role in providing emotional as well as instrumental support to mothers, which is especially important in view of the stress associated with the premature birth of an infant (Parke & Tinsley, 1982; Tinsley & Parke, 1983).

A word of caution in interpreting these shifts in the level of father involvement, as a result of either a c-section delivery or a preterm birth, is necessary. Although it is generally assumed that fathers in earlier eras would probably have reacted similarly in response to these medically related circumstances, this may not be the case. According to a life span perspective on fathering (Parke & Tinsley, 1984) consideration of both the cohort and time of testing need to be taken into account in evaluating father's role as a support agent.

Two factors may have altered the probability of fathers' increasing their care-giving participation in our current time period. First, the cultural shift in sex-role attitudes which have sanctioned father participation (Parke, 1981; Russell, 1982) may make it easier for fathers to increase their level of involvement. By contrast, in a more traditional era, characterized by more rigid sex roles for mothers and fathers, these medical circumstances may not necessarily have led to increased paternal involvement. Second, in light of decreased geographical proximity between families and extended kin, family-support systems that may have been utilized by mothers in such situations in the past may be less available. In turn, this increases the likelihood of father participation. Support for this argument comes from Bloom-Feshbach (1979), who found that the use of social networks for child-care activities is negatively correlated with the father's involvement in this type of activity. This finding suggests that father participation in the current historical period under circumstances such as a c-section delivery or a preterm birth may, in part, be due to the decreased availability of extended kin. Thus, several societal trends may be converging to create a situation in which, both some barriers to participation are lowered, and the necessity of father involvement is raised. In turn, these changes make the increases in father participation in the current period more likely. In summary, these findings underscore the relevance of changes in the medical sphere for understanding father's role as a support figure.

The Impact of Delayed Childbearing

Another factor which is associated with shifts in the father's level of participation is the timing of the onset of parenthood. Over the last decade, two different patterns have emerged. First, there has been a dramatic increase in the number of women beginning parenthood during adolescence. At the same time there was an increase in the number of women who were postponing childbearing until their 30s. Between 1970 and 1979, the number of first babies born to women between 30 and 34 years of age doubled. A detailed discussion of adolescent fathers as support figures is beyond the scope of this paper. (For reviews, see McCluskey, Killarney, & Papini, 1983; Parke, Power, & Fisher, 1980). In general, early onset of fatherhood is associated with decreased involvement of men as direct care-givers. However, there is both considerable variability in adolescent father involvement and evidence that father support can have beneficial consequences for both the infant and the adolescent mother (Furstenberg, 1976).

A variety of contrasts exists between becoming a parent in adolescence and initiating parenthood 15 to 20 years later. When childbearing is delayed, both men and women have made considerable progress educationally and occupationally, their person identities are more firmly established; their marital relations may be more stable. Recent evidence suggests that women are more likely to continue to pursue their outside work careers when childbearing is delayed—especially among women who adopted this delayed childbearing strategy in the 1970s (Daniels & Weingarten, 1982). In contrast, women who begin their parenting career in their early 20s are less likely to simultaneously pursue an outside career and raise a family. According to these investigations, delayed childbearing has clear implications for the father's role as a support figure within the family. In their study, three times as many late-timed fathers, in contrast to their early-timed counterparts (those in their early to mid-20s), had regular responsibility for some part of the daily care of a preschool child. Other evidence is consistent with the finding of greater father involvement when childbearing is delayed. Bloom-Feshbach (1981) found that the older a father is at the time of the birth of his first child, the more he is involved in the practical aspects of infant care-taking.

However, some other aspects of the father role are altered as well. Father's participation in physical play with infants and young children is negatively related to paternal age (MacDonald & Parke, 1986). On the other hand, the age of the father was not associated with expressive-nurturant aspects of the father–child relationship (Bloom-Feshbach, 1979). Possibly such central aspects of the father-infant relationship as father–infant attachment may not be altered by the father's age (Parke & Tinsley, 1984). This hypothesis merits empirical exploration.

The impact of shifts in father's role as a support figure in the care-giving arena on mothers and infants is not yet clear. However, it is possible that the increase in paternal care-giving responsibility assumed by fathers in late-timed families may account in part for the optimal and involved mother–infant interaction patterns observed among late-timed primiparous mothers (Ragozin, Basham, Crnic, Greenberg, & Robinson, 1982). Studies which include assessments of both father–and mother–offspring interactions as well as measurement of fathers' and mothers' supportive roles in early and late-timed childbearing families are necessary.

Finally, more attention needs to be given to the ways in which patterns of father support as a consequence of delayed childbearing have changed across historical time. As Parke and Tinsley (1984) note: "Presumably, the decision to delay the onset of parenthood was easier in the 1970s than in earlier decades due to increased acceptance of maternal employment, less rigid role definitions for men and women, and the greater availability of support services such as day care which would permit a simultaneous family-career option" (1984, p. 24).

The Impact of Work Patterns on Father Support Role

Work–family relations have become of increasing interest in recent years (Bronfenbrenner & Crouter, 1982); in this section, the impact of both women's and men's work patterns on father's role as a support agent in the family are explored. Although the change in rate of maternal employment is the most frequently researched issue, other issues such as men's work involvement and the impact of variations in work schedules will be explored as well.

Women's Employment and Father Support: What are the implications of the rise in the rate of women who work outside the home? Between 1950 and 1978, the maternal employment rate has more than tripled for married mothers of preschoolers, doubled for those with school-age children, and increased by one-half for those with no young children. Two findings are clear.

First, fathers increase the *proportion* of time that they devote to the total family workload when mothers are employed outside the home (Walker & Woods, 1976; Pleck, 1983). This increase, however, often emerges as a result of wives' reducing the amount of time they devote to housework and child care, rather than to increase in the absolute amount of time men devote to these tasks. These findings are not without significance because the impact of father participation with either his spouse or his children is likely to be different in families where father and mother are more equal in their level of family participation.

Second, there is some evidence for absolute increases in fathers' contribution to family work when wives are employed, especially in terms of father–child contact (Robinson, 1977). However, this varies with the age of the child, with father-child involvement increasing mainly in the case of infants (Walker & Woods, 1976) and young children (Russell, 1982). Interestingly, the quality of father support is different as well. According to Russell (1982), fathers with employed wives spent more time assuming *sole* responsibility for their children (i.e., caregiving to a child in the absence of a spouse) compared with fathers with nonemployed wives.

Finally, the impact of shifts in father participation as a result of maternal employment on either mothers or infants are not yet well understood (Hoffman, 1984). Nor is it known whether father support that is elicited as a consequence of maternal employment differs in its impact from father support which arises from other causes.

Finally, some problems plague this general area. In the current literature, cohort, time of testing, and age of children are often confounded. For example, in the studies that show that father participation is higher when infants and young children are involved, it is not clear whether this is due to only the age of the children or to a difference in the cohorts whose children are younger at the time of evaluation. Value shifts may elicit greater involvement in the current cohort of new parents, which may not have affected more seasoned parents. Moreover, once a pattern of father participation has been established, possibly these families will continue to participate more equally in childbearing.

If this analysis is correct, future surveys may indicate that father participation extends into later childhood age periods. Alternatively, fathers who are involved early may feel that they have contributed and consequently do less at later ages. The importance of considering the timing of the mother's employment as a determinant of the degree of father involvement is clear. Age of the child is not the only variable— however, other factors such as employment onset in relation to the family's development cycle as well as the reason for employment need to be considered.

Variations in Work Schedules: A variety of shifts have taken place in recent years that have resulted in either reduced work time or more flexible work-schedule arrangements. Two examples illustrate the possible ways in which these shifts may alter the father's supportive role. By altering the distribution of total work hours into 4 days rather than 5, Marklan (1976) found that men on the 4-day work schedule spent a significantly greater amount of time in child care. The men who worked four 10-hour days devoted nearly four more hours a week to child care than men on the 5-day schedule. Again, while it is possible that these changes in father's support role may provide the other with some relief from routine child care and thereby improve the mother–child relationship as well as the father–child relationship, these possibilities await empirical confirmation.

Flexible hours may be another vehicle for providing men more time for fathering and thereby for providing support to their spouses. Flexible hours, for example, may permit fathers to stay home later in the morning and assist their children in going to school or alternatively to be available to their children after school. Recent evidence (Bohen & Viveros-Long, 1981) found no evidence that either mothers or fathers who were on flex-time spent more time with their children than did workers on regular schedules. Workers on flex-time did report less conflict between home and work responsibilities than those on regular job schedules. However, the processes which mediated the reduced job–family strain were not evident from this investigation.

Other evidence is consistent with another aspect of this issue— namely, the relationship between time spent on paid work and time devoted to child care and play. In a comprehensive review of time-use studies, Pleck (1983) found a significant negative correlation between time spent on child care and paid work. In an Australian study, Russell (1981) found similar relationships between paid work and child care. However he found even stronger links between the time a father is at home and available to his children and participation in child-rearing than between paid work per se and child care. Moreover, the play/care-giving distinction again proved useful, because the relationship was stronger for involvement in play than in child care. Other evidence suggests that the work schedule is a more important determinant of paternal participation than the amount of time devoted to paid work. Men who were permitted to modify their work schedule without reducing their total work time spent 18% more time with their wives and children (Winnett & Neale, 1978). More importantly, the men who were permitted to vary their schedules daily were more involved in child-care tasks than other men who had flexible schedules but without the possibility of daily fluctuations. Further work is implicated, especially studies that avoid problems of self-selection and provide detailed reports of how mother and father family roles systematically shift as a result of flexible work arrangements.

Work Investment: Family and job responsibilities often conflict and compete for limited amounts of time and energy. In view of this tension between the worlds of work and home, it is not surprising that one of the determinants of father involvement in child care is the extent to which fathers are invested in their occupations. In a recent study, Feldman, Nash, and Aschenbrenner (1983) found a negative relationship between the importance that a new father attaches to his job and his level of involvement in care-taking and play with his infant at 6 months of age. However, age has been found to be a predictor of father involvement in child care (Bloom-Feshbach, 1981); it may be that men who are older are better established in their careers and are able to invest more in family concerns. Age and career issues are often confounded (Parke & Tinsley, 1984), and these issues merit systematic disentanglement in order to fully understand the contribution of either age or work investment to father's supportive role in the family.

In sum, a variety of factors, including shifts in ideology, medical practices, the timing of the onset of parenthood, and the nature and scheduling of men's and women's work all have a complex impact on the father's role as a support figure. Although these factors have been discussed separately, it is more likely that as they multiply they determine father's supportive function.

FATHERS AS RECIPIENTS OF SUPPORT

In view of the social, economic, and ideological changes that are promoting increased father involvement in the care and nurturance of infants and young children, it is important to examine both the availability and impact of sources of support for fathers.

Various sources of support that are available to fathers need to be distinguished; their separate contribution to fathering competence as well as their combined impact on fathering merits examination. First, intrafamilial sources of support need to be distinguished from support which resides outside the nuclear family unit. Spousal support which may assume the form of direct assistance to fathers in their execution of their parental role is the most common form. Indirect support from the spouse may flow from the emotional and social support provided through the marital relationship itself. Second, it is a central premise of our chapter that families and fathers need to be viewed within a broader set of social systems that exist outside the family (Parke & Tinsley, 1982; Tinsley & Parke, 1984). Moreover, the role played by informal as well as formal support systems merit separate consideration.

Finally, various kinds of support need to be considered that may have differing effects on fathers as parents and may be differentially available across various social-support agents. Emotional, social, physical, and informational support make distinctive contributions to fathering activities.

Intrafamilial Support

Fathering competence within the family is, in part, dependent on both the quality and quantity of maternal support as well as the overall quality of the marital relationship.

Just as paternal support relates positively to maternal competence, there is evidence that maternal support is similarly linked to the father's parenting competence. In the previously discussed study by Dickie and Matheson (1984), these investigators found that maternal emotional support and cognitive support were related to paternal competence. In fact, these investigators found that spousal support is a stronger correlate of competence in fathers than in mothers. The level of emotional and cognitive support successfully discriminated high- and low-competent fathers, but failed to do so in the case of mothers. In short, successful paternal parenting may be particularly dependent on a supportive intrafamilial environment. A number of factors may aid in explaining this relationship. First, there is prior evidence that father's level of participation is, in part, determined by the extent to which mothers permit participation (Dickie & Carnahan, 1980; Redican, 1976). Second, since the paternal role is less well articulated and defined than the maternal role, spousal support may serve to help crystallize the boundaries of appropriate role behavior. Third, men have fewer opportunities to acquire and practice skills which are central to care-giving activities during socialization and therefore may benefit more than mothers from informational (i.e., cognitive) support. Further research on this issue should be a fruitful vehicle for exploring the antecedents and constraints on performance of the fathering role.

Extrafamilial Support Systems

To understand the mechanisms by which support agents outside the family influence father functioning, informal and formal support systems need to be distinguished.

(a) *Informal support systems*: Informal support systems refer to: (1) Unstructured social networks, which consist of a person's relatives, friends, neighbors, co-workers, and other acquaintances who interact with the person; and (2) structured social-support systems which include a variety of neighborhood or community-based organizations or groups that are generally not officially generated, controlled, or funded by local or other government officials (Cochran & Brassard, 1979). Both of these types of social-support systems can help fathers in their parenting role by providing instrumental/physical and financial support, providing emotional/social support, and providing informational support.

Extended kin such as grandparents and other relatives often functioned as the primary informal support system for parents. While there has been a general shift in the structure of living arrangements from an extended to a self-contained nuclear family, the support functions of kin remain an important source of assistance to families, including fathers (Tinsley & Parke, 1984). Recent estimates indicate that families have relatively frequent contact with grandparents, for example—on the average of one to three times per week (Tinsley & Parke, 1984).

Do fathers utilize grandparents as sources of support? According to a recent study (Tinsley & Parke, 1987), fathers of 7-month-old infants did not differ from mothers in the extent to which they utilized grand-parents as sources of support. However, fathers did report higher levels of satisfaction with contact with their own parents (paternal grandparents) than with the wives' parents (maternal grandparents). Fathers as well as mothers rely upon extended kin during times of transition, change, and stress as well as on a day-to-day basis. Evidence suggests that fathers increase their contact with their own parents during pregnancy—especially their mothers (Bittman & Zalk, 1978). Fathers also increase their contact with other members of informal networks during pregnancy, especially friends who are already parents (Gladieux, 1978). Moreover, the availability of informal supports—either kin or nonkin, who can serve as provide support was linked with higher satisfaction for expectant fathers (Gladieux, 1978).

Families are particularly likely to rely on external social-support systems under conditions of high stress or family crisis. The birth of an infant prematurely constitutes one example of this type of situation. Recent evidence (Parke & Tinsley, 1984) indicates that parents are more likely to use social-support systems when their infants are born prematurely than when their infants are born at term. Although mothers and fathers use both informal as well as formal support systems when their infant is born prematurely, fathers overall utilize informal supports in these circumstances less than mothers. Instead, especially for informational purposes, fathers are more likely to rely on formal rather than informal support agencies. Although there is clear evidence (Unger, 1979) that mothers who have contact with informal support networks are more actively involved with their infants as assessed by Home Scale (Elardo, Bradley, & Caldwell, 1975), there is little information concerning the impact of informal support from extrafamilial sources on either paternal competence as a parent or on the infant's development. In view of paternal use of formal support systems, it is important to examine the role of formal agencies in supporting fathering.

Formal Support Systems. Two types of formal support systems need to be distinguished: (1) general and (2) specific to at-risk infants and families. *General* support systems refer to the types of formal support systems that are available to all members of the community, including such support systems as: health-care facilities for both adults and children; counseling services for individuals and families; employment agencies; educational opportunities; social work services to facilitate adoption and placement of infants and children; housing assistance; welfare assistance; and recreational facilities.

There are a variety of support systems of *special relevance* to at-risk infants and families. These programs serve both the educational function of providing child-care information as well as alleviating stress associated with premature or ill infants. Support systems that serve an educational function include: hospital-based courses in child care and child-rearing; nurse visiting programs; well-baby clinics; follow-up programs; and parent discussion groups. Some other supportive programs that offer stress relief are: family and group day-care facilities; baby-sitting services; mother's helpers; homemaker and housekeeping services; drop-off centers; crisis nurseries; and hot lines.

Evidence in support of the role of informal and formal support systems in regulating the father's ability to cope with at-risk infants is limited. In this section, some illustrative studies of the role of support systems in modifying father management of infant care and development is reviewed. Although some recent studies involve informal social-support systems, many of the studies have primarily involved modification of the formal support systems available to fathers and families. Finally, in some cases, informal and formal support are provided together, which underlines the interconnectedness of these two levels of social support for families.

MEDICAL SETTINGS AS SITES FOR FATHER INTERVENTION PROGRAMS

In recent years, a number of investigators have used either hospitals or physicians' offices to provide social support for parents. A number of studies of intervention in hospital settings have focused on the postpartum period as a convenient timepoint for initiating supportive services for parents of infants. Parents, including fathers, are accessible at this point, and often motivation for learning about infant development and care-giving skills is high during this period.

Intervention for fathers and mothers can assume a variety of forms. Recent work has shown that exposure to a demonstration of Brazelton Neonatal Assessment Scale has positive effects on the quality of mother-infant interaction (Widmayer & Field, 1980). In a more recent extension of this type of intervention to fathers, Beal (1984) exposed first-time fathers to a Brazelton demonstration on their 2- to 3-day-old infant. A control group of fathers received no intervention. To assess the impact of this brief intervention, father-infant interaction was assessed at 8-weeks postpartum. During the paternal-infant interaction session, the interaction patterns among the intervention group was characterized by a higher degree of father-infant mutuality. In addition, the fathers who received the BNBAS demonstration perceived their infants as less difficult than fathers in the control group. These findings suggest that both father-infant interaction patterns as well as paternal perceptions can be modified by this type of intervention. Because all of the fathers also attended prenatal classes and both labor and delivery, it would be interesting to assess whether this type of demonstration would be effective for less interested and involved fathers.

In fact, in another attempt to modify paternal behavior through a Brazelton demonstration, Belsky (1984) exposed either mothers or both fathers and mothers together to the Brazelton exam. A control group received only feedback from an examiner concerning their infant's performance on the BNBAS. On a later assessment of the impact of the intervention at 1 and 3 months of age, there was a positive effect on paternal behavior and the marital relationship for the fathers and mothers who rated the demonstration as interesting and engaging. Together, these studies suggest that this type of intervention may have value, but more attention needs to be paid to motivational factors as a possible qualifier of the utility of this type of intervention. Moreover, the long-term effects of this type of intervention have not yet been established.

Another approach involves direct teaching through the use of a film intervention. The effectiveness of this approach is illustrated by a recent hospital-based intervention designed specifically for fathers (Parke, Hymel, Power, & Tinsley, 1980). During the mother's postpartum hospitalization, one group of 16 fathers was shown a short videotape designed to increase father–infant interaction and care-taking involvement. In the videotape, three different fathers were shown successfully playing with, feeding, and diapering their babies. In addition, a narrator emphasized the wide range of newborn cognitive and social capacities as well as the active role fathers can assume in the early care and stimulation of infants. The videotape was designed to serve four purposes: (1) modification of father's sex-role attitudes concerning the appropriateness of infant care-taking for adult males; (2) provision of specific demonstrations of feeding and diapering; (3) provision of information concerning newborn infants' perceptual and cognitive capabilities; and (4) demonstration of a number of ways in which fathers can play with babies, emphasizing contingent responses to infant cues.

To assess the impact of the intervention, attitudinal and observational measures of father–infant interaction were secured in the hospital in the early postpartum period and in the home at 3 weeks and 3 months for both the film group of fathers and a group of 16 fathers who did not view the videotape. At 3 months, the typical level of father participation in routine care-taking activities in the home was also assessed. Results showed that fathers who viewed the film in the hospital increased their knowledge about infant perceptual abilities and believed more strongly that infants need stimulation more than fathers who did not see the videotape. In addition, for fathers of boys, viewing the film modified their sex-role attitudes concerning the appropriateness of their participation in care-taking activities. Based on diary reports of care-taking activities in the home, fathers who saw the film were more likely to diaper and feed at 3 months than fathers in the no-film control group.

The observational data revealed that the film modified father behavior in a variety of ways. The film was effective in increasing the amount of care-taking behavior exhibited during feeding, both in the hospital and at 3 months. The film significantly increased the stimulatory behavior of fathers of firstborn boys at the hospital period—but not at later time periods. Examination of father–infant behavior sequences showed that as the "film" fathers decreased their total amount of stimulation over the three timepoints, there was a concurrent increase in the probability of these behaviors being contingent on infant cues. Thus, as the infant's behavioral repertoire expanded over the first 3 months, "film" fathers changed from a highly stimulating interaction style to one that was highly contingent upon infant behavior.

A similar pattern emerged for affectionate behavior. There were no film effects in the hospital or at 3 weeks; but at 3 months, "film" fathers displayed more affection than control fathers during feeding, though control fathers were more affectionate than "film" fathers during play. Once again, examination of sequences revealed that this decrease in overall frequency was coupled with an increase in responsiveness. In spite of the lower amount of affection that "film" fathers displayed during play, the manner with which affection was displayed was more closely linked to infant signals for these fathers than for control fathers.

In summary, the film intervention significantly modified selected aspects of father behavior and attitudes both in the hospital and through the first 3 months of their infant's lives. Of particular interest is the finding that the level of father participation in feeding and diapering increased as a result of this very limited intervention even after a 3-month period—at least in the case of boys. The heightened impact of the film for fathers of boys merits comment. The most plausible explanation for this finding is a predispositional one. Because fathers are already differentially predisposed to interact more with male than female infants, the film served to strengthen these already existing tendencies. As discussed elsewhere, there is a substantial body of literature in support of the claim that fathers both expect to and do show higher involvement with male than female infants (cf., Parke, 1981; Pedersen, 1980). Similarly, previous social-influence literature suggests that it is easier to produce further change in a direction that is already favored than in a nonfavored direction (McGuire, 1968).

Further evidence of the effectiveness of a film intervention during the postpartum period comes from a recent study by Arbuckle (1983).

In this project, Arbuckle used a film intervention developed by Parke (1980). Entitled *Becoming a Family*, the film demonstrated the same behavior, such as feeding and diapering, playing and infant capabilities, as were included in the Parke et al. (1980) film intervention. In contrast to the earlier film, this film depicted *both* mothers and fathers actively engaged in care-giving and game playing. Assessment of the impact of the film 4 to 6 weeks later indicated that first-time fathers who saw the film in comparison to a no-film control group of fathers had greater knowledge of infant sensory and cognitive capabilities and were higher in their perception of the importance of providing infant affection and stimulation. Moreover, the experimental fathers reported higher levels of involvement in the daily care-giving of their babies 4 to 6 weeks after the intervention. No sex-of-infant differences were reported. In spite of the limitation of this study by the reliance on self-report measures, the similarity of the findings across these two film-intervention studies underscores the potential value of this approach for modifying paternal behavior. Further work is clearly justified; particularly important would be studies that isolate the effective components of these film-intervention programs as well as comparison of film interventions with other types of interventions such as medical staff instruction, discussion groups, or informational booklets. By addressing the relative effectiveness of different approaches, the most optimal and most cost-effective procedures for different groups will become evident.

Another set of studies illustrates the potential of health-care providers such as pediatricians to play a supportive role for parents of young children. Although these studies have focused on mothers, these types of interventions could provide a useful strategy for promoting father parenting competence as well. In a study by Chamberlin (1979), mothers who participated in an educational program concerning child development during pediatric well-baby visits increased their knowledge of child development and their perceptions of being supported in the care-giving role. A related study (Whitt & Casey, 1982) suggests that mothers who were provided with an office-based pediatric intervention program emphasizing physical and preventive child care, developmental norms, and information on infant communication abilities during well-baby exams demonstrated a more positive relationship with their infants. The potential of this type of intervention for fathers will depend, in part, on changes in the flexibility of work schedules, which would permit fathers to participate more regularly in pediatric follow-up visits to the pediatrician. Alternatively, intervention programs should be offered on a more flexible basis, such as evenings and weekends, to accommodate fathers.

Although the full potential of hospital and other health-care facilities as settings for providing support for fathers is not yet realized, the studies reviewed in these sections illustrate the value of these settings for modifying the parenting behavior of fathers as well as mothers.

NONHOSPITAL EXPERIMENTAL INTERVENTIONS

Successful intervention is restricted to neither the hospital postpartum period, as two recent experimental-intervention studies designed to increase the level of father competence and involvement have demonstrated.

In one study, Dickie and Carnahan (1980) provided training to mothers and fathers of 4- to 12-month-old infants in order to increase their competence. Utilizing Goldberg's notion of competence as parental ability to assess, predict, elicit, and provide contingent response experiences for their infants, these investigators provided eight 2-hour weekly sessions. Training emphasized individual infant variation, knowledge of the infant's temperament and cues, provision of contingent experiences, and awareness of the infant's effect on the parents. Fathers who had participated in the training sessions, in contrast to fathers who had not participated, increased their interactions with their infants; specifically, they talked, touched, held, attended more, and gave more contingent responses to infant smiles and vocalizations. The infants of the trained fathers sought interaction more than infants of fathers in the control group. However, mothers in the trained group decreased their interactions; in view of this fact, that training did increase the judgments of the spouses' competence, it is possible that the wives of the trained fathers encouraged "their" competent husbands to assume a greater share of the infant care and interactional responsibilities. Interestingly, this finding underlines the reciprocal nature of the mother-father relationship and provides further support for viewing the family as a social system in which the activities of one member has an impact on the behavior of other family members. Finally, these data are consistent with nonhuman primate findings that father–infant involvement varies inversely with the degree of maternal restrictiveness (see Redican, 1976; Parke & Suomi, 1981; for reviews).

As a number of recent studies suggest, efforts to modify father–infant interaction need not be restricted to young infants. Zelazo, Kotelchuck, Barber, and David (1977) selected 20 very low-interacting fathers and their 12-month-old firstborn sons for an intervention study. These fathers did little care-taking or playing and were present only occasionally when their child was awake. Twelve fathers received an intervention involving playing with their infants for ½ hour per day for 4 weeks in their homes. To facilitate the play interaction, a schedule of games and toys were provided for the father. Using a social learning strategy (cf. Bandura, 1977), the experimenters both demonstrated the games, toys, and styles of interaction and coached the fathers in these activities prior to the intervention period. A control group of eight low-interacting fathers received no intervention. To assess the impact of the intervention on the infant's behavior, a lab-based parent–infant interaction session was held before and after the training period. This consisted of a 20-minute free-play period, with both parents in the room reading, followed by a series of maternal and paternal departures. In comparison to the control group, infants in the experimental group increased their interaction with their fathers in the free-play session; these infant boys looked more at their fathers and initiated more interaction with them. Separation protest was not affected by the experimental intervention.

This was surprising in view of earlier reports that as father involvement increased, separation upset in the presence of a stranger lessened (Kotelchuck, 1972; Spelke et al., 1973). Although it was a pioneering study, there were a number of limitations. First, the fathers were instructed to initiate interactions in the lab sessions, and so it is unclear whether there were increases in father behaviors directed to their infants. Second, it is unfortunate that these investigators did not monitor the amount of interaction between fathers and infants in their homes as a follow-up to their intervention program. In spite of these limitations, the investigation further underlines the modifiability of the father–infant relationship. It also serves as a corrective reminder of the fact that modification of early social-interaction patterns are not necessarily limited to a particular "critical" period. As both Zelazo and his colleagues and many earlier intervention studies (Rheingold, 1956; Skeels, 1966) have demonstrated, infant responsiveness can be modified at a variety of age levels. A similar caution applies to the development of parental responsiveness to infants. Moreover, the early contact studies (cf. Klaus & Kennell, 1976, 1981) which suggested the importance of the immediate postpartum period for the facilitation of parental responsiveness to their infants have been seriously challenged (Goldberg, 1983; Lamb & Hwang, 1982). Instead, theorists are now recognizing the capacity of both parents and infants for continual adaptation to shifting social circumstances; in turn, this suggests that there is probably no critical time period for the formation of social relationships (Cairns, 1977).

Considerable care must be taken with the implementation of these support systems and the important issue of parent's rights needs to be considered. An implicit model of many intervention programs for fathers is the egalitarian rather than the more traditional family organization. However, the goal should not be to shift all families toward an egalitarian family arrangement. Instead, the goal should be to provide the quality and quantity of support that will enable each family to enact their roles competently within their own ideological framework. For some families this may mean minimal father participation; in other families this may mean shared responsibility between spouses. Too often, "more" is equated with "improvement"; however, in many families, increased father participation may cause conflict and disruption as a result of the threat to well-established and satisfying role definitions. Intervention, therefore, should be sensitively geared to the needs of individual families where the dynamics and ideology of the couple are given primary recognition.

CONCLUSION AND FUTURE DIRECTIONS

It is clear from our review that fathers are effective support agents for mothers in the postnatal period. Many questions remain concerning processes through which paternal support operates. For example, it is far from evident in the current literature which specific aspects of father support are most critical in effectively modifying maternal behavior. Physical, social emotional support often co-occur and the independent contribution of these differing types of paternal support merit careful examination. Similarly, a multifaceted definition of each of these forms of support is necessary if we are to move to a more process-based analysis of the effective components of these complex variables. In addition, greater attention needs to be given to the circumstances under which paternal support is elicited. While some progress has been made in identifying factors that determine paternal involvement, it is important to place this inquiry firmly within a life-span framework. This viewpoint will increase awareness of the impact of individual life trajectories in work, marital, and family spheres on how father and mother roles are defined. Moreover, the importance of monitoring secular changes in medical, social, and economic areas and an assessment of these shifts on the father's role as a support agent is underscored by a life-span approach.

Fathers as well as mothers require support, and in this chapter some of the possible avenues through which support can be provided are outlined. Again, many questions are left unanswered. Probably the most pressing need is for more research on the ways in which mothers provide support for fathers. It is clear that the husband–wife relationship is important, but the specific aspects of this relationship which affect men's role as fathers is unclear. Moreover, it is not yet evident whether mothers and fathers are affected in similar or different ways by a supportive or dysfunctional marital relationship. Of central importance is the mother's expectations concerning the father's role; more attention needs to be given to the mother's gatekeeper function (i.e., the extent to which mothers determine or control the degree of access that others have to care-giving and household tasks), and the degree to which mothers do in fact limit the degree of father involvement. The supportive and gatekeeping roles of mothers merit independent assessment.

The negative as well as the positive aspects of increased father involvement merit more attention. As fathers increase their involvement in care-giving as well as household tasks, the potential for more conflict between spouses may increase as well. Do mothers resent father involvement in domains that have traditionally been maternal domains? Better information concerning the negative impact of increased father participation would be helpful in the design and implementation of training programs for fathers and their families.

What are the most effective settings for intervention? Although hospitals have been a convenient context, other settings such as the home and workplace merit examination. Is the early postpartum period the most optimal time for intervention? Or is pregnancy or a few months postpartum more effective for producing lasting change in the father's role? The form of the support has received little systematic attention. Particularly if the development of programs aimed at widespread dissemination is a goal, more comparative work on the relative effectiveness of different types of supportive intervention for fathers is imperative. Finally, in spite of a long history of sociopsychological research on the importance of the identity of the change agent, little effort has been devoted to assessing the relative effectiveness of different types of intervention agents for fathers.

In spite of the host of unresolved issues, it is clear that fathers play an important supportive function within families. To discover better ways to assist fathers in being more effective contributors within the family is a goal that would benefit all members of the family system— mothers and infants as well as fathers.

REFERENCES

Arbuckle, M.B. (1983). *The effects of educational intervention on fathers' relationships with their infants.* Unpublished doctoral dissertation, University of North Carolina at Greensboro.

Bandura, A. (1977). *Social learning theory.* Englewood, NJ: Prentice-Hall.

Beal, J.A. (1984). *The effect of demonstration of the Brazelton Neonatal Assessment Scale on the father–infant relationship.* Paper presented at the International Conference on Infant Studies, New York.

Belsky, J. (1984). Mothering, fathering and the family triad: Exploring family system's processes. Paper presented at Conference on Transition to Fatherhood, Washington, DC.

Bem, S.L., & Lenney, E. (1976). Sex typing and the avoidance of cross-sex behavior. *Journal of Personality and Social Psychology, 33,* 48–54.

Bem, S.L., Martyna, W., & Watson, C. (1976). Sex typing and androgyny: Further explorations of the expressive domain. *Journal of Personality and Social Psychology, 34,* 1016–1023.

Bittman, S., & Zalk, S.R. (1978). *Expectant fathers.* New York: Hawthorn.

Bloom-Feshbach, J. (1979). The beginnings of fatherhood. Unpublished doctoral dissertation, Yale University.

Bohen, H., & Viveros-Long, A. (1981). *Balancing jobs and family life: Do flexible work schedules help.* Philadelphia: Temple University Press.

Bottoms, S.F., Rosen, M. & Sokol, R.J. (1980). The increase in the cesarean birth rate. *New England Journal of Medicine, 302,* 559–563.

Bronfenbrenner, U. (1979). *The ecology of human development.* Cambridge, MA: Harvard University Press.

Bronfenbrenner, U., & Crouter, A. (1982). Work and family through time and space. In S.B. Kamerman & C.D. Hayes (Eds.), *Families that work: Children in a changing world.* Washington: National Academy Press.

Brown, J.V., & Bakeman, R. (1980). Relationships of human mothers with their infants during the first year of life: Effects of prematurity. In R.W. Bell & W.P. Smotherman (Eds.), *Maternal influences and early behavior.* Holliswood, NY: Spectrum.

Cairns, R.B. (1977). Beyond social attachment: The dynamics of interactional development. In T.A. Alloway, P. Pliner, & L. Krames (Eds.), *Attachment behavior.* New York: Plenum.

Chamberlin, R.W. (1979). *Effects of educating mothers about child development in physicians' offices on mother and child functioning over time.* Paper presented at the annual meeting of the American Psychological Association, New York.

Cochran, M.M., & Brassard, J.A. (1979). Child development and personal social networks. *Child Development, 50,* 601–616.

Conway, E., & Brackbill, Y. (1970). Delivery medication and infant outcome: An empirical study. *Monographs of the Society for Research in Child Development, 35,* 24–34.

Daniels, P., & Weingarten, K. (1982). *Sooner or later: The timing of parenthood in adult lives.* New York: Norton.

Dickie, J., & Carnahan, S. (1980). Training in social competence: The effect on mothers, fathers and infants. *Child Development, 51,* 1248–1251.

Dickie, J.R., & Matheson, P. (1984). *Mother–father–infant: Who needs support?* Paper presented at the annual meeting of the American Psychological Association, Toronto.

Elardo, R., Bradley, R., & Caldwell, B. (1975). The relation of infants' home environments to mental test performance from six to thirty-six months: A longitudinal analysis. *Child Development, 46,* 71–76.

Entwisle, D.R., & Doering, S.G. (1980). *The first birth.* Baltimore: Johns Hopkins University Press.

Feldman, S.S., Nash, S.C., & Aschenbrenner, B.G. (1983). Antecedents of fathering. *Child Development, 54,* 1628–1636.

Furstenberg, F. (1976). *Unplanned parenthood.* New York: Free Press.

Gladieux, J.D. (1978). Pregnancy—The transition to Parenthood. In W.B. Miller & L.F. Newman (Eds.), *The first child and family formation.* Chapel Hill, NC: Carolina Population Center.

Goldberg, S. (1983). Parent–infant bonding: Another look. *Child Development, 54,* 1355–1382.

Grossman, F.K., Eichler, L.S., & Winickoff, S.A. (1980). *Pregnancy, birth and parenthood.* San Francisco: Jossey-Bass.

Harris, J.M., Veit, S.W., Allen, G.J., & Chinsky, J.M. (1974). Aide-resident ratio and ward population density as mediators of social interaction. *American Journal of Mental Deficiency, 79,* 320–326.

Hawthorne, J.T., Richards, M.P.M., & Callon, M. (1978). A study of parental visiting of babies in a special care unit. In F.S.W. Briblecombe, M.P.M. Richards, & N.R.C. Robertson (Eds.), *Early separation and special care nurseries.* London: SIMP/Heinemann Medical Books.

Henneborn, W.J., & Cogan, R. (1975). The effect of husband participation in reported pain and the probability of medication during labor and birth. *Journal of Psychosomatic Research, 19,* 215–222.

Herzog, J.M. (1979). Disturbances in parenting high-risk infants: Clinical impressions and hypotheses. In T.M. Field (Ed.), *Infants born at risk: Behavior and development.* New York: SP Medical and Scientific Books.

Hoffman, L.W. (1984). Work, family and the socialization of the child. In R.D. Parke, R. Emde, H. McAdoo, & G.P. Sackett (Eds.), *Review of Child Development Research* (Vol. 7). Chicago: University of Chicago Press.

Klaus, M.H., & Kennell, J.H. (1976). *Parent–infant bonding*. St. Louis: Mosby.

Klaus, M.H., & Kennell, J.H. (1981). *Parent–infant bonding* (2nd ed.). St. Louis: Mosby.

Kotelchuck, M. (1972). *The nature of the child's tie to his father*. Unpublished Ph.D. dissertation, Harvard University.

Kotelchuck, M. (1976). The infant's relationship to the father: Experimental evidence. In M.E. Lamb (Ed.), *The role of the father in child development* (pp. 329–344). New York: Wiley.

Lamb, M.E., & Hwang, C. (1982). Maternal attachment and mother–infant bonding: A critical review. In M.E. Lamb & A.L. Brown (Eds.), *Advances in developmental psychology* (Vol. 2). Hillsdale, NJ: Erlbaum.

Lamb, M.E., Frodi, A.M., Hwang, P., Frodi, M., & Steinberg, J. (1982). Attitudes and behavior of traditional and nontraditional parents in Sweden. In R. Emde & R. Harman (Eds.), *Attachment and affiliative systems: Neurobiological and psychobiological aspects*. New York: Plenum.

Leiderman, P.H., & Seashore, M.J. (1975). *Mother–infant separation: Some delayed consequences. Parent–infant interaction.* Amsterdam: Elsevier North Holland.

Lewis, M., & Feiring, C. (1981). Direct and indirect interactions in social relationships. In L.P. Lipsitt (Ed.), *Advances in infancy research* (Vol. 1). Norwood, NJ: Ablex.

MacDonald, K., & Parke, R.D. (1986). Parent–child physical play: The effects of sex and age of children and parents. *Sex Roles, 7–8,* 367–378.

Maklan, D. (1976). *The four-day workweek: Blue collar adjustment to a nonconventional arrangement of work and leisure time.* Unpublished Doctoral Dissertation, University of Michigan.

Marton, P., Minde, K., & Perrotta, M. (1981). The role of the father for the infant at risk. *American Journal of Orthopsychiatry, 51,* 672–679.

McCluskey, K.A., Killarney, J., & Papini, D.R. (1983). Adolescent pregnancy and parenthood: Implications for development. In E.C. Callahan & K.A. McCluskey (Eds.), *Life-span developmental psychology: Non-normative life events*. New York: Academic Press.

McGuire, W.J. (1968). The nature of attitudes and attitude change. In G. Lindzey & E. Aronson (Eds.), *Handbook of social psychology*. Vol. 3. Reading, MA: Addison-Wesley.

Minde, K., Trehub, S., Corter, C., Boukydis, C., Celhoffer, L., & Marton, P. (1978). Mother–child relationships in the premature nursery: An observational study. *Pediatrics, 61,* 373–379.

Murray, A.D., Dolby, R.M., Nation, R.L., & Thomas, D.B. (1981). Effects of epidural anesthesia on newborns and their mothers. *Child Development, 52,* 71–82.

Parke, R.D. (1981). *Fathers*. Cambridge, MA: Harvard University Press.

Parke, R.D., Hymel, S., Power, T.G., & Tinsley, B.R. (1980). Fathers and risk: A hospital based model of intervention. In D.B. Sawin, R.C. Hawkins, L.O. Walker, & J.H. Penticuff (Eds.), *Psychosocial risks in infant–environment transactions*. New York: Brunner/Mazel.

Parke, R.D., & O'Leary, S.E. (1976). Father–mother–infant interaction in the newborn period: Some findings, some observations and some unresolved issues. In K. Riegel & J. Meacham (Eds.), *The developing individual in a changing world: Vol. II. Social and environmental issues*. The Hague: Mouton.

Parke, R.D., O'Leary, S.E., & West, S. (1972). Mother–father–newborn interaction: effects of maternal medication, labor and sex of infant. *Proceedings of the American Psychological Association*, 85–86.

Parke, R.D., Power, T.G., & Fisher, T. (1980). The adolescent father's impact on the mother and child. *Journal of Social Issues, 36*, 88–106.

Parke, R.D., Power, T.G., & Gottman, J.M. (1979). Conceptualizing and quantifying influence patterns in the family triad. In M.E. Lamb, S.J. Suomi, & G.R. Stephenson (Eds.), *Social interaction analysis: Methodological issues*. Madison: University of Wisconsin Press.

Parke, R.D., & Sawin, D.B. (1975, April). *Infant characteristics and behavior as elicitors of maternal and paternal responsibility in the newborn period*. Paper presented at the biennial meeting of the Society for Research in Child Development, Denver.

Parke, R.D., & Sawin, D.B. (1980). The family in early infancy: Social interactional and attitudinal analyses. In F.A. Pedersen (Ed.), *The father–infant relationship: Observational studies in the family setting*. New York: Praeger Special Studies.

Parke, R.D., & Suomi, S.J. (1981). Adult male–infant relationships: Human and non-human primate evidence. In K. Immelmann, G.W. Barlow, L. Petrinovich, & M. Main (Eds.), *Behavioral development: The Bielefeld Interdisciplinary Project*. New York: Cambridge University Press.

Parke, R.D., & Tinsley, B.R. (1982). The early environment of the at-risk infant: Expanding the social context. In D. Bricker (Ed.), *Intervention with at risk and handicapped infants: From research to application*. Baltimore: University Park Press.

Parke, R.D., & Tinsley, B.R. (1984). Fatherhood: Historical and contemporary perspectives. In K. McCluskey & H. Reese (Eds.), *Life span development: Historical and generational effects*. New York: Academic Press.

Pedersen, F.A. (1975). *Mother, father, and infant as an interactive system*. Paper presented at the annual meeting of the American Psychological Association, Chicago.

Pedersen, F.A. (Ed.). (1980). *The father–infant relationship: Observational studies in the family setting*. New York: Praeger Special Studies.

Pedersen, F.A., Cain, R., Zaslow, M., & Anderson, B. (1980, April). *Variation in infant experience with alternative family organization*. Paper presented at the International Conference on Infant Studies, New Haven, CT.

Peterson, G.H., Mehl, L.E., & Leiderman, P.H. (1979). The role of some birth-related variables in father attachment. *American Journal of Orthopsychiatry, 49*, 330–338.

Pleck, J.H. (1983). Husbands' paid work and family roles: Current research issues. In H.Z. Lopata & J.H. Pleck (Eds.), *Research on the interweave of social roles: Vol. 3. Families and jobs*. Greenwich, CT: JAI.

Radin, N. (1982). Primary caregiving and role-sharing fathers. In M.E. Lamb (Ed.), *Nontraditional families*. Hillsdale, NJ: Erlbaum.

Ragozin, A.S., Basham, R.B., Crnic, K.A., Greenberg, M.T., & Robinson, N.M. (1982). Effects of maternal age on parenting role. *Developmental Psychology, 18*, 627–634.

Redican, W.K. (1976). Adult male–infant interactions in non-human primates. In M.E. Lamb (Ed.), *The role of the father in child development*. New York: Wiley.

Rendina, I., & Dickerscheid, J.D. (1976). Father involvement with first-born infants. *Family Coordinator, 25*, 373–379.

Rheingold, H.L. (1956). The modification of social responsiveness in institutional babies. *Monographs of the Society for Research in Child Development*, 21 (63).

Richards, M.P.M., Dunn, J.F., & Antonis, B. (1977). Caretaking in the first year of life: The role of fathers' and mothers' social isolation. *Child: Care, Health and Development*, 3, 23–26.

Robinson, J.P. (1977). *How Americans use time*. New York: Praeger.

Russell, G. (1978). The father role and its relation to masculinity, femininity and androgyny. *Child Development*, 49, 1174–1181.

Russell, G. (1981). Shared-caregiving families: An Australian Study. In M.E. Lamb (Ed.), *Non-traditional families*. Hillsdale, NJ: Erlbaum.

Russell, G. (1982a). *The changing role of fathers*. St. Lucia, Australia: University of Queensland Press.

Russell, G. (1982b). Shared-caregiving families: An Australian study. In M.E. Lamb (Ed.), *Non-traditional Families: Parenting and child development*. Hillsdale, NJ: Erlbaum.

Russell, G., & Radin, N. (1983). Increased paternal participation: The fathers' perspective. In M.E. Lamb & A. Sagi (Eds.), *Fatherhood and family policy*. Hillsdale, NJ: Erlbaum.

Skeels, H. (1966). Adult status of children with contrasting early life experiences. *Monographs of the Society for Research in Child Development*, 31 (3).

Sosa, R., Kennell, J.H., Klaus, M.H., Robertson, S., & Urrutia, J. (1980). The effect of a supportive companion on perinatal problems, length of labor and mother–infant interaction. *New England Journal of Medicine*, 303, 597–600.

Switzky, L.T., Vietze, P., & Switzky, H. (1979). Attitudinal and demographic predictors of breast-feeding and bottle-feeding behavior in mothers of six-week-old infants. *Psychological Reports*, 45, 3–14.

Szalai, A. (Ed.). (1972). *The use of time: Daily activities of urban and suburban populations in twelve countries*. The Hague: Mouton.

Tinsley, B.R., & Parke, R.D. (1983). The person–environment relationship: Lessons from families with preterm infants. In D. Magnusson & V. Allen (Eds.), *Human development: An interactional perspective*. New York: Academic Press.

Tinsley, B.R., & Parke, R.D. (1984). Grandparents as support and socialization agents. In M. Lewis (Ed.), *Beyond the dyad*. New York: Plenum.

Tinsley, B.R. & Parke, R.D. (1987). Grandparents as interactive and social support agents for families with young infants. *International Journal of Aging and Human Development*.

Unger, D.G. (1979). *An ecological approach to the family: The role of social networks, social stress and mother-child interaction*. Unpublished masters thesis, Merrill-Palmer Institute.

Vietze, P.M., MacTurk, R.H., McCarthy, M.E., Klein, R.P., & Yarrow, L.J. (1980). *Impact of mode of delivery on father– and mother–infant interaction at 6 and 12 months*. Paper presented at the International Conference on Infant Studies, New Haven, CT.

Walker, K., & Woods, M. (1976). *Time use: A measure of household production of family goods and services*. Washington, DC: American Home Economics Association.

Whitt, J.K., & Casey, P.H. (1982). The mother–infant relationship and infant development: The effect of pediatric intervention. *Child Development*, 53, 948–956.

Widmayer, S.M., & Field, T.M. (1980). Effects of Brazelton demonstration on early interactions of preterm infants and their teenage mothers. *Infant Behavior and
Development, 3*, 79–89.

Winnett, R.A., & Neale, M.S. (1978). *Family life and the world of work: A preliminary
report of the effects of flextime.* Paper presented at the annual meeting of the
American Psychological Association, Toronto.

Yogman, M.W. (1981). Development of the father–infant relationship. In H. Fitzgerald,
B. Lester, & M.W. Yogman (Eds.), *Theory and research in behavioral pediatrics*
(Vol. 1). New York: Plenum.

Zelazo, P.R., Kotelchuck, M., Barber, L., & David, J. (1977). *Fathers and sons: An experimental
facilitation of attachment behaviors.* Paper presented at the biennial meeting
of the Society for Research in Child Development, New Orleans.

CHAPTER 6
Stressful Life Events, Social Supports, and Parent–Child Interaction: Similarities and Differences in Single-Parent and Two-Parent Families

Marsha Weinraub
Barbara M. Wolf
Temple University

Other chapters in this volume (Crockenberg, Ch. 1, Crnic & Greenberg, Ch. 2) and elsewhere (Belsky, 1984; Cochran & Brassard, 1979) consider the mechanisms by which stress and social support systems may affect characteristics of the parent–child interaction and subsequent child development. In this chapter, we consider a small but increasingly prevalent family type—single-parent families. Preliminary data (Weinraub & Wolf, 1983) have suggested that parent–child interactions in these families may be especially influenced by stress and particular characteristics of the social-support system. Here we provide more complete data on a larger sample of these families and explore not only the relationships between social supports, life stress events and parent–child interactions, but also the relationships of these variables to child outcome. Such an approach enables us to consider (1) how stressful life events and social-support variables may differentially affect families of differing structures and needs, (2) the underlying process by which stressful life events and social-support variables influence child de-

This study was partially supported by Grant Number R01 MH/HD 32189 from the National Institute of Mental Health and from several grants from the Temple University Biomedical Research Support Fund. The authors are grateful for assistance in all aspects of this research from Susan Ansul, Sally Haimo, Sharon Marchon, Alan Sockloff, Susan Cohen, Linda Roberts, and others who have worked in the Infant Behavior Laboratory. This study could not have been done without the input, cooperation, and support from the families who participated in this project. Requests for reprints should be sent to Marsha Weinraub, Department of Psychology, Temple University, Philadelphia, Pennsylvania 19122.

velopment, and (3) the *direct* and *indirect* effects of each of these variables on child outcome.

INCREASING PREVALENCE OF SINGLE-PARENT FAMILIES

One of the most dramatic changes over the last decade in the composition of family units is the increasing number of female-headed families. Between 1970 and 1984 the number of single-parent, female-headed families more than doubled (Rawlings, 1984). This change in family composition exceeds the percentage of change attributable to divorce and seems to reflect increasing births to single mothers. From 1970 to 1982, a period during which births to married women fell 11%, the number of births to single women increased 79% (Ventura, 1985). In 1984, births to unmarried mothers accounted for 21% of the total live births (National Center for Health Statistics, 1986).

Interestingly, women showing the greatest increases in the rate of births are single women between the ages of 35 years of age and older. Because the number of women aged 35 to 39 is increasing with the aging of the post–World War II "baby boom" generation, the total number of births in this group is rising along with the unmarried women's birth rate (percentage of single women giving birth).

Thus, the population of single mothers is changing. With demographic changes in the population, changes in prevailing attitudes about women's roles, and increasing tendencies of women to postpone marriage to pursue educations and careers, more women are being faced with the issue of whether or not to bear children out of the traditional context of the two-parent family.

Unfortunately, psychologists have little relevant information to help single women predict the potential effects on their children. Much of the available information about the effects of growing up in families without fathers has been collected from families in which the fathers' absence was due to separation, divorce, or death. Marital conflict and trauma due to the associated losses (financial as well as social and emotional) may account for many of the differences observed between children in single-parent and two-parent families (Herzog & Sudia, 1973; Rutter, 1981; Svanum, Bringle, & McLaughlin, 1982).

As many authors have observed (see, for example Lewis & Weinraub, 1976; Parke, 1979; and Weinraub, 1978), father absence is a variable that can affect children in a variety of direct and indirect ways. Direct effects of father absence include those relating to the reduced social attention, stimulation, and modeling resulting from the absence of a second, and particularly male, parent (Weinraub, 1978). Indirect effects of father absence include those resulting from increased social and financial stresses on the mother, and those resulting from the mother's loss of the social and emotional supports provided by a second adult (Herzog & Sudia, 1973; Saunders, 1983; Weiss, 1979). As psychologists turn their attention toward understanding the ways in which *indirect* effects of the father, in his absence as well as his presence, influence mother–child interactions and subsequent child outcome, interest has been directed toward the larger issue of the effects of stressful life events and social supports on maternal behavior.

STRESSFUL LIFE EVENTS AND SOCIAL SUPPORT IN SINGLE-PARENT FAMILIES

Life circumstances common to single-parent families, such as increased daily stresses, more chaotic home life, task overload, decreased financial resources, and reduced social supports, may influence marital adjustment, parenting behavior, and subsequent child outcome. In single divorced mothers, financial stress predicts increased maternal demands and child-rearing restrictions (Colletta, 1983). For both married and single mothers, environmental stress and significant life changes have been shown to be associated with harsher maternal discipline, including physical abuse (Gil, 1970; Justice & Justice, 1976; Gaines, Sandgrund, Green, & Power, 1978) and with attachment problems in young children (Vaughn, Egeland, & Sroufe, 1979). Social and practical supports for parents have been linked to maternal attitudes, adjustment, confidence, and self-esteem (e.g., Crnic, Greenberg, Ragozin, Robinson, & Basham, 1983; Gaines et al., 1978; Melges, 1968; Abernathy, 1973; Barret, 1978) as well as to maternal nurturance, discipline style and ability to appropriately stim-ulate the child (Gaines et al., 1978; Minturn & Lambert, 1964; Pascoe, Loda, Jeffries, & Earp, 1981; Unger & Wandersman, 1985; Weiss, 1979).

In addition to the potential *negative impact* on parenting behaviors, environmental stress and life-event changes have been associated with somatic problems, emotional/behavioral disorders, and learning diffi-culties in children from both single-parent and two-parent homes (Billings & Moos, 1983; Eiduson, 1983; Gersten, Langner, Eisenberg, & Orzek, 1974; Kurdek & Blisk, 1983; Richman, 1977; Sandler & Block, 1979). Yet, since life events may necessitate adjustments in both the parent's and child's daily life, it is uncertain whether the child behavior problems associated with life changes are the direct result of stress on the child or the indirect result of the negative impact of stressful life events on the psychological and parenting functioning of the parents.

In this chapter we examine the influence not of *father absence per se* on child outcome, but how being in a family without a father can affect the mother's experiences of stress and social support. Do these differential experiences with stressful life events and social supports affect her interactions with her child; and if so, how? Are the effects of stressful events and social supports intricately interrelated, or can their separate effects be evaluated both on the mother–child interaction and on subsequent child outcome?

A subset of the data to be described here was previously reported by us in *Child Development* in 1983. In that article, we reported data from 14 single and 14 matched two-parent families showing that single-parent mothers tended to have fewer social contacts, work longer hours, and receive less emotional and parenting support. They tended to have less stable social networks and experience more stressful life changes. Most significant were the findings that different variables predicted optimal mother–child interaction in the two groups. Variables predicting optimal mother–child interaction in single-parent families were fewer stressful life events, *reduced* social contact, and increased parenting support. Predicting optimal interaction in two-parent families were fewer stressful life events, satisfaction with emotional support, and the availability of household help. Three variables—social contact, household help, and employment—differentially predicted mother–child interactions in the two groups.

In this report we provide information from a larger group (38 mother-child pairs); we explore the independent contributions of stressful events and social supports; and, most importantly, we investigate the effects of these variables not only on the mother–child interactions, but also on child outcome measures.

Participants. The sample consisted of 38 mother-child pairs—19 children from single-parent families, and 19 children from two-parent families. We defined "single mothers" as women who had raised their child since the child's birth or shortly thereafter without the presence of a male father figure in the home. Of the 19 single mothers in our sample, nine were never married and had made a conscious decision to raise their child on their own prior to their child's birth. Four of these women had made a conscious choice to become pregnant; one had used artificial insemination. Ten of the single mothers (five mothers of sons) had been separated or divorced prior to or very soon after the child's birth.

In four single-parent families, the father had lived at home with the child for a short period. In three cases—two girls and one boy—the father had lived at home for 1 month, for 4 months, and for 6 months respectively. In the fourth case, the father lived at home with his son for 15 months. We did not see this child in our study until he was 4½ years of age, so he had lived for the last 3 years in a single-parent family.

We recruited single and married mothers from letters to pediatricians, posters in health clinics, day-care centers, women's centers, and parenting organizations. In addition, we placed advertisements in local newspapers, in newsletters of single-parent organizations, and made announcements on local radio stations. For each single-parent child who was eligible, we made every effort to select a two-parent child who was matched on each of the following variables: child race, sex and age, maternal age, education, profession, and hours employment. In two cases, two parent matches were neighbors recommended by the single-parent families.

Each family status group included nine boys and 10 girls. The mean age of the children was 36.7 months, ranging from 27 to 55 months. The ages of boys and girls from single- and two-parent families were not significantly different. The majority of children were singletons; in addition, there were four firstborn children from two-parent families (two girls and two boys), and there were two girls who were second borns from single-parent families. All of the mothers in the sample were white. In the single-parent sample, one boy and one girl had black fathers. Ages and educational levels of single and married mothers were not significantly different. The mean age of the mothers was 32.9 years, ranging from 23 to 44 years. Four mothers had high school degrees, 10 mothers had 2 or more years of college, eight mothers had college degrees, and 16 mothers had graduate/professional training.

Certainly, this sample of families is not representative of the population of single or married families. On the average, our mothers are older, better educated, and of higher professional levels than those in the general population. However, we chose these families because we wanted to avoid the problems of social class and income differences that often confound comparisons of single- and two-parent families. (See Svanum & Bringle, 1982, for a discussion of these issues.) For the most part, our families represent the middle-class ideal—educated, professional, and financially secure. With demographic variables equal between single- and two-parent families, how are these families different?

There were some important variables on which we were unsuccessful in our matching process. Significant differences were found in the number of hours per week single mothers were employed as compared with married mothers (33.7 hours vs. 17.5 hours, F (1, 36) = 11.46 $p < .001$). Only one single mother, but six married mothers, were not employed outside the home. Two single parents were employed fewer than 20 hours per week, three were employed between 20 and 35 hours per week, and 13 were employed full time (more than 35 hours per week). In contrast, five married mothers were employed fewer than 20 hours per week, four were employed between 20 and 35 hours per week, and only five of 13 employed married mothers were employed full time. Although the single-parent mothers were employed more hours per week than the married mothers, the mean per person income for single-parent households was less than that of two-parent families ($7,309 vs. $9,022, 1980 dollars). This difference, however, was not a statistically significant one, and reflects the large variation in family income within both groups.

PROCEDURES

There were three visits with each mother and her child. On each of the first and second visits, we saw mothers and their children for about an hour and a half in the laboratory. We collected measures of parent–child interaction, children's gender-role development, children's intelligence, and children's responses to strangers. On the third visit, we visited the parents' homes and interviewed the mothers concerning their experiences and attitudes in a variety of areas. Questionnaires were distributed after each lab visit and collected on the subsequent visit. In this chapter, we report only information concerning parent–child interaction, stress, social support, and related measures of child outcome. Effects on gender development are not reported here.

MEASURES

Mother–child interaction. We used a structured laboratory task to assess the quality and frequency of mother–child interactions. The task, modified from one used by Diana Baumrind (1967), yielded information concerning maternal control, maternal communications, and child compliance with maternal demands.

A female graduate student introduced the task. She demonstrated a number of labeling, categorization, and sequencing activities that could be done with the cuisinaire rods. These activities involved the exploration of concepts of size, shape, and color for younger children; and for older children, the concept of number. The mother was instructed to choose some activity or activities with the rods that would be an appropriate and engaging learning experience for her child. Opposite the table where the mother and child were working were a number of interesting and distracting toys. The mother was asked to keep her child from playing with these very tempting toys until after the learning task was completed. After 10 minutes, the mother and child were signaled to return the rods to their case.

Videotapes of the interaction episodes were scored using a 5-point rating scale adapted from Baumrind (1967). The revised scale yielded a total summary score as well as summary scores based on from four to nine items. *Maternal control* included items measuring the mother's attempts to have her child conform to the rules of the task and the extent to which she gave effective directions. *Maternal maturity demands* measured the extent of the mother's demands on her child, given the child's age, to perform intellectually and to act maturely and independently. *Maternal nurturance* measured the mother's responsiveness to the child's frustration level, interests, activities, and physical needs as well as the mother's displays of affection and absence of her displays of hostility. *Mother–child communication* measured the ease and spontaneity of the mother's verbal and nonverbal communications and the extent to which the mother acknowledged her child's communications. The *child's compliance* measured the degree to which the child responded easily and freely to the mother's requests and to her activities with the rods, as well as the degree to which the child was actively oppositional or inattentive. This last measure was considered one of the child outcome measures.

Alpha coefficients among the items making up the summary scores ranged from .72 to .93, indicating internal consistency of items in each category. Interrater reliability estimates were obtained by having the coders independently code nine of the same tapes. Correlations between raters for scores in each category were—maternal control: .98; maternal maturity demands: .75; mother-child communications: .64; maternal nurturance: .93; and child compliance: .97.

Baumrinds's findings with the original rating instrument suggest that, despite the artificiality of the laboratory task, the cuisinaire rod task is a reliable and valid measure of mother–child interactions. In her research, Baumrind found that observers' ratings of maternal behaviors correlated highly with ratings of maternal behavior at home and children's social competence at school.

Child Outcome. We obtained several indicators of child outcome: children's intelligence as measured using the Peabody Picture Vocabulary Test (PPVT), children's compliance with maternal requests as measured in the laboratory on the first visit (see preceding), and children's at-risk scores as measured by the Child Behavior Form (CBF, Lorion, 1983). This last questionnaire was completed by all mothers between the first and second laboratory visits.

The Child Behavior Form (CBF) is a 28-item preschool developmental screening measure designed to identify preschool and kindergarten children "at risk" for educational and/or psychosocial problems (Lorion,

Barker, Cahill, Gallagher, Passons, & Kaufki, 1981). The 28 behavioral items are scored on a checklist by parents or teachers using a 5-point rating scale of frequency of occurrence. The questionnaire can be used to obtain four scores: three factor scores of Aggressiveness, Readiness to Learn, and Moodiness, and a Total Summary Score, reflecting the "at risk" nature of the child for educational and/or social-emotional problems. Initial research with 570 preschool children has indicated acceptable internal consistency and interrater reliability (Lorion et al., 1981). Evidence of construct validity was suggested by the form's ability to discriminate between children in regular and special education programs, after controls for age and social economic status were used (Lorion et al., 1981). The CBF has been used as an initial evaluation tool in an early-intervention program to prevent emotional and learning problems in children (Lorion, Hightower, Work, Shockley, & Clapp, 1983).

Stressful Life Events. We used a modified version of the Holmes and Rahe (1967) Social Readjustment Rating Scale (SRRS) to measure frequency of stressful life events. This 53-item checklist contained the original 43 potentially stressful life events listed by Holmes and Rahe, and an additional 10 items covering life changes in activities and relationships relevant to women in this age range. Each mother was instructed to check the life events that occurred in the preceding 12 months. The total stress score for each mother was the number of items checked. Because previous researchers (Caplan, 1981; Dohrenwend & Dohrenwend, 1981; Gore, 1981) have suggested that both social supports and an individual's own personal resources and coping style affect the individual's subjective perception of the stressfulness of life event changes, subjective rating measures of the stressfulness of these events were not used. In this way, we hoped to avoid confounding measures of stressful life events with measures of social support.

Social Supports. To measure the nature and extent of maternal social supports, we developed the *Social Network Form.*[1] The questionnaire covers five areas: (1) social contacts, (2) emotional supports, (3) parenting supports, (4) practical help with child-care and household tasks, and (5) satisfaction with the supports received. The questionnaire asks respondents to list the four friends and relatives they see most frequently and then to rate the extent to which each of these relationships are intimate, supportive, and helpful. While many questions request in-

---

[1] Copies of the Social Network Form and information for scoring can be obtained from the authors.

formation about the four people initially listed, several allow consideration of others as well.

We obtained five summary scores from the questionnaire. *Total social contacts* measured the frequency of monthly social contacts a mother had with the individuals she saw most frequently. This score included contacts with each person individually, in groups, or by telephone or letter. *Emotional supports* measured how frequently the mother confided in and obtained emotional support from each of these four people, as well as from parenting groups and other organizations (church, women's organizations, etc.). *Parenting supports* measured the extent to which the mother valued the parenting beliefs of the people she saw most frequently, and the extent of parenting support she received from groups and organizations. Measures of *practical* help with child care and with *household chores* were each summary scores based on the number of hours of help the mother obtained weekly. Mother's *satisfaction with the support* she received *emotionally* and as a *parent*, involved the mother's rating of the adequacy of the support she received in each area.

Alpha coefficients were computed to determine the internal consistency of individual items making up the summary scores of social contacts, emotional support, parenting support and help with childcare and household responsibilities. Alpha coefficients ranged from .65 to .95, indicating acceptable cohesiveness of items making up the different summary scores.

Test-retest reliability of the SNF was calculated using 10 graduate students or graduate student wives, all of whom were mothers. The SNF was administered twice over a 2- to 3-week period. Test-retest correlations were acceptable.

STUDY RESULTS

Differences between Parent–Child Interactions and Child Outcomes in Single- and Two-Parent Families

There were few parent–child interaction or child-outcome differences between our single- and two-parent families. Single-parent mothers were less demanding of their children ($F = 5.29$, $p \leq .02$), but this overall family status effect was qualified by an interaction between family status and child sex ($F = 4.00$, $p \leq .05$). Only with sons were single-parent mothers less demanding. Overall, for the total parenting score, single mothers of sons scored lower than two-parent mothers or single-parent mothers of daughters ($F = 5.47$, $p \leq .03$). This suggests that parent–child interactions are less optimal for single mothers of sons than for other groups.

Only two of the six child outcome measures showed single-parent children to be different from two-parent children. Single-parent children tended to be seen more frequently by their mothers as aggressive ($F = 3.94$, $p \leqslant .055$). Also, sons of single-parent mothers were rated by the laboratory observers as being less compliant with their mothers' requests than other children ($F = 4.06$, $p \leqslant .05$). There were no differences between single- and two-parent children in intelligence, readiness to learn, moodiness, or total at-risk scores.

Table 1 presents the relationships between parental behaviors and child outcomes for the sample as a whole and for single- and two-parent samples separately. Except for intelligence scores, where parent–child interaction measures were not predictive of child outcomes in single-parent families, and except for emotionality scores, higher parent–child interaction scores were predictive of better child outcome for both single- and two-parent groups. Not only do these correlations demonstrate important relationships between parenting behavior and child outcome, they also lend validity to our selection of parenting behavior and child-outcome measures. The lack of correlation between single-parent behavior and child intelligence scores is puzzling, but suggests that single-parent children are affected to a larger extent by experiences outside the mother–child interaction, as we discuss later in this chapter.

Similarities and Differences in Stressful Events and Social Supports for Single- and Two-Parent Families

Single parents tended to experience more stressful life events than two-parent families (mean score for single parents = 9.26, mean for two parents = 6.58 events, $F = 2.57$, $p \leqslant .058$, one tailed test). Subsequent analysis of these stressful events scores indicated that single-parent mothers had significantly more stressful events in the areas of employment and changes in daily routines, whereas two-parent mothers were more likely to have stressful events relating to pregnancy. (See Ansul & Weinraub, 1984, for details.)

Single-parent mothers also experienced fewer social supports than two-parent mothers. These data are presented in Table 2. Single parents received less emotional support, received less support in their parenting role, felt their parenting supports were less adequate, tended to confide less in their frequent social contacts, and received less emotional and parenting support from groups and organizations in the community.

Table 1. Relationship between Parenting Behaviors and Child Outcome Measures (Partial Correlation Controlling for Child's Sex and Age)

Maternal Behavior		PPVT IQ	Child Response to Mother's Requests	CBFI Aggressiveness	CBF2 Readiness to Learn	CBF3 Emotionality	CBF Total at Risk
				Child Outcome Measure			
Maternal control	All	.37*	.85**	-.40*	.29[1]	-.10	-.41**
	SP	.06[b]	.79**	-.34[1]	.26	-.28	-.30
	2P	.73**	.88**	-.39[1]	.35[1]	-.10	-.42*
Maturity demands	All	.19	.56*	-.31*	.29[1]	-.11	-.34*
	SP	-.06	.54*	-.29	.14	-.14	-.29
	2P	.42*	.49*	-.25	.42*	-.16	-.31
Parent–child communication	All	.19	.71**	-.40*	.26[1]	-.11	-.37*
	SP	.11[a]	.53*	-.48*	.22	-.34	-.41[1]
	2P	.66**	.90**	-.33[1]	.27	-.04	-.31
Maternal nurturance	All	.07	.53**	-.44**	.20	-.28[1]	-.42**
	SP	-.18	.41[1]	-.57*	.26	-.52*	-.50*
	2P	.44*	.58**	-.28	.09	-.24	-.28
Total parenting	All	.26[1]	.83**	-.48**	.31*	-.19	-.48**
	SP	-.10[b]	.72**	-.55*	.29	-.44*	-.49*
	2P	.71**	.88**	-.40[1]	.34[1]	-.17	-.42*

[1] p ≤ .10 (one tailed test); *p ≤ .05 (one tailed test); **p ≤ .01 (one tailed test).
[a] = z test of differences between correlations for single- and two-parent samples, p ≤ .10.
[b] = z test of differences between single- and two-parent samples, p ≤ .05.

Table 2. Differences in Social Supports between Single and Married Mothers

		Single Mothers	Married Mothers	F Family Status[a]	F Sex
Total social contacts	Boys	82.56	96.78		2.41[1]
	Girls	106.00	138.50		
Total emotional support	Boys	62.53	75.86	7.91**	2.89[1]
	Girls	70.50	84.38		
Sense of emotional support	Boys	3.89	4.33		7.80**
	Girls	3.60	3.20		
Total parenting support	Boys	30.33	40.56	6.15**	
	Girls	33.52	39.30		
Sense of parenting support	Boys	3.89	4.33	3.84*	2.34[1]
	Girls	3.40	4.00		
Extent confide	Boys	1.67	2.33	3.07*	
	Girls	1.80	2.40		
Emotional support from groups	Boys	2.78	3.67	8.43**	
	Girls	2.80	5.10		
Parenting support from groups	Boys	2.44	3.78	8.41**	
	Girls	2.90	4.80		

[a] test for family status are one-tailed; all others are two-tailed.
[1] $p \leq .10$; *$p \leq .05$; **$p \leq .01$.

Relationships between Stressful Life Events and Social Supports

We checked to see whether there were relationships between the frequency of mothers' stressful life events and their experiences with emotional and parenting supports. These data are presented in Table 3.

For single parents, there were no significant relationships between the frequency of stressful life events and social-support measures, even though most of these correlations were in a negative direction. However, for married mothers, frequent stressful life events were more related to the mother's perception of less adequate emotional and parenting supports. Differences in the correlations between sense of emotional support and number of stressful live events for single- and two-parent mothers' approached significance ($z = 1.6$, $p \leq .10$).

How can we interpret this inverse relationship for married mothers between stress and social supports? There are a number of possibilities, but perhaps relevant here is the difference in the relationships for single and married parents, the nature of the stresses they experience, and the relationship of their stressful life events to individuals in their social-support system. The single mother's stresses are most frequently related to changes on the job or changes in her daily routines. Such individually experienced events are not likely to affect the availability of providers in the social system, though they could negatively affect the mother's perception of their adequacy. In contrast, the stressful life events most commonly experienced by married mothers—pregnancy, buying a house, changes in daily routine—are also likely to have a negative impact on the most significant member of her support system—her husband. His ability to be sensitive and responsive to his wife's emotional and parenting needs may be affected by stressful events they both experience. Thus, for married mothers, more than for single mothers, increased stressors may be jointly experienced by the most critical member of the social-support system and may therefore to a significant extent affect the availability of emotional and parenting supports.

Relationships between Stress, Social Supports, and Parent–Child Interactions

Even more important than the relationships between stressful life events and social supports is the relationships between each of these variables and maternal behavior in interaction with her child. Statistical controls were used to consider the independent effects of stressful life events and social supports. In order to examine these relationships most parsimoniously, we chose one variable from the set of social-support measures and one variable from the set of parent–child interaction measures. Total parenting support was selected as an indicator of social support because it was highly correlated with all other measures (r's > .3) and because it seemed most directly pertinent to parental behaviors. As our measure of maternal behavior in the parent–child interaction, we selected a composite score (scores across all 4 interaction measures summed), total parenting behavior. This composite score was correlated highly

Table 3. Correlations between Stress and Social Supports for Single and Married Mothers (Child Age and Child Sex Partialed)

	Stress Events			
Social Support	Single Mothers	Married Mothers	Difference between Correlations	All Parents
Sense emotional support	.10	−.43*	p ≤ .10	−.18
Total emotional support	−.21	.08		−.16
Sense parenting support	−.25	−.64**	p ≤ .05	−.38**
Total parenting support	−.19	−.40[1]		−.29*

[1] p ≤ .10; *p ≤ .05; **p ≤ .02.

Table 4. Relationships between Stress, Parenting Supports, and
Maternal Behavior in Parent–Child Interactions (with Child Age and
Sex Partialed)

	Single Mothers	Married Mothers	Total (Controlling for Family Status)
Stress→Maternal behavior (Controlling for parenting support)	−.53*	−.02	−.40**
Parenting support→Maternal behavior (Controlling for stress)	.40[1]	.37[1]	.32

[1]p ≤ .10 (two-tailed tests); *p ≤ .05 (two-tailed tests); **p < .01 (two-tailed tests).

(r's > .7) with the component scores. Correlations between stress, support and mother–child interaction measures are presented in Table 4.

As Table 4 indicates, frequency of stressful events affects maternal behavior in parent–child interactions, but only in single-parent families. The overall correlation (r = −.40, p ≤ .01) is due solely to these effects of stressful events on parent–child interactions in single-parent families. The differences between the correlations for single- and two-parent families approaches significance (p ≤ .10). Social supports, however, tend to contribute to more optimal parent–child interactions for both single- and two-parent families, and the effect for the total sample is significant (r = .32, p ≤ .05). Regardless of family status, the more mothers received support in their role as parents, the more optimal was their behavior in interaction with their child.

The difference in the correlations between stress and maternal behavior for single and married parents is of particular interest. Not only do single mothers tend to have slightly higher incidences of stressful events, but these stressful life events are more likely to affect their interaction with their child. The differing relationships between all three variables—stressful life events, parenting support, and parenting behavior—are presented graphically in Fig. 1.

For single mothers, frequency of stressful life events and total parenting support are unrelated, but both affect the mother's behavior with her child. However, for married mothers, parenting supports and stressful life events tend to be correlated, but stressful life events do not independently affect the mother's interaction with her child. Stressful life events tend to affect the availability of parenting support, which may then impinge upon her parenting behavior.

These data suggest that, for married mothers, the social supports that she receives, though they may be related to stressful life events in her life, may nevertheless serve to *buffer* the effects of stressful events on her parenting behavior. This buffering action may occur in two ways. First, fathers may provide emotional support, nurturance, and advice concerning parenting behavior, thereby preventing events from becoming serious strains on the mother's interactions with her child (e.g., Lewis & Weinraub, 1976; Pederson, Yarrow, Anderson, & Cain, 1979). Second, as alternative care-givers, fathers may also be able to take over some of the mother's parenting functions temporarily while mothers withdraw from the family situation and recover from the disorienting effects of stressful life events. Although this temporarily increased role of the father in interaction with his child due to his wife's experience of stress may affect the marital relationship, it may also serve to diffuse the effects of the mother's stress on her interaction with her child. In these ways, stressful events may have less effect on the mother–child relationship in two-parent families than they do in single-parent families.

These findings are similar to those of Crockenberg (1981) and Crockenberg and McCloskey (1985) in which stress and social supports had greater effects on the mother's sensitivity to her child with infants of difficult temperament. Perhaps stress is more apparent in some families than others, and perhaps this *vulnerability* to stress, this ability to be affected by stress, is what defines a high-risk family (Goldberg & Kearsley, 1983).

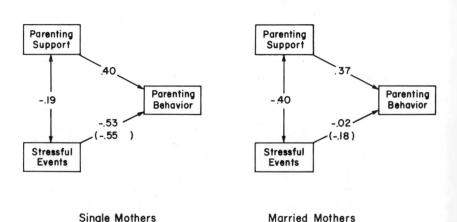

Single Mothers   Married Mothers

Figure 1 Relationships among stressful life events, parenting supports, and parenting behavior for single and married mothers. Correlations between parenting support and parenting behavior control for stressful life events; correlations between stressful life events and parenting behavior control for parenting support. In parentheses are correlations without these controls. All correlations are partialled for child age and sex.

Effects of Stressful Events on Child Outcome

Our data so far indicate that the frequency of stressful events affects mother–child interactions, at least in single-parent families. In addition, we have shown that parent–child interactions for both single- and two-parent families predict child outcome. Thus, life events may indirectly affect child outcome, particularly for single-parent families, through their disruptive effect on the mother's interaction with her child. However, can stressful life events, also *directly* affect the child's functioning in our single- and two-parent families?

In Table 5 are correlations between the frequency of stressful life events in the mother's life and child outcome measures, controlling for the effects of maternal behavior in interaction with her child. For children in single-parent homes, more frequent stressful life events tended to be negatively associated with lower children's intelligence scores ($r = -.34$, $p \leqslant .10$), lower readiness to learn ($r = -.33$, $p \leqslant .10$), and increased moodiness ($r = -.36$, $p \leqslant .10$). No such relationships were observed for children in two-parent families. Although these are only trends, they suggest that stress may have direct effects, independent of its effects on the mother–child interaction, for single parent children.

These results suggest a potentially greater vulnerability of children in single-parent families to the disruptive effect of stressful life events in the mother's life, above and beyond the indirect effects of stress on the mother's parenting behavior is held statistically constant. This finding is quite different from the findings of Crnic et al. (1983) regarding social support influences. Crnic and his colleagues showed that relationships between maternal social support and infant functioning disappeared

Table 5.   Relationships between Stressful Life Events and Child Outcome, Controlling for Maternal Behavior in Parent–Child Interactions (Child Age and Sex Partialed)

Stress→Child Outcome (Controlling for Maternal Behavior Interacting with Child)	Single Mothers	Married Mothers	Total (Controlling for Family Status)
Intelligence	$-.34^{1}$	.05	$-.11$
Aggression	.29	$-.24$	.07
Readiness to learn	$-.33^{1}$	.05	$-.15$
Moodiness	$.36^{1}$	$-.09$	.10
At risk	.26	$-.27$	.05
C Compliance	.00	$-.08$	.00

when maternal behavior was controlled for, suggesting that social support operates solely through its effect on maternal behavior. Whereas social support may influence the child indirectly through its effect on the mother's behavior, stressful life events may have a direct as well as indirect effect on the single-parent child. Indeed, as children grow older, the stressful events in the mother's life may have an increasingly significant direct effect on the child.

These findings appear to parallel those of Hodges, Wechsler, and Ballantine (1979) with children from divorced homes. Hodges, et al. suggested that children from divorced homes might be especially sensitive to parental functioning and to the cumulative effects of stress. When added to the impact of divorce, additional environment stressors, including such events as geographic moves and reduced finances, placed divorced children at greater risk for developing psychological difficulties. Children in single-parent homes may be placed doubly at risk when exposed to life events, directly as well as indirectly, through their primary care-giver's ability to care for them. Stressful life events may result in learning and emotional difficulties for the child at a time when the single parent is herself less able to effectively cope with and respond to the child's difficulties. In light of the relationships presented in Fig. 1, these findings suggest that effective social support may be particularly critical for single parents to counteract the negative effects of stressful events. Of course, the small size of our sample and the weak relationships on our data suggest caution in these interpretations.

Summary of Findings

Our data reveal very few overall differences in parent–child interactions or child outcome in single- and two-parent families. However, single mothers differ from two-parent mothers in their greater tendency to be exposed to stressful life events and their experience of fewer emotional and parenting supports. Although differences in the number of stressful life events are minimal, their effects are quite different in the two-family groups. Stressful life events affect the single-parent child indirectly through their influence on maternal parenting behavior in interaction with the child and possibly even directly by influencing the child's cognitive functioning, ability to learn, and emotional stability. For both single- and two-parent families, social support had a positive effect on optimal parenting behavior. But for married mothers, social support may have served a buffering effect, diluting or diffusing the effects of stress both on the mother's behavior with her child and the child's outcome.

Implications

These findings have practical implications. Single parents planning families should be aware of the important influence stressful life events can have on the child, and may want to take steps either to reduce stressful life events or to develop increased coping skills to avoid the impact of stress on her behavior with her child and on the child. Likewise, single parents may want to prepare in advance for supplemental emotional and parenting supports. This is not an easy task for two reasons: Single-parent mothers are often limited in the amount of time and emotional energy they have for relationships outside their own family, and communities rarely offer formal parenting supports for this unique group of women. Single mothers will be especially benefited by research aimed at increasing the effectiveness of parental coping strategies and research illuminating the process by which social supports influence maternal behavior and child outcome.

Our findings also have implications for a number of highly complex conceptual issues currently being addressed in the literature. First, what is the relationship between frequency of stressful life events and adequacy of social supports? Our data suggest that the relationship between these variables may be complicated by the extent to which members of a social-support system share stressful life experiences. The critical importance of the marital relationship in predicting parenting behavior (e.g., Crnic, et al., 1983; see Belsky, 1984, and Belsky & Vondra, in press, for excellent reviews of these data) may be partially explained by the multiple roles the marital relationship plays. Marital partners share stressful life experiences and emotional and parenting support systems. In addition, the marriage both reflects and influences the continuing personality development of each partner. The relationship of stress and social supports may be especially difficult to untangle in functioning social systems.

Second, our data suggest that social support may have direct effects on the mother's behavior with her child, as indicated by the situation with single-parent families; as well as indirect effects on maternal behaviors, as indicated by the situation with two-parent families. For married mothers, social supports may serve to buffer the mother's interactions with her child from the effects of stress. "Buffer" here is used in a different context from the interactive sense used by Cohen and Wills (1985). In our data, social supports may "buffer" the effects of stress by preventing them from affecting the mother's interactions with her child. A similar effect is reported by Brown and Harris (1978), where the presence of an intimate relationship seemed to protect women from experiencing depression following serious life events.

Third, as researchers become more sophisticated concerning social support, we become more aware of the need to identify specific aspects of social support which may differentially influence the behaviors in question (Shinn, Lehmann, & Wong, 1984). In this presentation, we may have been successful in identifying social support as an influence on parenting behavior because we focused specifically on parenting supports as they influenced parenting behavior (but see Weinraub & Wolf, 1983, for a fuller presentation). Unfortunately, the use of maternal ratings of parenting supports opens our findings to the possibility of serious confounding. Mothers having more difficulty in parent–child interactions may have been less likely to report confidence in the parenting beliefs of the people they saw most frequently and in the extent of support they received in their roles as parents. Perhaps only longitudinal research can circumvent such difficulties.

Two important issues are not addressed by our data but may nevertheless have significantly influenced our results. First, we focused on the frequency of life stress events and the nature of social supports at a given time in mothers' lives, just prior to our observation of maternal behavior. More important than the status of life stress and social support may be their *dynamics*. Future studies may want to consider the extent to which social-support systems are *dynamic*—i.e., they expand to meet the individual's changing needs under different conditions. This property of elasticity or expandability requires further attention, and may be especially important as it applies to specific discrete life stress events, as opposed to ongoing chronic stressful conditions.

Second, the process by which stress and social supports are predictive of parenting behavior cannot be unrelated to characteristics of the mother's personality and emotional sensitivity. By now a number of researchers have begun to consider how an individual's personality and status characteristics may affect that individual's exposure to life stress and access to social supports (Belsky, 1984; Rook & Dooley, 1985; Vaux, 1985). Again, because of the intricate and dynamic relationships between personality, experience, and social relationships, long-term longitudinal investigations may be required to assess the separate and related contributions of each.

REFERENCES

Abernathy, V.D. (1973). Social network and response to the maternal role. *International Journal of Sociology and the Family, 3*, 86–92.

Ansul, S. & Weinraub, M. (1984). *Single parent families: Effects of stress and parent* child interaction on children's responses to strangers. Paper presented at the International Conference on Infant Studies, New York.

Barrett, R.K. (1978). A study of the effects of maternal self-esteem on maternal caregiving behavior and relational esteem in the family system. Dissertation Abstracts International, 39 (2-B), 1040.

Baumrind, D. (1967). Child care practices anteceding three patterns of preschool behavior. Genetic Psychology Monographs, 35, 43–88.

Belsky, J. (1984). The determinants of parenting. Child Development, 55, 83–96.

Belsky, J., & Vondra, J. (in press). Lessons from child abuse: The determinants of parenting. In D. Cichetti & V. Carlson (Eds.), Current research and theoretical advances in child maltreatment. Cambridge, MA: Cambridge University Press.

Billings, A.G., & Moos, R.H. (1983). Comparisons of children of depressed and nondepressed parents: A social-environment perspective. Journal of Abnormal Psychology, 11, 463–486.

Brown, G.W., & Harris, T. (1978). Social origins of depression: A study of psychiatric disorder in women. New York: Free Press.

Caplan, G. (1981). Mastery of stress: Psychosocial aspects. American Journal of Psychiatry, 138 (4), 413–420.

Cohen, S., & Willis, T.A. (1985). Social support and the buffering hypothesis. Psychological Bulletin, 98, 310–357.

Colletta, N.D. (1983). Stressful lives: The situation of divorced mothers and their children. Journal of Divorce, 6 (3), 19–31.

Crnic, K.A., Greenberg, M.T., Ragozin, A.S., Robinson, N.M., & Basham, R.B. (1983). Effects of stress and social supports on mothers and premature and full-term infants. Child Development, 54, 209–217.

Crockenberg, S.B. (1981). Infant irritability, mother responsiveness and social support influences on the security of infant–mother attachment. Child Development, 52, 857–865.

Crockenberg, S.B., & McCloskey, S. (1985). Predicting infant attachment from early and current behavior of mothers and infants. Paper presented at the biennial meeting of the Society for Research in Child Development, Toronto.

Dohrenwend, B.S., & Dohrenwend, B.P. (1981). Stressful life events and their contexts. Monographs in Psychosocial Epidemiology (Vol. 2). New York: PRODIST.

Eiduson, B.T. (1983). Conflict and stress in nontraditional families: Impact on children. American Journal of Orthopsychiatry, 53 (3), 426–435.

Gaines, R., Sandgrund, A., Green, A.H. & Power, E. (1978). Etiological factors in child maltreatment: A multivariate study of abusing, neglecting, and normal mothers. Journal of Abnormal Psychology, 87, 531–540.

Gersten, J.C., Langner, T.S., Eisenberg, J.G., & Orzek, L. (1974). Child behavior and life events. In B.S. Dohrenwend & B.P. Dohrenwend (Eds.), Stressful life events. New York: Wiley.

Gil, D.G. (1970). Violence against children: Physical child abuse in the United States. Cambridge, MA: Harvard University Press.

Goldberg, S., & Kearsley, M. (1983). Introduction to the special issue on high risk infants. Child Development, 54, 1083–1085.

Gore, S. (1981). Stress-buffering functions of social supports: An appraisal and clarification of research methods. In B.S. Dohrenwend & B.P. Dohrenwend (Eds.), Stressful life events and their contexts. Monographs of Psychological Epidemiology, 2, 202–222.

Herzog, E., & Sudia C. (1973). Children in fatherless families. In B.M. Caldwell & H.N. Ricciuti (Eds.), Review of child development research (Vol. 3). Chicago: University of Chicago Press.

Hodges, W.F., Wechsler, R.C., & Ballantine, C. (1979). Divorce and the preschool child: Cumulative stress. Journal of Divorce, 3 (1), 55–67.

Holmes, T.H., & Rahe, R.H. (1967). The social readjustment rating scale. Journal of Psychosomatic Medicine, 11, 213–218.

Kurdek, L.A., & Blisk, D. (1983). Dimensions and correlates of mother's divorce experiences. Journal of Divorce, 6 (4), 1–23.

Lewis, M., & Weinraub, M. (1976). The father's role in the child's social network. In M.E. Lamb (Ed.), The father's role in child development (pp. 157–184). New York: Wiley.

Lorion, R.P., Barker, W.F., Cahill, J., & Gallagher, R., Passons, W.A., & Kaufki, M. (1981). Scale development, normative and parametric analysis of a preschool screening measure. American Journal of Community Psychology, 9, 193–208.

Lorion, R.P., Hightower, A.D., & Work, W. (in press). The basic academic skills enhancement program: Translating prevention theory into action research. Journal of Community Psychology.

Lorion, R.P., Work, W.C., & Hightower, A.D. (in press). A school-based multi-level preventive intervention: Issues in program development and evaluation: Personal and Guidance Journal, 62, 479–484.

Melges, F.E. (1968). Postpartum psychiatric syndromes. Psychosomatic Medicine, 30, 95–108.

Minturn, L., & Lambert, W.W. (1964). Mothers of six cultures: Antecedents of child-rearing. New York: Wiley.

National Center for Health Statistics, Advanced Report of Final Natality Statistics. (1984). Monthly Vital Statistics Report, Vol. 34, No. 6, Supplement September 20, 1985.

Parke, R.D. (1979). Perspectives of father–infant interaction. In J.D. Osofsky (Ed.), Handbook of infant development. New York: Wiley.

Pascoe, J.M., Loda, F., Jeffries, V., & Earp, J. (1981). The association between mother's social support and provision of stimulation to their children. Developmental and Behavioral Pediatrics, 2 (1), 15–19.

Pederson, F.A., Yarrow, L.J., Anderson, B.J., & Cain, R.L. (1979). Conceptualization of father influences in the infancy period. In M. Lewis & L. Rosenblum (Eds.), The child and its family. New York: Plenum.

Rawlings, S. (1985). Household and family characteristics: March 1984 (Series P 20 #398, U.S. Bureau of Census). Washington, DC: U.S. Government Printing Office.

Richman, N. (1977). Behavior problems in preschool children: Family and social factors. British Journal of Psychiatry, 131, 523–527.

Rook, K.S. & Dooley, D. (1985). Applying social support research: Theoretical problems and future directions. Journal of Social Issues, 41, 5–28.

Rutter, M. (1981). Maternal deprivation reassessed (2nd edition). Hammondsworth, U.K.: Penguin.

Sandler, I.N., & Block, M. (1979). Life stress and maladaptation of children. American

Journal of Community Psychology, 7, 425–440.

Saunders, B.E. (1983). The social consequences of divorce: Implications for family policy. *Journal of Divorce, 6,* 1–17.

Shinn, M., Lehmann, S., & Wong, N.W. (1984). Social interaction and social support. *Journal of Social Issues, 40,* 55–76.

Svanum, S., Bringle, R.G., & McLaughlin, J. (1982). Father absence and cognitive performance in a large sample of six- to eleven-year-old children. *Child Development, 53,* 136–143.

Thompson, E.H., Jr., & Gongla, P.A. (1983). Single-parent families: In the mainstream of American society. In E.D. Macklin & R.H. Rubin (Eds.), *Contemporary families and alternative lifestyles.* Beverly Hills, CA: Sage.

Unger, D.G. & Wandersman, L.P. (1985). Social support and adolescent mothers: Action research contributions to theory and application. *Journal of Social Issues, 41,* 29–45.

Vaux, A. (1985). Variations in social support associated with gender, ethnicity, and age. *Journal of Social Issues, 41,* 89–110.

Ventura, S. (1985). Recent trends and variations in births to unmarried women. Paper presented at the biennial meeting of the Society for Research in Child Development, Toronto.

Weinraub, M. (1978). Fatherhood: The myth of the second-class parent. In J. Stevens & M. Mathews (Eds.), *Mother–child, Father–child relationships,* Washington, DC: National Association for the Education of Young Children.

Weinraub, M., & Wolf, B. (1983). Effects of stress and social supports on mother–child interaction in single and two-parent families. *Child Development, 54,* 1297–1311.

Weiss, R. (1979). *Going it alone: The family life and social situation of the single parent.* New York: Basic Books.

PART II

RESEARCH
ON INFORMAL SYSTEMS
OF SUPPORT FOR PARENTING

CHAPTER 7

Parent-Infant Support Groups: Matching Programs to Needs and Strengths of Families

Lois Pall Wandersman
University of South Carolina

Adjusting to life with a newborn can be challenging, joyful, stressful, exhausting, demanding, and exciting. Most parents adjust to parenthood by trial and error—with lots of trials and many frustrating errors. In the months after the birth of a baby, parents often feel isolated, unsure of themselves, and unprepared for their new tasks (Grossman, Eichler, & Winickoff, 1980). Parents and professionals have developed a variety of support programs to meet the needs of new parents for education and support. Types of programs include unstructured mutual-help groups (Cronenwett, 1980), parenting skills training groups (Dickie & Gerber, 1980), couple discussion groups (Cowan & Cowan, 1981), and home visits by paraprofessionals (Dawson, Robinson, & Johnson, 1982) or professionals (Olds & Roberts, 1981). The programs vary widely in goals, target groups, leaders, structure, curriculum, and intensity.

The purpose of this chapter is to analyze what we now know about support for parents and infants, and what directions might lead to more effective support. First I describe my experiences with three parent-infant support programs and what we can learn from them. Second, I analyze some basic assumptions of parent-infant support programs and review the evidence for them. Finally, I suggest an approach to matching support programs to the strengths and needs of families. My goal in this chapter is to encourage parents and professionals to realistically analyze what kinds of programs can have what kinds of benefits (and costs) for what kinds of parents.

LESSONS FROM THREE PARENT-INFANT SUPPORT PROGRAMS

In 1974, when I was a graduate student studying developmental psychology, my husband and I had our first baby. At the time there were few formal resources for family support. Parenting was assumed to come "naturally" for "normal" families. The first months were a whirlwind of joy, baby bouncing, and exhaustion. With our families far away and few friends with children, it was difficult for us to evaluate how well we were coping with our demanding new challenges.

As the months went by and we grew more confident, my husband and I began inviting parents of newborns to informal discussions about the adjustment to parenthood. What emerged from these discussions was a remarkable similarity between parents in their progressions of feelings, concerns, and triumphs as their babies developed. Parents were visibly relieved to discover that they were not the only ones having difficulty coping, that their problems were normal, and that many problems would ease as their babies got older. We became convinced that many parents felt a need for education and support. I felt that my training in theories of human development and in research could be applied to scientifically study ways to meet the needs of families. I've spent the years since then studying how parents and babies adjust, and in developing and evaluating programs to support and educate new parents. A brief description of these three programs and what I've learned from them will highlight some of the problems, limitations, and potential that are common in parent-infant support programs.

1. Family Development Parenting Groups

The Family Development Parenting Groups (FDPGs) were developed "to make the difficult job of parenting less isolated and more rewarding through information, sharing experiences, and social support" (Wandersman, 1978, p. 121). We envisioned an exciting chain reaction in which reduced anxiety would lead to improved marital interaction, optimal parenting, and more responsive babies.

The FDPGs were designed to support new parents through: (a) reinforcement and encouragement; (b) respect for individual styles of parenting, needs, and values; (c) information that parents could add to their coping skills; and (d) discussions of advantages and disadvantages of approaches. Groups met for 6 consecutive weeks to develop cohesiveness in the early and intense period of adjustment, then 4 consecutive months to include later issues of family development. Meetings focused on basic topics that we had found in the informal meetings to be important to couples in the adjustment to parenthood. Topics included the parent-infant relationship, the marital relationship, infant health and nutrition, cognitive and social development, socialization, and effective parenting techniques. Information was tailored to the concerns of the particular group, and participants were encouraged to share experiences and alternative solutions to problems and to make choices based on their own family's needs, values, and temperaments. The approach did not promote a particular "correct" way to bring up children, nor aim to change parents' values.

The project was publicized at a variety of classes for expectant parents, and couples indicated interest in being contacted by the project after delivery. Of the parents who expressed interest, about half participated in the groups and filled out questionnaires (N = 23 wives, and 18 of their husbands), and half (N = 24 couples) chose not to attend groups and only filled out questionnaires. Generally, the parents were white, middle-class, in their mid-20s, and had been married an average of 4 years. Most of the babies were between 2 and 3 months of age at the start of the groups. Group participants filled out questionnaires at the start and completion of the group, and the contrast group filled out questionnaires at parallel times. Measures included general well-being and mood, marital satisfaction, child-rearing attitudes, infant temperament, parental sense of competence, and division of household and child-care responsibilities. Results showed improvement for all respondents over the first year, with few significant advantages for FDPG participants (Wandersman, 1980; Wandersman, Wandersman, & Kahn, 1980).

Participants reported high levels of subjective satisfaction with the groups, and reported that they felt the groups had positively affected the way they felt about themselves and their expectations for themselves as parents and their interactions with their babies (Wandersman, 1978). Participants attended regularly, formed baby-sitting pools, contacted each other outside of meetings, formed lasting friendships with members of the group, and recommended the group to friends.

Should we conclude from the lack of significant differences in adjustment between participants and nonparticipants that the FDPGs had little impact? In retrospect, it seems naïve of us to have expected that 10 discussions on a wide range of issues would lead to changes in deeply ingrained attitudes and patterns. The groups were aimed at providing support, not at producing lasting change in complex behaviors and attitudes such as attachment to the infant or marital satisfaction. The participants joined, wanting to meet other new families, to learn about babies, and to gain ideas. They did not come because they were dissatisfied with their parenting behaviors or marital interaction and wanted to change their behavior. The FDPGs served families that were functioning well. Marital satisfaction and parental sense of competence and well-being were high even before the start of the groups. The groups served their intended purpose of improving the way participants felt about themselves and their expectations for themselves and their babies.

Comments on the group evaluations indicated that participants felt the support from the group increased their confidence and reduced their anxiety as parents.

In a population that is satisfied with its family functioning, increasing the frequency of social contacts with similar peers in a stressful transition period may be a worthwhile goal in itself. The increased supportive contacts may be perceived by participants as matching their temporary needs. Behavior change may not be a goal of the participants and may be very difficult to achieve.

In a target group that is functioning less adequately, or that is at risk for future problems, focusing a support program on behavior change would be more appropriate. In higher-risk groups, such as teenage parents, parents are faced with additional stress and may have fewer personal and maternal resources for adaptation. Facilitating effective problem-solving and parenting skills would be aimed at preventing adverse consequences for the parent (e.g., low educational achievement and income) and for the child (low educational achievement). To explore this idea, I developed an educational support group program for adolescent mothers who are at risk for parenting problems. I wanted to study who participated and how participation affected their parenting competence.

2. Babies and Mothers Growing Together

The "Babies and Mothers Growing Together" groups were aimed at supporting the development of competence in teenaged mothers and their infants by: (a) emphasizing the important influence of young mothers on their babies' development; (b) providing information about the needs and development of babies; (c) modeling and encouraging positive styles of interaction with babies; and (d) discussing and supporting the coping and adjustment of the young mothers.

Each group of mothers and babies met for approximately 10 sessions (six weekly, then four monthly) beginning in the first months after birth. Sessions combined discussions, films, speakers, baby exercises, and making baby toys. Topics included the adjustment to motherhood, responsiveness to baby, nutrition, accident prevention and illness care, mother's own development and family planning, and positive reinforcement and discipline. Observing the changing interaction of the babies with other babies, other mothers, and new objects was an integral and favorite part of each session.

Prenatal interviews were conducted with 48 pregnant, low-income adolescents to assess their knowledge, attitudes, social support, and health prior to randomly assigning them to parenting group or control conditions. At 1 and 8 months postpartum, mothers were interviewed and mothers and babies were observed at home to assess subjective satisfaction, attitudes toward parenting, social support, knowledge about babies, observed parenting competence (HOME: Home Observation for Measurement of the Environment [Caldwell & Bradley, 1978]), and the infant's developmental status using the Bayley Scales of Infant Development (Bayley, 1969).

Analysis of the prenatal interviews showed that different patterns of project participation were related to the needs and resources of the mothers (Wandersman, 1983b). Of the 48 mothers who were interviewed prenatally, 20 could not be contacted for, or refused to participate in, the postpartum assessments prior to the intervention. White mothers were more than twice as likely to drop out of the project as black mothers. Mothers who dropped out had reported lower support from their families on the prenatal interview than those who stayed in the project. Much effort went into trying to keep these mothers in the project, but they often left a tangle of frequent moves, disconnected phones, or unanswered calls that we could not penetrate. While this dropout rate is high, it is quite common in high-risk samples (e.g., Johnson & Breckenridge, 1982; O'Connor et al., 1982; Slaughter, 1983) and is one of the thorniest problems in intervention research (Gray & Wandersman, 1980; Wandersman, 1982, 1983a).

Although mothers were randomly assigned to parenting group or control, they actually selected their own levels of participation. Of the 16 mothers who were randomly assigned to the parenting groups, nine attended at least three sessions (x = 6.5 sessions) and seven attended zero to two sessions (x = 0.4 sessions). Twelve control mothers participated only in data collection at each point. Compared to the mothers who were invited to the parenting groups but did not come, parenting group participants were younger, had less knowledge about babies, and were rated by the prenatal interviewers as showing high promise of being good mothers. In other words, group participants were young and scared, in need of information about babies, and motivated to be good mothers.

The mothers who came to the group sessions rated their satisfaction with the group and their learning from the group very highly. From 1 to 8 months after the birth, group participants showed increases in their provision of good environments for their babies (group M HOME gains = 8.3, control = 3.45) and on knowledge of babies (group M knowledge gain = 2.9, control = 1.2) that were more than doubled the gains in the control group (Wandersman, 1983b).

The sample in this pilot study is very small. The results suggest hypotheses to study further rather than providing definitive conclusions.

These preliminary results suggested the hypothesis that parenting groups can be effective in increasing knowledge and improving the mother–child interaction of very young black adolescent mothers with adequate family support. Significant differences were not found between groups in the mental or motor development of babies at 8 months. We can hypothesize, however, that based on the gains made by parenting group mothers in the HOME, that group participation will positively affect the later development of the children by helping mothers to provide more stimulating, verbal and developmentally appropriate environments for their children (Bee et al., 1982). However, other approaches to support are needed to effectively reach and maintain participation in older and white adolescents and those with low family support. To try to reach these young mothers, we explored the effectiveness of a more intensive home-visiting approach beginning prenatally.

3. Resource Mother Program

The overall goal of the Resource Mother Program is to support the development of health and competence for rural teenaged mothers and their babies. The specific aims include: (a) increasing appropriate use of medical and social services; (b) reducing perinatal complications; (c) improving maternal child-rearing attitudes and parenting behaviors; (d) promoting maternal confidence and sense of control; and (e) promoting infant competence.

Resource Mothers identify pregnant teenagers in their communities and visit monthly to teach prenatal care and parenting, to facilitate use of medical and social services, and to provide support. The Resource Mothers are five experienced mothers who were selected after multiple interviews from more than 100 applicants for their social competence, warmth, empathy, tolerance, and knowledge of community resources. Several of the Resource Mothers are young or single mothers themselves. They were extensively trained for three weeks and participated in continued weekly training and supervision by a team of professionals.

The Resource Mother functions as a teacher, model, reinforcer, friend, and facilitator. The Resource Mother focuses on the strengths of each mother and her environment, and encourages support from the mother's social network. The structured curriculum for each home visit is geared to the young mother's changing interests and needs and uses a concrete, goal-centered approach that is individualized for each mother. The content of each home visit includes discussion of the mother's adjustment, monitoring progress with medical and social services, and education about a specific area of prenatal or infant care. Educational topics were designed to involve the mother in learning and planning; for example, planning an adequate diet, planning for labor, ways of teaching baby. The Resource Mother's visits emphasize the importance of the young mother in influencing the development of her baby.

To assess the effectiveness of the Resource Mother program in improving the health and competence of teenage mothers and their babies, pregnant teenagers were randomly assigned to Resource Mother home visits (RM; N = 345 mothers) or a small comparison group (C; N = 54). In the comparison, teenagers were contacted approximately once every 3 months to monitor progress and make referrals, but they did not get the systematic education and support of the Resource Mother group. Interviewers who did not know the mother's group visited a subsample of mothers at home when the baby was 1 month (N = 93) and 8 months (N = 96). Mothers were interviewed about their feelings and attitudes about parenting, sources of social support, and health. Mothers and babies were observed interacting and the quality of stimulation for the baby rated on the Home Observation for the Measurement of the Environment (HOME, Caldwell & Bradley, 1978).

Our results (Unger & Wandersman, 1985) show that the rate of low birth weight has been consistently lower in the Resource Mother group than in the comparison group (RM = 9.56%, C = 14.81%). Low birth weight is a major problem for teenage mothers and is associated in this group with increased risk of infant mortality and developmental problems.

The Resource Mother program has also shown an impact on the young mother's adjustment to parenthood. At 1 month postpartum, young mothers with Resource Mother visits are more likely to be back in school, providing a good-quality environment for their babies, eliciting responsive interacting from their babies, and taking their babies for health care. At 8 months, they are less anxious and know more about babies than monitored mothers.

We cannot determine from this research how Resource Mothers could affect the rate of low birth weight and the adjustment of young mothers. We suspect that the Resource Mother's effectiveness is not due to any single behavior, but rather to flexibility in meeting a teenager's particular needs. For some teenagers that might mean an emphasis on improving nutrition and speeding the application for nutritional supplements. For another teenager the Resource Mother might help find a stable place to live and help get her to the doctor. Another teenager might benefit from being encouraged to watch, play, and talk with new babies. In any case the lower rate of low birth weight and improved adjustment in the Resource Mother group suggests that the individualized behavioral focus may have potential for improving developmental outcomes in this high-risk group. Follow-up evaluations of these families would be useful to determine if there is a lasting impact.

There are several lessons that can be learned from these programs. Parent-infant support can meet the needs of some new parents for education and support. While most parents who participate in support programs feel satisfied with support, their increased confidence may not lead to quantifiable changes in attitudes or behavior. Parental behaviors and attitudes are influenced by a wide range of deeply ingrained causes—including ability, unconscious factors, cultural values, network controls, family patterns, and ecological and family constraints (Harman & Brim, 1980). Increased supportive social contacts may increase parents' satisfaction in a difficult transition, but may have limited impact on parenting behaviors that are enmeshed in parents' personalities and social systems.

A certain level of personal resources (confidence, social competence, social support) is necessary for people to be able to participate and benefit in reciprocal support relationships (Fein, 1979). Different types of programs may appeal to and benefit different parents. A group program that emphasizes supportive contacts may be most appropriate for parents who are relatively skilled in their parenting and have adequate economic and personal resources to interact actively with the group. A home-visiting program that emphasizes encouragement for the individual and specific parenting skills may be more appropriate for parents with less-adequate parenting skills and less ability to participate actively in a support group by sharing ideas, reinforcing other participants, and generalizing information to their own situation. Program designers need to attempt to increase the degree of fit between program goals and the objective and subjective needs of target parents.

The analysis of these three programs suggests that parent-infant support programs have the potential to benefit parents in the adjustment to parenthood. However, we need to develop more realistic expectations. In the next section we draw on the experiences illustrated in these programs and on other research as we examine the assumptions and evidence of effectiveness of parent-infant support programs.

ASSUMPTIONS OF PARENT-INFANT SUPPORT PROGRAMS

The Family Resource Coalition, a recently formed national organization of family-support programs, summarizes seven principles that underlie family-support programs. In this section we consider the evidence in relation to these seven principles of parent-infant support programs.

1. Support: Family resource programs recognize that parenthood is an extremely complex and demanding job in today's society, and that families need support

in order to effectively cope with the personal and social pressures that can disrupt family life. (Family Resource Coalition, 1982, p. 2)

Members of the Family Resource Coalition emphasize different aspects of providing support to families in their definitions of support:

a. reciprocal relationships—"... being interconnected with others in ways that are mutually satisfying ..." (Weissbourd, 1982, p. 8);
b. communication—"... overcoming isolation and opening up channels of communication ..." (Callahan, 1982, p. 9);
c. responsiveness—"... responding directly to real needs ..." (Dean, 1982, p. 9);
d. teaching—"... providing them with information on child growth and development ..." (Rodriguez, 1982, p. 10);
e. acceptance—"... believing that *all* parents are doing the best they can ..." (Raney, 1982, p. 11); and
f. encouragement—"... enabling parents to get pleasure out of the process of being parents ..." (Elkin, 1982, p. 17).

Each of these perspectives reflects an important component of the sensitive *provision* of support. The provision of support *seems* like it should be helpful to new parents. Little is known, however, about how the provision of support is *perceived* by families, and how it fits with their needs and with their informal systems of support.

Recent research reveals that support is a complex, multidimensional concept. Support can be defined in terms of: (a) the sources of support (e.g., kin, neighbors, group members) and the structure of the social network (e.g., dense–sparse); (b) the subjective appraisal of quality of support (e.g., satisfaction) and need for support (e.g., isolation); or (c) the quantities of specific behavioral activities (e.g., material and physical assistance, intimate interaction, guidance, feedback, social participation) (Barrera, 1981). Different dimensions of support are not highly related (Barrera, 1981) and have different relationships to adjustment (Wandersman, Wandersman, & Kahn, 1980; Colletta, 1981). Whether an individual seeks and uses support in a stressful period depends not just upon support availability, but on the person's competence in eliciting support and on coping strategies used in the past (Heller & Swindle, 1983).

Short-term support programs do not replace the existing network and are unlikely to diminish its important influence. Support programs interact with the existing network and may sometimes augment contacts and emotional support. Support programs may augment the support from the social network by working with the individual on ways to effectively elicit and use support, by working with the network to provide support better suited to the individuals needs, or by adding similar others (e.g., group members) to the network. However, support groups may also conflict with the existing network to increase stress. The impact of a few support-group sessions may simply be trivial in relation to the impact of the ongoing network.

Support is not a "treatment performed on subjects." Rather, support is a transaction in which the program leaders and participants influence each other, develop norms and expectations, and determine what they will accomplish. The participants themselves seek, perceive, or do not accept support. For example, McGuire and Gottlieb (1979) reported increases in social support for participants in a group led by one doctor, but not in a group led by a different doctor. We do not know, however, the actual differences between the groups in leader characteristics, participants' characteristics, or content. How does variation between groups in leaders' styles, warmth or knowledge, in the participants' enthusiasm, needs or strengths, or in the content of questions, answers and topics, affect parents' perceptions of the program and its impact? Powell (1983) emphasizes the importance of understanding the process of support programs. His program analyzes: (a) the relationship between parents' program experiences and changes in child and family behavior; and (b) the relationship between parents' program experiences and staff and family characteristics. This type of analysis of the interaction between program and participants is crucial to understanding how support impacts the lives of families. Rather than assuming that families need support, we need to assess what kinds of support parents need, from which sources, when in the transition, and with what effects on their satisfaction and adjustment.

2. *Building on Strength:* Family resource programs assume that support should build upon the strengths that whole families and individual family members already have. (Family Resource Coalition, 1982, p. 2)

A key element to success in working families is certainly the emphasis on their strengths rather than their weaknesses. Yet an emphasis on strengths can sometimes be perceived by families as an attempt to whitewash their very real concerns and stresses (Bromwich, 1981). Many families have important deficits—not enough money, food, skills, intelligence, or warmth. These deficits are not erased when we focus on strengths. In fact, their deficits may be more painful if we encourage families who are under stress to take control when few resources are available to them. In his summary of the Yale Bush Conference on "Family Support Programs: The State of the Art," Moroney cautioned that family-support programs should not become a panacea or a substitute for other resources that parents need (Weiss, 1983). Family-support programs can become advocates for basic resources.

3. *Prevention:* Family resource programs also assume that support should serve a preventive function. They offer early and continuing support to families with the express purpose of strengthening the family unit and preventing family dysfunction. (Family Resource Coalition, 1982, p. 2)

The prevention of problems before they occur makes economic, ethical, and practical sense. Most support programs aim to prevent a wide range of problems—family violence, school failure, repeat pregnancy—to name just a few. Only a few programs, however, have evaluated changes in behavior or prevention of problems. Many of these demonstration programs have shown short-term beneficial effects on family functioning. Examples of beneficial effects include greater maternal warmth and skill (Dawson et al., 1982); less marital dissatisfaction (Cowan & Cowan, 1981); fewer accidents, feeding problems, and paternal nonparticipation (Larson, 1980): higher developmental status of the infant (Beller, 1979); and more appropriate and contingent responsiveness of parents (Dickie & Gerber, 1980). A long-term follow-up of several parent education and support programs in the preschool period by the Consortium on Developmental Continuity demonstrated a reduced probability for program participants of special education or retention in grade (Lazar, Hubbell, Murray, Rosche, & Royce, 1977). Early intervention can even be cost effective in reducing the number of parents dependent on government support (Naylor, 1982).

The finding that very different programs can positively affect parent-child interaction and children's development suggests that the key to success lies less in specific curricula or structure and more in shared characteristics. Successful parent-support programs share a belief in: (a) the parents' desire to do the best for their children; (b) the importance of the parents' behaviors for their children's development; and (c) the importance of even the earliest children's behaviors. Rescorla and Zigler conclude:

It would seem that a crucial effect of interventions is that the recipients come to believe that the service providers value them as people and consider their development and achievement as an important goal worth striving for. Perhaps of equal importance, the intervention helps parents to see that their own behaviors are important in influencing the course of their children's educational, social, and emotional development. (Rescorla & Zigler, 1981, p. 12)

The results suggest that high quality parent-infant support programs have the potential to prevent family dysfunction. In this period of limited funding, parent-infant support programs cannot survive on the value or ethics of providing support for parents. Reduced incidence of family dysfunction must be documented by programs to justify the cost effectiveness of support. Examples of quantitative measures of cost effectiveness that have been used include incidence of special education or grade retention, rate of low birth weight and neonatal intensive care, welfare support to parents or subsequent birth rate.

4. *Parent Education:* In order to assist families in their childrearing role, family resource programs provide parents with information on child development and parenting issues. (Family Resource Coalition, 1982, p. 2)

Professionals strongly agree that parents need education about child development and parenting (Lane, 1976; Huntington, 1979). However, there are several reasons to be cautious about parent education. Clarke-Stewart (1981) summarizes the major lines of research that have been used as a basis for parent education programs and concludes that the evidence for making recommendations is shaky:

All point in the same direction: the environment, particularly parental behavior, does seem to have an effect on development throughout childhood (not just early childhood), and the kind of parental behavior that is most predictive of good child developmental outcomes is stimulating, consistent, moderate, and responsive. But this evidence is not incontrovertible. Each line of research has serious limitations. (Clarke-Stewart, 1981, pp. 52–53)

Extreme care is needed before leaping from research based on small numbers and flawed designs to recommendations for all families. For example, Lamb and Hall (1982) question the scientific evidence for the critical importance of early postpartum contact between mother and newborn. They suggest that the widespread belief in the magic of early contact may lead to guilt for families who do not have early contact and to ignoring other important aspects of the early bonding process and of family formation.

The dangers of overgeneralizing from research are greatest when recommendations for one group are based on research with another race, ethnic group, income group, age, sex, or family structure. For example, Baumrind (1972) found that while negative consequences of authoritarian child-rearing patterns are expected from white norms, black authoritarian families produced the most self-assertive and independent girls. The search for general principles can lead to recommending behaviors that are inappropriate in a particular context. Rather than giving advice, a more effective strategy might be to teach parents to be "scientists" who try out behaviors in different situations, observe the response, and evaluate the results for themselves. In other words, a mother who was concerned about spoiling her infant might be taught to observe whether the child was more content or required more attention on days when picked up immediately or on days when picked up after extended crying.

Even when we agree on some facts about child development, parent educators sometimes forget that learning is an active process of assimilation and accommodation. Parent educators do not simply add information into a void. Parents sort, fit, and modify new information according to their assumptions, values, and level of reasoning about the parent-child relationship (Newberger & Cook, 1983). For example, parents who see their role as organized around their own needs may be uninterested in information about the child's needs. Levels of parental awareness may be deeply ingrained, not controlled by conscious choice, and sustained by longstanding patterns of interaction (Harman & Brim, 1980), and may be difficult to change—even by direct intervention (Sandy, 1983). Parent education, then, is an interaction in which we try to understand, and educators and parents come to share each other's perceptions and understandings.

Thus, while our intentions in providing parent education are noble, we must be careful not to present guesses, opinions, and correlations as facts. We must not leap to suggest that what is good for one group will have good consequences in a different context. And we must determine how the facts we do present are perceived, processed, judged, and acted upon by the parents.

5. *Community Ties:* Family resource programs place their efforts to provide support in the context of community life. Since they recognize the dangers of isolation and the value of personal and social networks, they try to bring families in closer contact with each other and with community resources. (Family Resource Coalition, 1982, p. 2)

One of the important contributions of parent-child support programs is their realization that programs must work together and with the family's informal network to support families. This can lead to increased cooperation and coordination between programs and community resources (Badger & Burns, 1980).

Interventions in social networks can be risky, however. McGuire and Gottlieb (1979) found that participants in postpartum support groups increased their frequency of discussion of child-rearing matters with members of their own networks, but this was not accompanied by lower levels of reported stress or by more positive ratings of their well-being. Gottlieb (1981) suggests caution in increasing contact when the network is not equipped to offer support or they recommend unproductive or self-defeating coping strategies.

Increasing contact with other families can be harmful if it leads to increased demands, conflict, or dependency. Belle (1981) reported that poor mothers with large networks and frequent interaction felt more stressed than mothers with smaller networks. In our research, teen mothers who were more mature and prepared for their newborns and had *less* family support were providing a better environment for their babies at 1 month than teens who were more dependent on their families (Unger, Wandersman, O'Reilly, & Adams, 1983). Large networks and frequent contact can create pressure for reciprocation and conformity.

The importance of independence and privacy for adjustment can be overlooked by focusing only on support. When intervening in communities and social networks, one cannot do "just one thing," and we must be very aware of the potential for conflict within networks or for inadvertently upsetting the balance within a system.

6. *Peer Support:* Family resource programs recognize the value of support, based on the shared experience of parenthood, that parents give to and receive from each other. (Family Resource Coalition, 1982, p. 2)

The benefits of peer support have been proposed from many perspectives, including: (a) mutual help groups aimed at the mastering of developmental tasks can be a primary prevention strategy to reduce maladjustment and promote positive growth (Goldston, 1977); (b) social support can buffer the stress of transitions, and can facilitate coping through help, resources, and caring (Cobb, 1976); (c) reference groups of similar others can provide role models and standards for self-evaluation (Festinger, 1954); and (d) accurate information and support can lead to more appropriate parenting behaviors (B. White, 1975) and coping skills (R. White, 1974).

Leaders of parent-support programs generally agree that the informal interaction and sharing between parents is a crucial and often favorite component of their programs (Huntington, 1979; Cronenwett, 1980). Nevertheless, the effectiveness of peer support has not been unequivocally demonstrated. In studies of the informal networks of parents of infants, support from peers has been found to be less influential on parenting or adjusting than support from family or spouse (Colletta, 1981; Crnic, Greenberg, Ragozin, Robinson, & Basham, 1983; Unger et al., 1983).

Support programs have not yet demonstrated either that support from peers in their programs actually augments the support from the informal networks of parents, or that augmenting peer support can lead to higher satisfaction, better adjustment, or improved parenting (Wandersman et al., 1980, Wandersman, 1982; Gottlieb, 1981). Clearly, many parents seek and enjoy interaction with similar peers. A comparison of mothers of toddlers in home-visiting and group-discussion programs by Slaughter (1983) showed greater gains by discussion-group mothers in ego development and in teaching interactions in play with their children. The results indicate the potential of peer-group support to influence adjustment and parenting. However, the small sample, nonrandom assignment (randomized by neighborhood), and high rate of attrition emphasize the need to replicate the results and study how support is related to behavior change. For example, the attrition of half of the discussion group (more dropouts than in home-visiting or control group) underline the need to understand roles of personality, motivation, competence, need for support, and existing support in moderating the use and influence of peer support.

We need also to be aware that peer support can sometimes have negative consequences. Peers can sometimes threaten the shaky confidence of some new parents by suggesting that there may be other ways to do things or that others are coping more effectively. In the FDPGs, one mother whose baby cried continuously felt that, in spite of all the group's encouragement, there was something wrong with her for not being able to soothe her baby as well as other mothers could soothe theirs. Peers may also pressure participants to conform to group norms or may encourage participants to become dependent for problem solving or encouragement. Peer norms may also conflict with norms of the parents' existing social networks, creating conflict or tension for the parents.

Before we can accurately evaluate the results of providing support for new parents, we need to evaluate whether support is being provided and perceived, and then whether participants feel more confident, relaxed, and helped. Measures of the subjective and behavioral processes of support need to be developed and refined that include the following components: (a) interaction process (degree of interaction, sharing experiences, advice, or reinforcement from members of the group); (b) information acquisition (accuracy of parenting or child-development information and how to get it); (c) instrumental support (degree of help from others, baby-sitting pools, play groups); (d) emotional support (feelings of reduced isolation and anxiety, enjoyment of parenting); and (e) network augmentation (additions to the network, frequency of interaction). Measures need to distinguish components of social support as well as specify the special needs for support in the transition to parenthood.

7. *Open Door:* Family resource programs also recognize that all families need support. Thus, they open their doors to all members of a target population regardless of their sex, race, economic status, religion, or ethnic origins. (Family Resource Coalition, 1982, p. 2)

Parent-support programs should be available to all who seek them. Yet very few parents knock on our doors (Rosenberg, Reppucci, & Linney, 1979; Harman & Brim, 1980). Perhaps we need to think creatively of ways to make our doors more accessible and less threatening. Support can be an approach to families as well as a program that parents must join for a specified time. Encouragement, child-development information, peer interaction, and referral can be incorporated into many community settings, including day-care centers and schools, libraries and community centers, churches, hospitals, and health departments. Support for families should not be isolated in a few family-support programs, but should be part of the training, philosophy, and approach of all who work with families.

MATCHING SUPPORT TO FAMILY STRENGTHS AND NEEDS

Our discussion thus far has highlighted the potential of high-quality family support programs to have lasting beneficial effects for parents and children. We have also underscored the risks of expecting support programs to be a panacea that can solve all problems for all families. In the past we have often tried to develop a model program that would demonstrate how well it works, and then could be widely implemented (e.g., Headstart). But families vary tremendously in their structures, values, needs, and resources. To support families, we need to ask, "What works, *when, for whom, how,* and *why?*" (Weiss, 1983, p. 5).

Little systematic data have been reported about how support programs are actually put into action, what motivates parents to attend, what goes on during sessions, and how parents perceive the groups and their own roles in them. Rosenberg et al. (1979) suggested that lack of attention to problems of implementation may be a major factor in the limited success of human service programs. In documenting the problems that their program had in getting referrals and attracting parents, they concluded that the success of a program may hinge on the process of selling the program to agencies and potential participants. The problem that all support programs have in recruiting participants and maintaining attendance may indicate the need to develop more sophisticated ways to inform parents about the benefits of participation. Powell (1983) suggests the importance of direct contact between program staff and target parents. Badger (1981) emphasizes the importance of timing the approach right after birth, when mothers are feeling anxious and excited. Recruitment problems, however, may not be solved simply by improving recruitment techniques. By not joining, parents may be indicating that they do not like or need the programs, or that the programs do not fit their needs.

The problem of attracting participants will not be solved by asking, "Why don't more parents participate?" We need to address the question, "What kind of parents attend what kind of programs under what conditions?" For example, Badger (1981) reported that white Appalachian mothers attended groups less than black mothers, and suggested husband disapproval as a possible reason. In our FDPGs, husbands who participated in the groups reported higher marital adjustment and fussier babies at the start of the group than did contrast fathers (Wandersman, 1980), reflecting a combination of high support and high need. These findings suggest the importance of the family ecology in determining group participation. Knowing the characteristics of people who choose not to attend particular types of programs can help us to pinpoint the program to those it attracts and to explore other kinds of programs to reach those who want support but do not participate. More research is needed on the roles played by other family members, networks, neighborhoods, cultural values, and other characteristics of the ecology of families in influencing participation in different kinds of groups for parents.

Evaluation of parenting groups should move from the pre-post questionnaires to measures of the *process* of support and its short- or long-term effects for families with different characteristics (Ramey, Sparling, Bryant, & Wasik, 1982). Prior to group formation, extensive measures of the strengths, needs, and attitudes of parents and their networks are essential to determine the interaction of the program with the participants. Evaluations need to include a range of subjective and objective measures of the support process and behavioral effects.

We need to document what goes on in support programs and how different parents interact with the program. What topics are discussed and what recommendations are made? Do parents share feelings and experiences? Which parents drop out? In order to understand the effects of support programs, we need to understand what the programs do, and for whom. Programs can be analyzed from several perspectives, including: (a) organization and structure (e.g., number of sessions, topics, leader's role and training); (b) aggregate profile of participants (e.g., age,

marital status, socioeconomic status, personality, and social characteristics of participants); and (c) social climate of relationships, personal
development, and system maintenance (cohesiveness, leader support,
expressiveness, independence, task orientation, self-discovery, anger
and aggression, order and organization, leader control, innovation) (Moos,
1975). Although behavioral analysis of the interaction in groups is expensive and time consuming, we may be able to devise shortcuts to
determine the important characteristics of groups and how they are
linked to the characteristics of participants. Logs, ratings, or interviews
completed by leaders, participants, or observers can point to group
factors that may interact with the characteristics of parents and their
environment to influence their impact on participants.

   To understand the *effects* of the program, we should be less concerned
with main effects than with interactions. At least three basic process
questions need to be addressed to understand how interventions interact
with people and their environments: (a) Who participates in the program
and how are they involved? (b) What is the structure and content of
the intervention and how does it vary with different leaders and participants? (c) How does the intervention affect different kinds of participants? By using basic concepts and theories about the factors and
contents that influence development, we can add to our understanding
of the contextual influences on development while increasing our understanding of how interventions interact with families (Wandersman,
1983a).

   For too long, scientists have viewed variations in program delivery,
parent involvement, and family effects as annoying noise that distracts
from main effects of programs. Heroic efforts have been made to reduce
program variations and attrition. Of course, programs must make every
effort to maintain program quality and parent involvement. Rigid experimental controls, however, can obscure the messages that families
try to communicate through their varying types of involvement and
response to the program. Variations in program delivery, parent involvement, and family effects are not likely to be random. Attrition
may appear random when we look at insensitive measures (e.g., SES,
IQ) that do not explain why a participant drops out. We need to study
how variations in programs and parent participation relate to the patterns
of needs, strengths, stresses, resources, and attitudes of families. Then
the noise will become a message that can educate us about how our
programs interact with the lives of families. The challenge is to find
ways to read the messages that families are communicating to us. Ultimately, our goal is to have a diversity of supportive parent education
programs so that a particular program can be matched to the needs and
strengths of a particular family.

REFERENCES

Badger, E. (1981). Effects of parent education programs on teenage mothers and their offspring. In K.G. Scott, T. Field, & E. Robertson (Eds.), *Teenage parents and their offspring*. New York: Grune & Stratton.

Badger, E., & Burns, D. (1980). *Promoting infant development: A coalition model for community service delivery*. Paper presented at the annual meeting of the American Psychological Association, Montreal.

Barrera, M., Jr. (1981). Social support in the adjustment of pregnant adolescents. In B. Gottlieb (Ed.), *Social networks and social support*. Beverly Hills, CA: Sage.

Baumrind, D. (1972). An exploratory study of socialization effects on black children: Some black-white comparisons. *Child Development, 43*, 261–267.

Bayley, N. (1969). *Bayley scales of infant development: Birth to two years*. New York: Psychological Corporation.

Bee, H.L., Barnard, K.E., Eyres, S.J., Gray, C.A., Hammond, M.A., Spietz, A.L., Snyder, C., & Clark, B. (1982). Prediction of IQ and language skill, from prenatal status, child performance, family characteristics, and mother–infant interaction. *Child Development, 53*, 1134–1156.

Belle, D. (1981). *The social network as a source of both stress and support to low-income mothers*. Paper presented at the biennial meeting of the Society for Research in Child Development, Boston.

Beller, E.K. (1979). Early intervention programs. In J.D. Osofsky (Ed.), *Handbook of infant development*. New York: Wiley.

Bromwich, R. (1981). *Working with parents and infants*. Baltimore: University Park Press.

Caldwell, B.M., & Bradley, R.H. (1978). *Administration manual: Home observation for measurement of the environment*. Little Rock: University of Arkansas.

Callahan, B. (1982). What do we mean by support? *Family Resource Coalition, 1* (4), 8–9.

Clarke-Stewart, K.A. (1981). Parent education in the 1970s. *Educational Evaluation and Policy Analysis, 3*, 47–58.

Cobb, S. (1976). Social support as a moderator of life stress. *Psychosomatic Medicine, 38*, 300–314.

Colletta, N.D. (1981). *The influence of support systems on the maternal behavior of young mothers*. Paper presented at the biennial meeting of the Society for Research in Child Development, Boston.

Cowan, C.P., & Cowan, P.A. (1981). *Couple role arrangements and satisfaction during family formation*. Paper presented at the biennial meeting of the Society for Research in Child Development, Boston.

Crnic, K.A., Greenberg, M.T., Ragozin, A.S., Robinson, N.M., & Basham, R. (1983). Effects of stress and social support on mothers and premature and full-term infants. *Child Development, 54*, 209–217.

Cronenwett, L.R. (1980). Elements and outcomes of a postpartum support group. *Research in Nursing and Health, 3*, 33–41.

Dawson, P., Robinson, J.L., & Johnson, C.B. (1982). Informal social support as an intervention. *Birth to Three, 3* (2), 1–5.

Dean, S. (1982). What do we mean by support? *Family Resource Coalition, 1* (4), 9–10.

Dickie, J.R., & Gerber, S.C. (1980). Training in social competence: The effect on mothers, fathers and infants. *Child Development, 51,* 1248–1251.

Elkin, M. (1982). What do we mean by support? *Family Resource Coalition, 1* (4), 11.

Family Resource Coalition. (1982). *Statement of philosophy, goals and structure.* Chicago: Individual authors not cited.

Fein, G. (1979). *Socio-cultural issues: Privacy, needs, and benevolence.* Paper presented at the biennial meeting of the Society for Research in Child Development, San Francisco.

Festinger, L. (1954). A theory of social comparison process. *Human Relations, 7,* 117–140.

Goldston, S. (1977). Defining primary prevention. In G.W. Albee & J.M. Joffe (Eds.), *Primary prevention of psychopathology: Vol. I. The issues* (pp. 18–23). Hanover, NH: University Press of New England.

Gottlieb, B. (1981). Preventive interventions involving social networks and social support. In B. Gottlieb (Ed.), *Social networks and social support.* Beverly Hills, CA: Sage.

Gray, S., & Wandersman, L.P. (1980). The methodology of home-based intervention studies: Problems and promising strategies. *Child Development, 51,* 993–1009.

Grossman, F.K., Eichler, L.S., Winickoff, S.A., with Anzalone, M.K., Gofseyeff, M.H., & Sargent, S.P. (1980). *Pregnancy, birth and parenthood.* San Francisco: Jossey-Bass.

Harman, D., & Brim, O.G., Jr. (1980). *Learning to be parents: Principles, programs and methods.* Beverly Hills, CA: Sage.

Heller, K., & Swindle, R.W. (1983). Social networks, perceived social support and coping with stress. In R.D. Fellner, L.A. Jason, J. Moritsugu, & S.S. Farber (Eds.), *Preventive psychology: Theory, research and practice in community intervention.* Elmsford, NY: Pergamon.

Huntington, D.S. (1979). Supportive programs for infants and parents. In J.D. Osofsky (Ed.), *Handbook of infant development.* New York: Wiley.

Johnson, D.L., & Breckenridge, J.H. (1982). The Houston Parent-Child Development Center and the primary prevention of behavior problems in young children. *American Journal of Community Psychology, 10,* 305–316.

Lamb, M.E., & Hall, E. (1982). Bonding. *Childbirth Educator, 2* (1), 18–23.

Lane, M.B. (1976). *Education for parenting.* Washington, DC: National Education Association of Young Children.

Larson, C.P. (1980). Efficacy of prenatal and postpartum home visits on child health and development. *Pediatrics, 66,* 191–197.

Lazar, I., Hubbell, V.R., Murray, H., Rosche, M., & Royce, J. (1977). *Summary report: The persistence of preschool effects: A long-term follow-up of fourteen infant and preschool experiments* (DHEW Publication No. (OHDS) 78-30129). Washington, DC: Government Printing Office.

McGuire, J.C., & Gottlieb, B.H. (1979). Social support groups among new parents: An experimental study in primary prevention. *Journal of Clinical Child Psychology, 8,* 111–115.

Moos, R.H. (1975). *Evaluating correctional and community settings.* New York: Wiley.

Naylor, A. (1982). Child day care: Threat to family life or primary prevention? *Journal of Preventive Psychiatry, 1* (4), 431–441.

Newberger, C.M., & Cook, S.J. (1983). *The study of cognition in parenthood: The parental awareness measure.* Paper presented at the biennial meeting of the Society for Research in Child Development, Detroit.

O'Connor, S., Vietze, P., Sherrod, K., Sandler, H.M., Gerrity, S., & Altemeier, W.A. (1982). Mother–infant interaction and child development after rooming-in: Comparison of high-risk and low-risk mothers. *Early Intervention Programs for Infants. Prevention in Human Services, 1* (4), 25–43.

Olds, D., & Roberts, J. (1981). *An ecological perspective on providing support to parents of infants.* Paper presented at the biennial meeting of the Society for Research in Child Development, Boston.

Powell, D.R. (1983). Individual differences in participation in a parent-child support program. In I. Sigel & L. Laosa (Eds.), *Changing families.* New York: Plenum.

Ramey, C.T., Sparling, J.J., Bryant, D.M., & Wasik, B.H. (1982). Primary prevention of developmental retardation during infancy. *Prevention in Human Services, 1,* 61–81.

Raney, A. (1982). What do we mean by support? *Family Resource Coalition, 1* (4), 10–11.

Rescorla, L.A., & Zigler, E. (1981). The Yale Child Welfare Research Program: Implications for social policy. *Educational Evaluation and Policy Analysis, 3,* 5–14.

Rodriguez, G. (1982). What do we mean by support? *Family Resource Coalition, 1* (4), 10.

Rosenberg, M.S., Reppucci, N.D., & Linney, J.A. (1979). *Problems of implementation: Parent education for high-risk families.* Paper presented at the annual meeting of the American Psychological Association, New York.

Sandy, L.R. (1983). *Parent intervention and the development of parental awareness.* Paper presented at the biennial meeting of the Society for Research in Child Development, Detroit.

Slaughter, D.T. (1983). Early intervention and its effects on maternal and child development. *Monographs of the Society for Research in Child Development, 48* (4, Serial No. 202).

Unger, D.G. & Wandersman, L.P. Social support and adolescent mothers: Action research contributions to theory and application. *Journal of Social Issues* 1985, *41,* 29–45.

Unger, D., Wandersman, L.P., O'Reilly, B.K., & Adams, C.T. (1983). *Prenatal prediction of obstetrical complications and early adjustment of young mothers.* Paper presented at the annual meeting of the Southeastern Psychological Association, Atlanta.

Wandersman, L.P. (1978). Parenting groups to support the adjustment to parenthood. *Family Perspective, 12,* 117–128.

Wandersman, L.P. (1980). The adjustment of fathers to their first baby: The roles of parenting groups and marital relationship. *Birth and the Family Journal, 7,* 155–162.

Wandersman, L.P. (1982). An analysis of the effectiveness of parent-infant support groups. *Journal of Primary Prevention, 3,* 99–115.

Wandersman, L.P. (1983a). *New directions for studying the interaction between parent education and family characteristics.* Paper presented at the biennnial meeting of the Society for Research in Child Development, Detroit.

Wandersman, L.P. (1983b). *A support program for adolescent mothers: Who participates and effects.* Paper presented at the annual meeting of the American Psychological Association, Anaheim, CA.

Wandersman, L.P., Wandersman, A., & Kahn, S. (1980). Social support in the transition to parenthood. *Journal of Community Psychology, 8,* 332–342.

Weiss, H. (1983). Yale Bush Conference highlights—Family support programs: The state of the art. *The Networker, 4* (4), 4–6.

Weiss, H.B. (1983). *Strengthening families and rebuilding the social infrastructure: A review of family support and education programs.* Charles Stewart Mott Foundation.

Weissbourd, B. (1982). What do we mean by support? *Family Resource Coalition, 1* (4), 8.

White, B. (1975). *Reassessing our educational priorities: Official report of the National Conference on Parent/Early Childhood Education, Denver, Colorado, May 1975.* Washington, DC: U.S. Office of Education.

White, R.W. (1974). Strategies of adaptation. In C. Coehlo, D. Hamburg, & J. Adams (Eds.), *Coping and adaptation.* New York: Basic Books.

CHAPTER 8
Stability and Growth in Parent-Support Services: A National Survey of Peer Support for Parents of Premature and High-Risk Infants

Deborah Spitz Cherniss
University of Medicine and Dentistry of New Jersey

Many professionals have recognized the need felt by parents of premature or sick newborns for contact with other parents who have shared this crisis (Enriquez, Harrell, & Putnam, 1980; Erdman, 1977; Garrand, Sherman, Rentchler, & Jung, 1978; Mangurten, Slade, & Fitzsimmons, 1979). This sense has been confirmed by studies that have explored parents' desire for peer contact, and the positive effects of such contact. Leiderman (1975) found that when asked who would be most helpful to them, the first choice of parents with babies in the neonatal intensive-care unit (NICU) was other parents. Minde and his colleagues (1980) found that 7 to 10 weeks' participation in a peer-support group increased mothers' visiting and interacting with their premature infants, and their sense of competence in their new parenting roles. Further, when compared with controls 3 months after discharge, these mothers continued to

A comprehensive list of parent-support groups for parents of premature and high-risk infants is available in the Resource Directory of Parent Care, Univ. of Utah Medical Center, 50 N. Medical Dr., Rm. 2A210, Salt Lake City, UT 84132; (801) 581-5323. This list includes the active groups represented in this study, but is not limited to them.

The author gratefully acknowledges the assistance of Martha Ogburn, RN, MS, Matthews, NC, and of Joanne Williams, Parents of Prematures, Houston, TX. Their help in locating groups and resource materials was essential to the development of this project. Cary Cherniss, PhD, contributed substantially with professional expertise and personal support. In addition, a great debt is owed to all those parents and professionals who took the time to participate in this survey.

show more involvement with their babies and more confidence in their parenting.

The far-reaching importance of such positive effects is underscored by research on later development of preterm and low-birthweight infants. As Caputo, Goldstein, and Taub (1979) and Jacob (1984) document, many studies have linked preterm birth with serious developmental disabilities such as mental retardation, epilepsy, hearing and vision defects, and a continuum of motor impairments ranging from cerebral palsy to gross motor delays and awkwardness, to more subtle fine motor difficulties.

However, many preterms experience only mild developmental consequences of their difficult births, and many show no obvious residual effects. This issue is addressed in extensive reviews of the literature by Desmond, Wilson, Alt, & Fisher (1980) and Sameroff and Abbe (1978), who conclude that the environment has a profound effect on the preterm child's development. As Sameroff and Abbe state, ". . . attempts to predict intelligence or retardation . . . have proven inadequate using the single constitutional variable of premature birth. . . . Poor outcomes are clearly not the result of prematurity itself, since children of identical gestational periods, raised in *good environments*, show few consequences of the problem" (p. 201, my italics). Further, in looking at a variety of prenatal, natal, and neonatal complications, Parmalee, Kopp, and Sigman (1976) point out the difficulty of identifying children at risk for later disabilities. They suggest that when handicapping conditions are present, one major reason for differences in development "is that environmental factors may have a stronger influence . . . than [do] early biological events" (p. 179).

THE "GOOD ENVIRONMENT"

What then constitutes the "good environment" that can be so crucial to positive outcomes? Researchers have framed it in broad terms, consistently suggesting that it is linked to socioeconomic factors (Cohen, 1981; Parmalee & Haber, 1973; Sigman & Parmalee, 1979). In addition, a number of authors emphasize the parent-child relationship as the context in which a child's early deficits are ameliorated or amplified (Butterfield & Miller, 1984; Desmond et al., 1980; Thomas & Chess, 1980; Sameroff, 1981; Sigman, Cohen, & Forsythe, 1981).

When describing this context, writers have identified three elements that have special significance for social support of preterm and high-risk parents. First, there is the parents' perception of the child (Sameroff

& Abbe, 1978). This includes their initial view of the child either as simply small and immature, or as peculiar and damaged, and their subsequent ability to adjust their perceptions of the child's vulnerability as he matures.

Second, there is the preterm's contribution to the parent-child relationship, expressed in his reactions to the environment (Escalona, 1984). Given the immaturity and lability of a preterm's central nervous system, this may mean, for example, that even "good parenting" is inadequate to calm a disorganized infant. And if the parents do not understand the neurological causes of their baby's behavior, they may interpret it as a rejection or as a negative reflection on their own abilities to parent.

Finally, there is the issue of emotional support available to parents as they deal with the stress of preterm birth and their early interactions with their infant. As Herzog (1979) reports, mothers most negatively affected by preterm birth felt that they were deprived of social support and that they lacked the emotional resources to nurture their infants.

Thus, while various writers have taken different perspectives on the psychological and social environments necessary for optimal development of preterm and high-risk infants, when put together their work makes a compelling picture of the "good environment." It is one that would include economic and social supports for the family; the parents' positive attitude toward their unusual newborn; their understanding of the needs and behavior of a preterm or high-risk infant, their ability to accommodate to these, and, in doing so, to feel competent in their parenting role; and emotional support for the trauma, grief, and anxiety they have experienced.

THE ROLE OF PARENT-TO-PARENT SUPPORT SERVICES

In a sense, parent-support programs can be viewed as existing to create and establish that vital good environment for the families they serve. These programs take two basic forms. Some offer groups run by professionals who bring together parents simultaneously sharing the experience of a difficult birth and its aftermath. The focus of these services is primarily on having new parents help each other by expressing their fears and questions, under the guidance of a professional (although such groups may involve contact with a "veteran" parent who has "graduated" from the NICU, as did the groups in the study by Minde et al. [1980]). Additionally, Enriquez et al. (1980) suggest that these services may be aimed at offering information to help parents understand their baby's behavior and appearance, increase their involvement with their infant, and improve parent-staff relationships by sensitizing staff to parents' needs.

In contrast to such services, many programs for parents of preterm and high-risk infants take the form of "mutual aid networks" (Boukydis, 1984), in which parents who have survived the experience reach out to those who have just suffered it. These programs bring together veteran and new parents through support-group meetings and/or individual contacts.

Boukydis (1982, 1984) highlights the practical and emotional contributions that can be made by veteran parents: they not only have a unique empathy, and can validate new parents' feelings of anger, guilt, and confusion, but they also can serve as models who have coped adequately with these feelings. They can guide the bewildered parent by interpreting the "lore and lingo" of the NICU, and they can share the specific solutions they found to overwhelming situations. Frequently they offer the special benefit of continuity of contact that begins within the NICU and then extends past its walls. Finally, by bringing together individuals who share an unusual and unhappy experience, they offer a response to the problem of social isolation.

In addition to these benefits described by Boukydis, it would seem that parent-to-parent support programs also can positively affect parents' attitudes toward their children and their sense of mastery as care-takers: by having contact with parents whose children have moved beyond their difficult beginnings, new parents can put into perspective their infant's appearance and behavior, seeing these as transient and part of a continuum of developmental maturity. And contact with veteran parents also can suggest that the new parents, like the veterans who experienced similar feelings of helplessness and anxiety, can become competent in their care-taking role.

Thus, whether parent-support services are offered under the guidance of hospital staff or through a "self-help" program based on mutual aid; whether they are offered in a group format or from one individual parent to another; there are many ways in which they can contribute to the "good environment" associated with positive outcomes of preterm and high-risk births. And for these reasons, it seems clear that parent-to-parent support has a special place in services for premature and high-risk infants and their families.

What has not been clear is the nature and extent of the parent-support services that have burgeoned over the past 10 years (Cherniss, 1984; Williams, 1981). The purpose of this study was to survey such groups in order to learn about their origins, structures, and services. In the following report the majority of existing groups are profiled, and a central question is addressed: what factors seem related to the survival, stability, and growth of parent-support services for parents of preterm and high-risk infants?

BACKGROUND TO THE STUDY

This project began evolving in 1981 as an exploration of information and services available to parents of premature infants. At that time the only nontechnical information that could be obtained on the parents' experience of premature birth was first-person accounts in popular magazines. The original goal of this study was to make accessible to new parents of preterms some of the knowledge and wisdom earned by those who already had lived through this difficult experience.

However, as information was collected it became clear that other writers were addressing the needs of individual parents, systematically gathering and publishing material on coping with events faced during an infant's hospitalization, as well as handling questions about the baby's survival and development (Harrison & Kositsky, 1983; Henig & Fletcher, 1983; Lieberman & Sheagren, 1984; Nance et al., 1982).

Further, in collecting this information it was learned that support groups designed to help parents of prematures existed, but in isolation. These groups seemed to have a wealth of knowledge to share, not only on the issues vital to new parents, but also for parents and professionals interested in creating services.

Thus, the goal of the study changed from providing material for individual parents and the professionials concerned with helping them cope, to learning about the support groups that seemed to hold so much promise for parents' emotional health in a preterm baby's first days and months.

Defining the Population

Once it was determined to look at parent-support groups, the intent was to study programs for parents of premature infants. It became clear, however, that very few groups limited their focus to preterm births. Instead, most programs defined their services as being for parents whose babies had "special needs," or were "at risk," or simply "sick." Some groups dealt with particular problems, like apnea, which might occur even if the newborn was not premature; others offered services to any parents whose newborn was hospitalized, whatever the reason; and still other groups served all new parents, and tried to address the needs of parents of premature and high-risk infants within this broader context.

Despite such differences in the infant population served, all of these groups shared the goals of helping new parents deal with anxieties about their at-risk baby's survival. Thus, it was decided that the sample would be made up of any groups that emphasized support services to parents of newborns with special needs, whether or not the infants were premature. As a corollary to this, the sample would not include groups that focused primarily on other needy parent populations (e.g., parents of developmentally disabled children) when these groups dealt only occasionally with infants.

It is important to note that although the population was defined as "parent-support groups," this did not necessarily mean the groups were run by parents, nor that services were provided in a group format. First, the kind of service, not who provided it, was the deciding factor. Thus, services organized and controlled by parents, by social workers, by nurses, by other professionals, or any combination of these, were included—as long as they offered support and information to parents of small or sick newborns. Second, many of these "groups" did not have meetings. Instead, their services were offered on a one-to-one basis. Thus, while they referred to themselves as parent-support groups, in fact they were groups of parents and professionals offering support in a variety of ways.

Similarly, the location in which services was based varied among the programs in this study. Most operated under the sponsorship of hospitals or community centers, but many were independent of any formal organization. Therefore, while location of service was not a factor in defining the sample, availability in terms of time and money was a criterion: groups that offered time-limited service (e.g., a 6-week discussion group) and/or asked a fee for this service, were not included. (Membership dues in a parent organization did not disqualify a group.)

In sum, the project population was made up of services that emphasized emotional and practical peer support to parents with preterm, sick, or high-risk infants, during hospitalization and after discharge. The services might be run by parents or professionals or both; be affiliated with a hospital or not; offer group meetings or individual counseling; but the services had to be free, and available on an ongoing basis.

Finding the Population

From this project's inception, finding the population to survey was an issue. When the study was conceived, there was no central source of information about such programs, no way to find out how many existed or where. Therefore, initial investigation involved locating a sample to study.

Groups were found largely through informal networks: inquiries made at hospitals with NICUs; letters sent to organizations such as the National Association of Perinatal Social Workers; notices placed in newsletters for professionals working with young families. As groups were identified, letters were sent requesting names of additional groups that might be known to them. When all sources had been tapped, 114 possible groups had been identified.

Selecting the Sample

A decision was made to send questionnaires to all contacts on the accumulated list. Frequently, only an individual's name and address were given, without a title or group designation. Thus, someone interested in beginning a support program would not be differentiated from the contact person for an established organization. It was not possible to know how many names on the list represented real groups, nor how many groups would fit the criteria for study.

The only way to determine this was to query all the groups. At this point, because it had become clear that little was known about the history and status of any of these services, it was decided to survey them all.

Data Collection

The survey data were collected primarily through questionnaires mailed to specific individuals identified as possible representatives of support groups for parents of premature and high-risk infants. Responses were supplemented by descriptive comments, letters, printed materials prepared by the groups, and, in some cases, phone interviews.

In January–February 1982, letters were sent out to 53 possible parent-support groups (the number identified at that time). Contacts were asked to respond by letter or phone to open-ended questions about their groups' origins and functioning. Twelve groups (27%) did so.

On the basis of these responses, a survey questionnaire was designed addressing the most salient issues defined by the "pilot" participants. The six-page survey allowed for both systematic and simple collection of data. As groups were identified, this questionnaire was sent with a cover letter describing the goals of the study and a stamped return envelope. Contacts were asked to return the questionnaire even if their groups had disbanded, in order to allow for comparison between groups that had survived and those that had not.

Response rate. During an 18-month period (January 1982 to June 1983) questionnaires were sent to 114 groups in the United States and

Canada. Of these groups, six could not be reached because of address changes; four contacts communicated that there were no such services in their areas. Five who responded did not meet study criteria. Of the 99 remaining groups, 63 (64%) responded, and they make up the study sample.

Respondents. On 29 of the questionnaires (46%), information was provided by professionals, on 32 (51%), by parents. One questionnaire included responses from both a parent and a professional, and the status of one correspondent was unknown.

Other sources of data. The survey data were obtained primarily through the questionnaires. In addition, almost half the respondents (44%, N = 27) sent samples of their newsletters, pamphlets, and/or newspaper articles describing their activities, and 49% (N = 31) offered extensive comments about their situations. Finally, 10 phone interviews supplemented written data. These additional sources of data were used to clarify and amplify questionnaire responses.

PROFILE OF GROUPS: DEMOGRAPHIC DATA

Location and Functioning of Groups

Every region of the continental United States was represented in this study. The location of groups was as follows (numbers in parentheses represent those groups contacted that did not respond): Northeast region = 4 respondents (0); Mid-Atlantic region = 5 (5); South = 9 (7); Midwest = 18 (0); Plains states = 3 (2); Mountain states = 5 (1); Southwest = 8 (3); Far West = 11 (5); Alaska = 0 (1); Hawaii = 0 (0); Canada = 0 (2).

Of the 63 respondents, 51 (81%) represented groups actively providing services. Eight groups (13%) reported that they were having difficulties, had curtailed their services, or were in the process of disbanding. Four questionnaires (6%) were returned by contacts who had been involved in groups that already had disbanded.

Type of Program

More than 90% (N = 59) of the programs offered contact between a veteran parent and a new one. Almost always this involved a sustained relationship; but occasionally the contact was informal, taking place in a lounge or group meeting. In addition to individual contacts, more than 60% (N = 39) of the programs also had opportunities for group discussion. (For more details on these activities, see "Emotional Support," following.)

Only three programs (5%) in this survey were based on meetings for new parents guided by a professional, without veteran parent involvement.

Age of Groups

The newest group had begun 1 month before the questionnaire was filled out; the oldest group had been functioning for 10 years. The mean age of the groups was 3.1 years; the mode and the median were 2 years.

Population Served

More than half the groups (52%, $N = 33$) defined their service population as the parents of any baby in the NICU. Another 28% ($N = 18$) served this population and any newborn with a special need, whether or not the child was in the NICU. Only six groups, 10%, focused their services on parents of preterms. (Two groups served parents of any newborn; two focused on particular difficulties—i.e., breast-feeding a hospitalized infant and apnea; and two groups did not provide this information.)

Transport

Intensive care for neonates is a regionalized service; certain hospitals throughout the country are designated as NICU centers for a large region or small one, depending on the area's population census. Because of this, in some places newborns at risk are transported from their community hospitals to medical centers with specialized personnel and equipment. This can mean that parents and infants are separated by as much as 1,000 miles.

Of the 49 groups who responded to this item on the survey, only three reported no transport into their hospitals. Four groups were based in home communities 20 to 150 miles from the nearest NICUS. For the

Table 1. Age of Groups

Age	Number of Groups
1 to 8 months	8 (13%)
1 to 2 years	22 (35%)
2½ to 3¾ years	11 (17%)
4 to 6½ years	12 (19%)
7 to 10 years	7 (11%)
Unknown	3 (5%)
Total	63 (100%)

46 groups dealing with transport, the range was 20 to 1,000 miles; the mean was 198 miles. Eight of these groups were 20 to 30 miles from the NICU; seven were 40 to 60 miles away; eight were 90 to 120 miles away; 10 were 150 to 200 miles away; seven were 250 to 300 miles away; four were 400 to 600 miles away; and two were 1,000 miles away from the NICU.

Hospital Affiliation

For most parents of premature or high-risk infants, the NICU is the focal point of interaction. Here they find not only professional staff who have helped with many anxiety-laden situations, but they also meet other parents dealing with similar questions and fears. Therefore it seems natural that most groups would be affiliated with the hospital where their members' children are receiving or recently received care.

In fact, 67% of the groups ($N = 42$) were affiliated with a single hospital. However, one-third of these did not serve that hospital exclusively. That is, although they were based at one hospital, they served parents from several: Twelve of these groups served two to four hospitals, and three served seven to 10.

When groups had no hospital affiliation, this sometimes was because an area had several NICUs and it was decided to share resources. In other cases, hospitals turned down the idea of a parent-support group, and parents were forced to begin on their own. In still others, the program originated through contacts made at local community or mental-health centers.

The 20 groups (32%) without hospital affiliation typically served several hospitals: only one worked with parents from a single hospital; eight groups served two to four hospitals; eight more served seven to 20 hospitals; and two of these nonaffiliated groups served 20 or more hospitals. (Data on number of hospitals served was not available for one group.)

PARTICIPATION OF PARENTS AND PROFESSIONALS IN PROGRAMS

Origin of Groups

Parents and professionals worked together initiating 13 of the groups (20%) in this study. Parents began 28 (44%), and professionals began 21 (33%).

When parents and professionals did work together, the initiative might come from either source: sometimes doctors, nurses and/or social workers approached parents; sometimes a parent expressed interest just at a point when a professional who shared that interest joined the staff; and sometimes, as one respondent wrote, "parents kept bugging the staff to get something going and [they] finally did."

It should be noted that in many of the cases where parents initiated the group, some support from hospital staff was likely. For example, two mothers who had helped each other through their simultaneous NICU experiences arranged a meeting with the unit's chief neonatalogist, head nurse, and social worker, and gained their support for creating a group. In another instance, five couples seeking information and support were referred to each other by a hospital social worker. Three groups, who indicated on the questionnaire that they had been started by parents, specifically mentioned "assistance from hospital staff," "initial help of a social worker," and "support from social work and nursing." Thus, while only 13 groups saw themselves as being joint enterprises of professionals and parents, it is likely that there was more interaction between staff and parents than the statistics suggest.

Involvement of Professionals, by Discipline. As already noted, one-third of the groups were begun by professionals who saw that the parents of their tiny patients needed emotional support. Social workers and nurses were almost equally involved in starting these groups, and both were involved twice as often as doctors: in the nine groups started by professionals working together, nurses and/or social workers were included in eight. (One involved a doctor and a staff member in a different field.) When doctors did participate, it most often was with other professionals—with or without parents.

Social workers were more likely to begin groups on their own or with other professionals than they were to begin with parents, whereas nurses were most likely to work with parents. They were the only professionals working with parents in five groups; social workers alone worked with parents in only two. In contrast, social workers began as many groups on their own as all other individual professionals combined.

Authority in Groups

Whatever the relative involvement of professionals and parents in a group's initiation, the data showed that this involvement did not necessarily remain the same as the group developed. In fact, there were some striking differences between initiation of groups and subsequent involvement in them.

Fewer than 25% of the groups had begun with sustained efforts of both parents and professionals. However, at the time of the survey, when the modal age of the groups was 2 years, almost 63% of the groups

Table 2. Professional Involvement, by Discipline

Group Initiated by	Doctor	Nurse	Social Worker	Other*
Professional working alone	1	4	6	1
Professional working with professionals of other disciplines	4	6	6	3
Professional working with other professionals and parents	3	4	4	
Professional working with parents	1	5	2	
Totals for each discipline**	9	19	18	4

*Other includes educational and developmental consultants; infant specialist; and a grant coordinator

**Totals show involvement of each discipline and do not add up to the study sample as there is overlap in categories including "professionals of other disciplines," i.e., a group started by a nurse and a social worker would appear under both social work and nursing.

were run with involvement of both professionals and parents. This involvement fell along a continuum, from minimal interaction and sharing of authority to regular consultation and shared responsibility.

Of special note were the nine groups in which authority was split: whereas the majority of groups shared responsibility in varying degrees, in these nine groups responsibility was rather sharply divided between parents and professionals. Typically, this meant the staff might be responsible for informing new parents of services and referring them to the group, but parents planned and carried out the activities. In such cases the graduate parents had no contact with new parents unless the staff arranged them, but the staff had little involvement in the kind of services the graduate parents provided.

In other groups, staff would be in charge of a special activity, such as a reunion, which was separate from ongoing services but provided under the auspices of the parent-support group. Thus, in these nine groups, both parents and professionals were involved, but in different, circumscribed areas of responsibility.

Core Participants. In an effort to understand more about who planned and carried out activities, a questionnaire item asked specifically how many parents and how many professionals were involved in this core aspect of group functioning. Unfortunately, many respondents did not provide numbers, or misinterpreted the question and indicated total group size rather than the number of core participants.

Keeping in mind the limitations of these data, from the 36 respondents who did accurately answer, it seemed that, as one would expect, most groups had more parents than professionals participating. There are, after all, many more parents in need of such services than there are professionals available to provide them.

Given that, however, the ratio of professionals to parents was very high. In 25% of these groups, there was a professional for every four to six parents involved in running the group; in another 25% there was a professional for every two to three parents; and four groups (12.5%) had two professionals for every three parents. Further, in some groups professionals equalled or exceeded parents in the core of involved participants. Typically this was in groups run by professionals, but in two cases there were more professionals than parents involved in groups run by parents.

How Parents Learn About Groups

Having the idea for a parent-support group, mobilizing staff and/or parent energy, and planning activities are merely preliminary steps. The target population—new parents in need of support—must be aware of this service if it is to have any reality.

There were four basic ways in which new parents learned about the support groups represented in this study: a veteran parent was available at the NICU to introduce the group; brochures were given to new NICU parents; staff verbally described the group; and/or there was publicity

Table 3. Professional/Parent Interaction in Running Groups

Parents control

All aspects:	10 (16%)
Consult occasionally with professionals:	7 (11%)
Consult regularly with professionals:	19 (30%)
Total:	36 (57%)

Professionals control

All aspects:	8 (13%)
Consult occasionally with parents:	2 (3%)
Consult regularly with parents:	3 (5%)
Total:	13 (21%)
Authority split:	9 (14%)
Unknown:	5 (8%)*
Total	63 (100%)

*Four of these groups had been started by professionals.

in the community (notices in doctors' offices; announcements in the media).

Most groups made their services known through a combination of these four means. Most frequently, however, groups relied primarily on two ways of reaching parents: through printed information in the NICU and through staff description to reinforce that information.

Almost 90% of the groups had introductory information about their services ranging from a simple, hand-lettered notice to elaborate packets containing brochures, newsletters, and a garment or toy for the baby. But only 60% ($N = 38$) were allowed by hospitals to give their information to all new NICU parents; whereas 16% ($N = 10$) were allowed to have brochures or notices only in waiting rooms or on hospital bulletin boards. The remaining groups relied on publicity in the community and on staff description of their services. And of these two means, staff's verbal description was far more certain to reach new parents in need of support.

Thus, the staff's description of a group was a major means of involving new parents in activities. In this role staff had three options: they could routinely tell all new parents about the group, as was reported in 35% of the programs ($N = 22$); they could be selective, discussing it with those whom they assessed as needing its services (done in 50% of the programs, $N = 32$); or they could have no involvement at all (in 10%, $N = 6$).

For those groups that had printed materials given to all new parents, staff involvement reinforced available information, perhaps giving it credibility. But for the groups that did not have literature automatically available, staff involvement seemed likely to be crucial in reaching new parents.

Initial Contacts. Out of respect for a parent's privacy, hospitals often will not give out information on a new NICU patient. Thus, many groups reported that before initial contact could be made by a graduate parent, the new parent would have to express some interest in the support program. In some cases, the presence of a volunteer parent in the NICU made this easier. Most groups, however, had to wait for some initiative from the new parents, even if that was simply their agreement to have the NICU nurse or social worker inform the group of their interest.

Once a group was aware that a new parent was interested in their services, they used three ways of engaging the parent in group activities: a call or visit by a veteran parent; an invitation to a regular meeting of the group; and/or the giving of a veteran parent's phone number so that the new parent might call when s/he wished.

No group in this study depended solely on giving a phone number to new parents. More than 75% of the programs (N = 48) made a personal call to the parents. Of these, 15 (24%) made only that initial call; nine (14%) also gave parents a number they could use when they wanted to make contact; 16 programs (25%) both called and invited the parents to a meeting; and eight groups (13%) did all three.

In contrast, for 11 programs (17%) invitations to meetings (probably verbally, by a staff person), were the primary introduction to the program, though in four of these groups (6%) a phone number also was given to the new parents in case they wished to speak to someone before the meeting.

ACTIVITIES AND SERVICES OFFERED BY GROUPS

To achieve their goals of helping parents of premature and high-risk infants, most support groups offered three basic services: individual emotional support; meetings that provided education and/or a chance for informal group discussion; and newsletters or other printed material. In addition, many groups participated in fund raising for the NICU, community education, special services for parents (e.g., grieving groups), and social activities for current and former NICU families. Finally, some groups developed unique, innovative programs or materials.

Emotional Support

This activity can be seen as the heart of parent-support services. Virtually all of them exist in order to help parents cope with the emotional stress, anxiety, and confusion, created by the birth of a high-risk or special-needs infant. Obviously, a prime way to achieve this is by providing a means for expressing grief, fear, and concerns about the infant's survival and subsequent development. And the means most favored by the groups in this study was the matching of new parents with "graduate" or "veteran" ones who had been through similar experiences.

Of the 62 groups who gave information on this topic, 55 (87%) reported matching parents on some basis, usually the infant's condition or the family's geographical location. In 16 groups (25%), matching was done based on the child's condition alone; and in four (6%), on the family's location alone. In 24 groups (38%) both criteria were used. In addition, one group used cultural background as a way of matching veteran and new parents, and two based pairing on parents' requests. (Eight groups did not give the bases on which their matching was done.)

Besides this pairing of new and experienced parents, groups had several other ways of offering emotional support. These included "warmlines" (numbers to call at almost any time for encouragement and information); support from professionals, usually social workers; and meetings for informal discussion.

Twenty-six groups (41%) used some combination of these services; but matching alone or in combination with other support was by far the most-offered form.

In sum, 90% of the groups operated on the assumption that sustained one-to-one contact between veteran and new parents was the best way to offer emotional support; and most believed that the best basis for pairing parents would be the similarity of the children's conditions.

Meetings

Regular meetings of any social service organization can provide a way in which new and prospective members meet experienced ones and gain a sense of the people and activities the group represents. For parent-support groups, meetings can make possible a nonthreatening introduction, a chance for a new parent to look over the participants before turning to them for more personal help.

At least once a month, 41 groups (65%) held meetings for members. Eight other groups (13%) met less often, from four to six times a year. Eleven groups had no meetings; and data were unavailable for three. These meetings served three primary functions: to provide education through presentations by professionals and parents; to give parents an opportunity to share their experiences through informal group discussion; and to attend to some organizational business.

In 32 (51%) of the groups, the two main functions—of education and informal discussion—were mixed or alternated. Seven groups (11%) used their meetings just for "rap" sessions, whereas three (5%) had only

---

Table 4.   Range of Individual Support Services Offered

2	Matching + Warmline + Professional
17	Matching + Warmline
7	Matching + Professional
31	Matching only
1	Warmline only
1	Informal discussion with veterans
3	Professional (+ Discussion with other new parents)
1	Unknown
63	

presentations by professionals. Another three of the groups used these meetings for organizational business, such as planning group activities or supervising their emotional-support providers.

Training for Support. Comments on the questionnaires suggested that the veteran parents who offered support to others did so from a wish to ease the kinds of burdens they themselves had experienced. And with so many new parents matched to veterans on the basis of their infants' conditions, to some extent the veterans were being asked to relive their own crises. In addition, whether support is offered through ongoing individual contact, a warmline, or informal discussion, the task of providing it to a new parent in crisis can demand a great deal of emotional energy. There are likely to be situations that would test the resources even of more detached and professionally experienced helpers.

Given the stresses veteran parents were likely to encounter, an important question became how much training, if any, they received before giving support to new parents.

Survey responses made it clear that training was required by most groups, and that professionals played a major role in it. Of the 60 groups known to offer emotional support, 42 (70%) indicated that they required some training. One group offered but did not require it; four groups planned to have it; and six groups did not have or plan to have such training. (In one group, an MSW provided all support; information was unavailable for six groups.)

Of the groups that did require training, 22 (52%) had written guidelines available. Almost 60% of these groups (N = 24) offered training sessions with both experienced parents and professionals instructing new volunteers. Where there was only one means of training, twice as frequently these were sessions with professionals alone (N = 13) rather than with experienced parents alone (N = 6).

Newsletters and Other Literature

Because some groups are based many miles from parents' home communities, meetings may not be a feasible way to reach those they hope to serve. Newsletters can do this, and they also can provide a link to the group after a child is discharged, thus helping to maintain the interest and involvement of veteran parents. Finally, by keeping professionals aware of the groups' services, newsletters also can contribute to support and credibility for a group.

Newsletters, however, require a fair amount of time, talent, and money. There must be people willing and able to plan and contribute material to them, handle layout and typing, and pay for the printing and mailing costs. Thus, while a newsletter can be an important part of a group's services, it is one of the hardest to provide.

Despite this, 28 of the groups (44%) did have newsletters. Only 16 groups (25%) managed to publish these newsletters on a monthly basis. Twelve groups (19%) published newsletters two to six times a year; another five (8%) planned to start them. But 28 groups (44%) had none, nor planned to have any.

On the other hand, 50 groups (79%) had leaflets or brochures to offer parents. These covered a range of issues during and after hospitalization, including breast-feeding a preterm infant, emotional bonding with a hospitalized infant, stimulating hospitalized preterms, and the feelings and rights of parents.

Other Services

In addition to these three basic services already described, the parent-support groups in this study also put effort into other, related activities.

Besides individual contacts and meetings, 26 groups (41%) provided *practical and emotional support to parents* through a variety of means. These included sending letters and pictures to out-of-town parents; making possible parental visits to the hospitalized baby by providing transportation or the money for it, offering housing to parents far from home, and baby-sitting with older children; making, giving, lending, or exchanging preterm clothing and equipment; and offering groups for grieving parents.

Seventeen groups (27%) had *social activities*, usually on an annual or biannual basis, including NICU reunions, nurses' teas, Christmas parties, and summer picnics. An equal number were involved in *education or political action*: this ranged from lobbying in state legislatures for better transport services or better medical coverage for NICU care to creating speakers' bureaus and presenting information on preterm birth and its emotional consequences to community and professional groups, and talking with high-risk parents *before* their child's birth. Finally, 11 groups (17%) did *fund raising for the NICU*, providing funds not only for equipment but also for furnishings, both within the NICU (rocking chairs) and in the lounges where anxious parents waited.

In all, 42 groups (67%) were involved in providing such services. Only three groups provided all four kinds of programs, but 19 offered some combination of them. Of the 20 groups that had only one service in addition to the basic three (support/meetings/newsletter), 10 invested their energies in additional parent support.

Innovative Programs and Materials

Beyond the varied services already described, several groups created unique activities and materials. Some of these required a great deal of institutional support, such as one hospital's predischarge room, where parents could be near the security of the NICU for the first night of full responsibility of their child. Some projects demanded enormous time and energy from at least a dozen determined group members—e.g., the writing and marketing of the first book published for parents of premature infants.

Other activities were smaller in scope but large in inspiration: the grandparents' pamphlet written by one group, the baby-book sheet for preterms created by another; the blood drive to set up a blood bank credit system for infants in an NICU; the recordings of parents' voices to play near transport infants; or the "shadow parenting" in which parents of high-risk infants exchanged baby-sitting after discharge.

Such projects were conceived and carried out both by large, established groups and smaller, newer ones. And in all cases, the originators were eager to share their ideas with those interested in creating or expanding services for parents of premature and high-risk infants.

CONTACTS POSTDISCHARGE

One NICU nurse specified what she saw as the parents' needs after their child came home, "Graduate parents have two different needs, depending on their child's status: to get the experience out of their system, or to deal with continuing problems." In fact, anecdotal responses suggested that both these needs exist simultaneously for many parents. Even those whose babies seem healthy have many questions about the normality of their infant's behavior and development.

Certainly, the data from this study support comments about the need for contact postdischarge. Forty-five groups (71%) reported that this was desired by parents, with an additional 10 saying the wish for contact varied among their members. Only two groups said that postdischarge contact was not usually desired. Therefore, to varying degrees, almost 90% of the groups provided some way of being involved after hospital discharge, and several groups existed specifically for this purpose.

There were two main ways of maintaining posthospital involvement: individual contact with an experienced parent, and continued contact with a group. Individual support was available in 50 of the groups (79%). Parents might continue contact with the veteran they had grown to know during their child's hospitalization; be given the name of another veteran; or given the number of a warmline. Frequently all these options were offered.

Continued participation in a group was available in 43 groups (68%). In 29 (46%), parents could return to the hospital group after discharge; in 14 (22%) parents could attend groups meeting in their home communities.

Overall, 56 groups (89%) had ways to offer service that extended after the infant's hospital discharge. More than half the groups made possible both group and individual contacts; 16 groups had only continued individual contacts; four had only group meetings open to graduate parents; and two offered social-work counseling.

Obstacles to Service

Frequently, however, offering the service was not enough: many groups voiced their frustration at not being able to reach parents after discharge. As one staff member, the coordinator for a group, wrote, "Regionalized intensive care sometimes creates problems for families [after discharge]. One of the most frustrating aspects of providing support to 'long-distance families'—most without resources and 'high risk' by definition—is the problem of maintaining contact." And a parent, who because of job transfers was involved in creating *two* parent-support groups, echoed these feelings: "Unfortunately, once a baby goes home, we generally lose contact with the family. Mostly this is because of the distance involved. . . . The biggest problem I see in parent-support groups is the follow-up. We've discussed the problem over and over again, and haven't come up with a solution."

Distance, however, is not the only obstacle to continued contact. Some groups noted that even if parents had concerns, after discharge they wanted to forget their experience in the hospital, and ongoing parent-support group contacts make that difficult. In other cases, parents were overwhelmed by practical and financial demands, and their anxieties shifted or extended to finding the resources they needed, including sitters who could adequately care for very small or handicapped infants, and so make it possible for the parents to attend meetings.

Ideas for Outreach. Despite the difficulties in providing support after discharge, many groups agreed with the professional who wrote, parents "need [even] more support at this stage." And, several respondents had ideas to share on how to deal with this dilemma.

One group, with babies transported to its state's single NICU, had created a network of volunteer parents in home communities. This meant that the organization concentrated effort on the more than 20 satellite groups operating around its state. They found it was most important and effective to have support in local communities, although this required coordination and communication over long distances and meant less energy could be invested in regular hospital-based meetings.

Another group was considering more interaction with pediatricians. This group had a very successful system of matching new and experienced parents while in the hospital, and thought that outreach after discharge would be facilitated by creating a matching system done through the pediatricians' offices, when parents came in with questions after their child's hospital discharge.

Yet another group, noting the difficulty in getting parents to meetings after their babies left the hospital, made as many individual contacts as possible before discharge. Then, their veteran parents would follow up with a phone call 1 month after discharge, and keep calling at mutually agreed upon intervals until the new parents felt comfortable with their baby.

The three groups in this study that focused on parents' needs after discharge based their services on community contacts. For example, one publicized its services in pediatric offices and had a support group designed especially for those "just going home," families in the first year after discharge. Another included practical assistance as a goal along with education and parent-to-parent support. This program made accessible not only clothing and equipment, but also a list of resources including respite and special needs child care, transportation services, medical care, and community agencies. Such a program component met a real need—and it also might involve families who were uncertain about continuing contact.

Finally, in addition to peer support, the third program offered home visits by a nurse from an early intervention program. The nurse could provide an expert source against which to measure an infant's behavior, and could reassure or offer ways to enhance development. All the parents served by this program had welcomed the nurse into their homes, thus making possible ongoing follow-up contacts.

GROUP CONTINUITY

One way of maintaining involvement in a group was to receive services after discharge; another was to give service by volunteering to act as a graduate parent for new ones. This would seem to be a basic need for support groups; without a small but constant influx of recruits, most groups cannot continue.

Despite this, when indicating what kind of involvement was available to parents after discharge, only 35 groups (55%) in this study included as an option "becoming involved in providing services to new parents." Five groups did not answer this item, but this means that at least the remaining 23 groups, or 36% of the sample, did not recruit volunteers from the parents they served.

This finding was very puzzling, considering that over time the involvement of new parents could be vital to the groups' survival. In order to understand how this factor, and those described earlier, might be related to a group's stability and survival over time, comparative analyses were done on the data. The results are presented in the next section.

COMPARATIVE ANALYSES: THE STABILITY AND SURVIVAL OF GROUPS

The Status Scale

In an effort to identify those factors related to group success, a "status scale" was developed. This 3-point scale was based on stability, growth, and innovation. "0" was assigned to any group that had disbanded or curtailed services, or that was experiencing problems in becoming established. In a few cases, programs in this category were providing services similar to those of programs in the next rating. The deciding factor was that the lower-ranked groups were having difficulties in carrying out what they had been doing, or in reaching the reasonable goals they had set.

Sixteen groups fit these criteria. Of these, four had disbanded completely; two had suspended services; three had curtailed services; and four had been in existence for one to two years but still were having trouble establishing services.

"1" was given to the 27 groups that showed stability. These programs had been in existence for at least a year, and in addition to providing emotional support to new parents, had maintained some of several basic services: regular meetings for members, a newsletter and/or other printed material, postdischarge follow-up care. This category included groups that had established some services and were adding others. Thus, a program that for 3 years had held weekly meetings and offered individual emotional support, and now was adding a newsletter, would be rated as stable, or a "1."

This rating contrasted with the highest rank, that which reflected not only stability, but also growth and/or innovation. The 13 groups ranked

"2" had established all services possible in their situations (e.g., they might not have in-hospital meetings because a hospital did not allow them); in addition, they had innovative activities or expanding programs. For example, they might have lobbied for legislation to increase insurance coverage for neonatal crises; or they might be extending their program to include satellite groups in distant communities. Finally, this category included the five groups that were *both* innovative and growing.

Using this scale, Chi-Square tests of significance were done on the data from all groups more than a year old at the time of the study. Seven groups, existing from 1 to 8 months when the survey was done, were not included. They were in a process of growth, and their stability could not be determined. However, the "0" category did include two groups that had ended after 6 months of efforts to establish services. They were included because a clear judgment could be made of their status.

Findings

Demographic Variables. First, the data analyses showed a very strong linear relationship between age and status, with the higher-ranking groups much more likely to be among the older ones ($\chi^2 = 36.3718$, $p < .001$, $df = 8$). Age was not a factor in determining status (except to exclude nascent groups that might have been assigned to any of the three categories). This finding therefore provides support for the validity of the status scale, at least as a measure of a group's ability to continue providing services over time.

Rankings did not differ significantly on any other demographic variable. There was no correlation between ranking and the parent population served (parents of preterms only, NICU infants, or all infants with special needs), nor with the distance that infants were transported. Neither was there an association between status and the groups' affiliation with hospitals, or the number of hospitals served.

Table 5. Status Rating Scale

Number of Groups/ (Percent of Sample)	Rating
13 (21%)	2 = Stability plus growth and/or innovation
27 (43%)	1 = Stability
16 (25%)	0 = Problems establishing or maintaining
7 (11%)	services; too new to be rated
63 (100%)	

Thus, there was no difference in status between groups that defined their infant populations more narrowly or broadly, that focused on parents living near or far from the hospital, or that sought to serve one hospital or to establish a broader base of community support by serving many. The data seem to suggest that there is no *single*, preferred decision to make as to what parent-infant population to serve, or what kind of institutional and community support to seek.

Parent and Professional Interaction. It was thought that the interaction of parents and professionals in support groups would be related to status. Specifically, the higher-ranking groups would reflect the joint efforts of parents and professionals working together, and this would be true for both the groups' origins and for their provision of ongoing services.

Contrary to expectations, in comparing group origins no significant difference in status was found between groups that had been started by parents alone, by professionals alone, or by both working together. However, in looking at ongoing services, there was a strong correlation between status and the regular interaction of parents and professionals: when parents and staff worked together, their programs were more likely to be in the higher-status category; less likely to be in the lower. And conversely, when parents and professionals did *not* interact regularly, their groups were much more likely to be in the lower status, and much less likely to be in the higher (χ^2 = 6.8782, p < .05, df = 2). Further, this was true not only in situations where parents alone or professionals alone were in charge of a group, but also in ones where parents and professionals each took responsibilities, but split them rather than working together (see Profile: Authority in Groups).

Thus, it seemed that though successful groups might be started without involvement of both parents and professionals, their survival and growth were enhanced by establishing a working relationship based on regular interactions.

Reaching New Parents. A weak trend was found between status and the availability of printed materials for new parents of premature or high-risk infants (χ^2 = 8.8839, p < .1, df = 4). The variance was accounted for by the lack of such literature for the lowest status, and the fact that both of the higher rankings had some form of program description, usually available in the NICU for all parents. Another analysis involved the relationship between status and staff's providing verbal description of the groups. There was no statistically significant difference between groups on this dimension.

In contrast, after parents had learned about the programs, there was a significant difference between groups in the way they made initial contact. Higher-ranking groups were much more likely to have their veterans make a personal call to interested new parents, and they never relied solely on the more distanced mode of an invitation to an open meeting. Lower-ranked groups were much more likely to do this (χ^2 = 6.8527, $p < .05$, $df = 2$).

Thus, while introduction to the group through written materials or staff descriptions did not seem strongly related to the program's success, the way in which an interested parent was first invited to participate appeared likely to be a factor of some importance.

Activities and Services. To some extent, activities and services were used in judging status. However, it was their existence not their frequency or format that were judged, and in analyzing the data several relationships were found between status and certain aspects of activities.

First, in provision of emotional support, there was a strong relationship between status and the pairing of new parents with veterans: all those groups that did *not* match veterans and new parents were in the lowest ranking (χ^2 = 9.0355, $p < .05$, $df = 2$). However, the bases on which matching was done had no relation to status: there was no statistically significant difference between groups bringing parents together because of similarity of their infants' conditions, geographical proximity, a combination of these, or other reasons. Clearly, the matching of new and veteran parents could be done in a number of ways; what was important was that it did occur.

On the other hand, there was no confirmation of the expectation that volunteer training would be associated with higher-ranking groups: analyses showed no statistical differences between groups that did or did not provide training for their volunteers.

There were two other areas of activity in which correlations with status were significant: frequency of newsletters, and format of meetings. Higher-status groups were more likely to have newsletters and to distribute them monthly (χ^2 = 15.8616, $p < .05$, $df = 8$). However, it was not clear whether having a newsletter enhanced a program's stability by contributing to communication within the group and creating credibility with professionals and the community, or whether more stable groups had the resources to organize and carry out such an activity.

There was only a weak correlation between status and frequency of meetings, with higher-ranking groups more likely to have them at least once a month (χ^2 = 9.1555, $p < .1$, $df = 4$). But, there was a strong relationship between status and the format of meetings. In fact, contrary to expectations, it became clear that the highest-ranked groups were much more likely to use their meeting times for purposes other than peer support: they were the only ones to devote this time solely to presentations by professionals, and also were much more likely to focus on business only. In contrast, no lowest-ranked group used meetings in this way, being much more likely to offer a combination of informal discussion and presentations by professionals (χ^2 = 10.5137, p < .05, df = 4).

The data thus suggested that programs ranking higher on stability and growth used their group gatherings for more than service provision, and were likely to spend them on issues of importance to group maintenance.

Postdischarge Services. Ninety percent of the groups offered services after the infants were discharged from the hospital. Some made possible continued involvement in a hospital-based group, others offered individual emotional support; still others offered a choice of both. No correlation was found between status and the possibility of ongoing group involvement; and there was only a weak trend between status and the availability of individual emotional support after discharge. However, there was a strong linear relationship between status and having the *choice* of both kinds of services: less than half of the lowest-ranking groups offered such a choice, while more than three-quarters of the highest-ranking groups did so (χ^2 = 9.487, p < .05, df = 4).

Further, analyses of parent and professional involvement in programs provided a finding that seemed significant both in terms of statistics and the successful functioning of groups: programs with both parents and professionals involved were more likely to offer a choice of postdischarge services. Programs run by parents alone were much more likely to have only individual contact after discharge, and programs run by professionals alone were more likely to have no postdischarge services at all (χ^2 = 18.1002, p < .01, df = 6). To the extent that having this choice contributes to a group's ability to serve new parents, this finding seemed to underscore the importance of parent and professional involvement for successful service provision.

Opportunity to Serve. Finally, it was thought that group status would be related to the opportunity for parents to serve as veterans once they had graduated from the stressful period following their infant's difficult birth and uncertain future. This factor was seen as being especially important to status, as it meant new people were being recruited to maintain services. It therefore was expected that having this opportunity would be correlated with higher status. This was so: higher-ranking groups were more likely to have such opportunities and less likely not to have them (χ^2 = 6.3637, p < .05, df = 2). Further, much of the variance was accounted for by the lower-ranked groups' not offering this option.

Interestingly, when recruitment was looked at in terms of parent and professional involvement, there was no difference between groups: although it seemed natural that parent-run organizations would be more likely to seek new volunteers, this was not so. Instead, there was a very strong linear relationship between age and recruitment ($\chi^2 = 16.3036$, $p < .005$, $df = 4$), with the older groups far more likely to recruit new volunteers. Thus, at least survival certainly seemed tied to ongoing efforts to involve new members in providing services.

DISCUSSION

The data in this survey suggests a picture of parent-support services that rank highest on a scale reflecting stability, growth, and innovation. In the foreground are parents and professionals working together, consulting regularly for the planning and provision of services. They reach out to parents in crisis through the matching of the new parent with a veteran who shares some aspect of their experience, and who initiate contact with a personal call.

These more successful groups then are likely to offer a variety of other services, such as group-discussion meetings and newsletters, and to provide a choice of ways to receive continued support after discharge. Finally, despite the spectrum of services offered, these groups do not expend all their energy on service: there is a place in their program for meetings devoted to business and the supervision of volunteers, and they seek new graduate members to sustain services over time.

In contrast, the less successful groups are less likely to have parents and professionals interacting together to plan and carry out activities, or to have a choice of services. They are less likely to match new parents with veterans, and more likely to rely on less personal means of inviting new parents to participate. Finally, they are less likely to set aside meetings to attend to group business or to recruit volunteers from the parents they served.

In planning research or action on a study such as this, it is important to remember the limitations of results based on correlational data analyzed with univariate statistics. First, it is impossible to know the direction of the correlation: is a program successful because it has certain services, or is it able to offer these services because it is successful? Second, univariate analyses cannot tell us if a cluster of factors are related to each other, or strongly influenced by a single variable. So, the central factor in having a successful group could be the educational background of the parents served: this might influence other variables that seem related to success, such as members' ability to contribute to a newsletter, their expectation that meetings are devoted to business, and their effective communication and positive interaction with professional staff.

However, taking into account the limitations in the data available from this project, several issues stand out as most salient to the creation and survival of parent-support services.

Obstacles to Collaborative Parent–Professional Relations

Some interaction between parents and professionals is an inescapable reality for support services focused on parents of preterm and high-risk infants: The fact that the newborn needs special medical care is, after all, the reason that parents need special social support. Information in this survey suggested that many groups realized they could benefit from the skills and commitment of both professionals and veteran parents, and that the most stable and successful groups involved parents and professionals in regular interactions. But for most groups obstacles remained to comfortable and cooperative working relationships.

In some instances, professionals who wanted to begin a program met with resistance from their colleagues. For example, in one hospital doctors would not support nurses' attempts to begin a group, and hospital administrators confiscated printed materials the nurses wanted to give new parents. In another case, a public-health nurse began a group, but found that although private pediatricians in her community made referrals to her, the local hospitals would not recognize the group she chaired as a "meaningful organization."

Then there were the programs in which professionals were not able to involve the parents they sought to help. In two situations social workers reported that their clients were wary of anything but activities affiliated with religious groups; and one found that parents accepted emotional support from the social worker but not from other parents. Another group started by professionals offered parents the opportunity to become involved in providing services; but in 3 years no parents had expressed an interest in doing so.

Far more common, however, were comments about veteran parents' difficulties in gaining acceptance by professionals. Occasionally this had to do with hospital politics. One group had to deal with staff resistance after the NICU head nurse took the group under her wing— and acted as if the organization were "a big secret . . . her own private little group." As this respondent noted, it was "so discouraging when we were ready and willing to be used and were not being used," and tensions between staff members were the reasons.

More typically, groups could not gain support from any hospital personnel. For one group, resistance from hospital staff led to seeking support from the local March of Dimes. But even with technical and financial aid from this respected organization, the group still met with resistance from the hospital. No referrals were made.

A parent from a group that was just beginning offered an explanation for this kind of situation: "The staff is not sure how much we are to be trusted in dealing with new parents. It is difficult for professionals to let go of any aspect of control." Such professional resistance to parent involvement was a theme played out even in well-established groups. Two thriving groups, each in existence more than 7 years, and each serving parents from several hospitals, still could not convince hospital staff even to distribute their literature. They depended on media publicity and informal reports of their services. And after 8½ years, another group was disbanding because "the enthusiasm from hospital staff which generated our group has deteriorated so badly that we cannot continue to draw from their resources. . . . The hospital staff assume they are meeting all of the needs of parents, and that our group has become an 'anachronism,' but parents coming to us for service tell us this is not so."

This last comment suggests another important issue in staff/parent relations: the varying perceptions of those involved. In several of the cases reported in this study, hospital staff wanted to meet parents' needs and thought that they were. But parents did not share this perception. The issue appeared again, in another context, when groups were reporting on the division of authority within a program. Here, contrary to the usual ratio of one professional to several parents, groups supposedly run by parents would report more professionals than parents involved in planning and carrying out services. And in one surprising instance, a group in which authority was seen as split between parents and professionals reported that 10 professionals and no parents did the planning and providing of services.

These findings raise some important questions about the perceptions of parents and professionals in these groups. One wonders if within programs there are significant variations in the parents' and the professionals' views of their interaction and relative authority. Do professionals feel they are sharing control, when in fact parents are not involved in decision making? Do parents want more guidance and support from professionals? And how can the best balance of authority and responsibility be developed and maintained?

This survey is descriptive; it does not look at the ways in which parent and professional relationships evolve, nor at the range of workable relationships that can exist. It does provide a clear picture of the inescapable importance of these relationships and of some of the obstacles that interfere with them. Whatever the balance of involvement and authority achieved by parents and professionals in a particular program, those wishing to establish services must give a great deal of attention to this pivotal issue.

Group Maintenance: Leadership and Availability of Volunteers and Professionals

All but three programs in this survey were based on individual contact between veterans and new parents. Thus it was surprising that only 55% of these included volunteering as an option for parents after their infants had graduated from the NICU. The data suggested that having such an option was related to both success and longevity in groups: recruitment of volunteers was more likely to occur among the higher-ranked programs, as well as among the ones that had survived the longest (these subgroups overlapped but were not identical).

Unfortunately, recruiting and retaining volunteers can be difficult even when the need is recognized. One respondent wrote, "The only trouble with our group is getting parents involved after their babies are 'well.' The parents really appreciate our visits at the hospital, but not enough for many of them to want to help someone else out." Another respondent whose group shared this problem offered a reason: "We are limited by the fact that our members have very young and often very ill children; therefore we are continually short of manpower. We have, at minimum, 20 good ideas . . . but we do not have the people to implement them."

Virtually all groups using veterans face the problem of having their volunteers meet the emotional needs of new parents while handling feelings about their own experience, and the responsibilities of their own young children. Further, for most volunteers in these programs, no matter how committed, involvement in a service for parents of preterm and high-risk infants is not a life's work. Parents find that their needs and interests change as their children grow. A child without severe disabilities becomes involved in nursery and elementary school activities, and a parent oriented toward community organizations is likely to shift energy to those more immediately serving his family. Or, the parent of a handicapped child puts her energy into supporting a group more directly related to the child's disability. Families move, or have new babies who do not require special care—and the availability of volunteers changes. And for similar reasons, the commitment of involved hospital staff also may shift: they too move, have babies, change jobs.

The impact of such predictable shifts in availability of individual volunteers and staff is especially critical when it involves someone in a leadership position. Several of the oldest groups, those in existence for 7 to 10 years at the time of the survey, had had no change in leadership. Some of these leaders were professionals who had remained at the same job, but some were parents who had committed themselves to managing the growing organizations they had helped found.

Laudable as this is, it may well have the paradoxical effect of making group survival even more difficult when that central figure moves on, for whatever reason. In fact, this is precisely what happened in two of the groups ranked highest at the time of the survey—one led by a parent, the other by a professional. Subsequently it was learned that when the professional moved to another city, and the parent's commitments changed, the vacuums in leadership led to one group's curtailment and the other's demise.

In the excitement and energy generated by a program's creation, it is tempting to expand services, both in what is offered and to whom outreach is made. It seems very important, however, that very early in a program's life, plans be made for recruitment of volunteers (cf. Weatherston et al., 1983), enlarging staff support, and identifying potential leaders. And, the fact that groups ranked highest in this study were likely to make use of their meeting time for business and program development suggests that it might be wise to set aside such time for dealing with issues of group maintenance and change.

Support During the Postdischarge Period

An infant's discharge from the hospital—the graduation from the tubes and monitors, round-the-clock noise and bright lights—does not mean an end to a parent's questions and concerns. Parents can say good-bye to the doctors and nurses whose care has made it possible to bring home a live baby. But the twin specters of the baby's traumatic birth or illness and of the possible damage these may portend ride home with the family. As one respondent wrote, "The homecoming period with my child was more difficult than the actual hospitalization. Homecoming was when all the 'support' vanished and friends expected me to get on with life now that the 'crisis' was over. These attitudes caused a great deal of mental anguish."

Material in this survey strongly suggests that special attention and energy be given to providing services for parents after their infant is discharged from the hospital. The impression conveyed by respondents, and confirmed by writers in the field, is that the period after hospital discharge is a particularly difficult one.

Earlier in this report (Profile: Postdischarge Services), both parents and professionals spoke of their concern and frustration in reaching parents after their babies had been discharged. The reasons for such concern have been comprehensively summarized by Desmond et al. (1980), who depict the parents' postdischarge plight: the support and security of the NICU are withdrawn and a new, possibly unknown doctor assumes responsibility for their fragile infant's care; the bills begin to arrive; the baby often is very demanding, crying a great deal, feeding slowly, sleeping little, and s/he may take months to adapt to a predictable sleep/wake pattern; the parents are likely to have unrealistic expectations for their baby's development, and these will be aggravated by the contributions of family and friends, who compare the infant with others and speculate about its future. In sum, these writers conclude that after a high-risk baby's homecoming, parents are likely to continue to be as emotionally stressed, socially isolated, and economically vulnerable as they were during the hospitalization—and now they also must cope with the constant needs of a very demanding infant.

It is a sad irony that at a time of such need, it becomes more difficult for groups to provide support to parents. Distance often interferes with continued contact, and economic and family pressures may make it hard for new parents to maintain involvement. As noted in the Profile section, programs in this survey tried varied outreach services, such as working with pediatricians to offer postdischarge service, providing practical assistance, and arranging home visits by public-health nurses. These and other innovative approaches certainly should increase the chances of reaching parents after their baby's discharge. Nevertheless, many of the neediest parents remain inaccessible.

Despite the difficulties in reaching parents after discharge, special efforts must be made: Postdischarge services can be vital to all parents of preterm and high-risk infants. As Sameroff and Abbe (1978) have said, "Until the child appears and acts in accord with the [parents'] views of normality, there is still the potential for later care-taking problems. For this reason the family requires follow-up care to assure that the [parents] will not be overwhelmed by a child who may give little satisfaction for meeting its many care-taking demands" (p. 223). In addition, they go on to emphasize an important point: "These problems are more likely to occur in those families with fewest economic, educational, or emotional resources to deal with such burdens" (ibid.). This statement highlights a final issue, that of serving parents from different backgrounds and circumstances, varying in their needs and resources.

Differences in Populations Served

Whether one is developing services in-hospital or postdischarge, attention to the values and living situations of the population served is crucial if the program is to reach those it hopes to help. In this survey, the parent population is defined only by the infant's status: NICU, preterm, etc. The study does not look at populations in terms of socioeconomic, cultural, and religious factors; not in terms of race, the mother's age and marital status. It seems likely that these factors can play a major role in a program's success in reaching parents—especially after discharge, when they no longer share the common meeting ground of the NICU.

Although parents from different socioeconomic, ethnic, and age groups obviously can develop very supportive relationships with each other, cultural values (including child-rearing practices and expectations of infant behavior), as well as economic constraints or options, may have a great deal to do with the relationship on which parent-to-parent support is built. In planning services it thus seems essential to carefully consider the population a hospital usually serves, and ways to address their particular needs (cf. Field et al., 1982).

Recommendations

For Groups. In addition to the issues already described here for consideration by those developing parent-support services, the results of this study offer a number of guidelines for program planning.

The data suggest that a successful group may begin in a number of different ways, with parents or professionals initially working alone, or with them working together; the group may serve parents whose infants' conditions are more narrowly or broadly defined; and it may work within or outside the hospital. But whatever its origin, affiliation, and goals, for its continued survival and growth it seems likely that it would do well to offer a choice in its services, to match new parents with veterans who have graduated from the grief and anxiety of having a baby who requires special care, and who reach out in a private, personal way to the parent in crisis. Finally, such a group would focus energy on finding these vital volunteers; and, perhaps most of all, would set a priority of involving parents and professionals in a collaborative relationship.

For Research. This study involved exploration of an area not previously charted. As such, it pursued certain promising paths, but also overlooked some important ones. Both those followed and those missed suggest avenues for future research.

Most basically, it seems necessary to identify populations in terms of socioeconomic status, mother's age, marital status, and racial and cultural background. However, even while placing the population in a large sociocultural perspective, there could be refinement in the identification of parents by infants' status. For example, one respondent commented on difficulties in having discussion groups bring together parents whose newborns were in critical condition, with those whose babies were well enough to be released. Each subgroup had its own particular anxieties and questions, and the mix was an uncomfortable one. Similarly, in postdischarge services there could be a difference in use depending on the child's prognosis as either handicapped or as essentially small but healthy. By both enlarging the scope and refining the focus on population, much can be learned about who is being reached and who may be underserved, what programs seem to best meet the needs of the hard to reach, and the relationship of a program's success to its target population.

Second, almost all areas mapped in this survey would be thrown into relief by a focus on process and the participants' perceptions. For example, when an infant enters the NICU, what is the process by which parents are informed of a program? When matching of veterans and new parents is done, how soon after the child's birth do contacts occur? Where and how often do they take place? What is their typical content? Do these contacts meet the expectations of new parents and of those providing the service?

In recruitment, what is the process of screening and invitation to participate as a volunteer? What kind of evaluation and supervision or consultation are available? Where does authority lie within a group? Is the explicit division of responsibility and decision making congruent with the participants' perceptions of it? How often do changes in leadership occur? Are they planned?

These are only some of the questions that ranged beyond the boundaries of this survey. However, with the descriptive data available here providing guideposts, it is hoped that further research will explore this ground in greater depth and detail.

REFERENCES

Boukydis, C.F.Z. (1982). Support groups for parents with premature infants in NICUs. In R.E. Marshall, C. Kasman, & L.S. Cape (Eds.), Coping with caring for sick newborns. Philadelphia: Saunders.

Boukydis, C.F.Z. (1984). The importance of parenting networks. Paper presented at First Annual Conference of Parents of Premature and High Risk Infants International, Inc.: "Parent Care for Parents of Critically Ill Newborns," Salt Lake City, Utah.

Butterfield, P.M., & Miller, L. (1984). Read your baby: A follow-up intervention program for parents with NICU infants. Infant Mental Health Journal, 5 (2), 107–116.

Caputo, D.V., Goldstein, K.M., & Taub, H.B. (1979). The development of prematurely born children through middle childhood. In T.M. Field, A.M. Sostek, S. Goldberg, & H.H. Shuman, (Eds.), *Infants born at risk: Behavior and development.* New York: SP Medical and Scientific Books.

Cherniss, D.S. (1984). *The resource directory.* Salt Lake City, Utah. Parents of Premature and High Risk Infants International.

Cohen, L. (1981). Examination of habituation as a measure of aberrant infant development. In S.L. Friedman & M. Sigman (Eds.), *Preterm birth and psychological development.* New York: Academic Press.

Desmond, M.M., Wilson, G.S., Alt, E.J., & Fisher, E.S. (1980). The very low birthweight infant after discharge from intensive care: Anticipatory health care and developmental course. *Current Problems in Pediatrics, X* (6), 1–59.

Enriquez, M.., Harrell, H., & Putnam, M. (1980). Role of parent groups in an intensive care unit. In E.J. Sell (Ed.), *Follow-up care of the high risk newborn—A practical approach.* Springfield, IL: Thomas.

Erdman, D. (1977). Parent-to-parent support: The best for those sick newborns. *American Journal of Maternal Child Nursing, 2,* 291–292.

Escalona, S. (1984). Social and other environmental influences on the cognitive and personality development of low birthweight infants. *American Journal of Mental Deficiency, 88* (5), 508–512.

Field, T.M., Widmayer, S.M., Ignatoff, E., & Stringer, S. (1982). Developmental effects of an intervention for preterm infants of teenage mothers. *Infant Mental Health Journal, 3* (1), 19–27.

Garrand, S., Sherman, N., Rentchler, D., & Jung, A.L. (1978). A parent-to-parent program. *Family Community Health Journal, 1,* 103–113.

Harrison, H., with Kositsky, A. (1983). *The premature baby book: A parent's guide to coping and caring in the first years.* New York: St. Martin's Press.

Henig, R.M., & Fletcher, A.B. (1983). *Your premature baby: The complete guide to premie care during that crucial first year.* New York: Rawson.

Herzog, J.M. (1979). Disturbances in parenting high-risk infants: Clinical impressions and hypotheses. In T.M. Field, A.M. Sostek, S. Goldberg, & H.H. Shuman (Eds.), *Infants born at risk: Behavior and development.* New York: SP Medical and Scientific Books.

Jacob, S. (1984). Psychological assessment of prematurely born infants and young children. *Infant Mental Health Journal, 5* (4), 221–236.

Leiderman, P.H. (1975). Parents of babies of very low birthweights. In R. Porter & M. O'Connor (Eds.), *Parent–infant interaction.* Ciba Foundation Symposium, *33.*

Lieberman, A., & Sheagren, T. (1984). *The premie parents handbook.* New York: Dutton.

Mangurten, H.H., Slade, C., & Fitzsimmons, D. (1979). Parent–parent support in the care of high risk newborns. *Journal of Gynecological Nursing, 8,* 275–277.

Minde, K., Shosenberg, N., Marton, P., Thompson, J., Ripley, J., & Burns, S. (1980). Self-help groups in a premature nursery: A controlled evaluation. *Journal of Pediatrics, 96* (5), 933–940.

Nance, S., Timmons, S., Bick, M., Kane, L., Kauffman, T., Nash, K., Pearson, S., Turney, P., Wafe, D., & Williams, J. (1982). *Premature babies: A handbook for parents.* New York: Arbor House.

Parmalee, A.H., & Haber, A. (1973). Who is the "risk infant"? *Clinical Obstetrics and Gynecology, 16,* 367–387.

Parmalee, A.H., Kopp, C.B., & Sigman, M. (1976). Selection of developmental assessment techniques for infants at risk. *Merrill-Palmer Quarterly, 22,* 177–199.

Sameroff, A.J. (1981). Longitudinal studies of preterm infants. In S.L. Friedman & M. Sigman (Eds.), *Preterm birth and psychological development.* New York: Academic Press.

Sameroff, A.J., & Abbe, L.C. (1978). The consequences of prematurity: Understanding and therapy. In H.L. Pick (Ed.), *Psychology: From research to practice.* New York: Plenum.

Sigman, M., Cohen, S.E., & Forsythe, A.B. (1981). The relation of early infant measures to later development. In S.L. Friedman & M. Sigman (Eds.), *Preterm birth and psychological development.* New York: Academic Press.

Sigman, M., & Parmalee, A.H. (1979). Longitudinal evaluation of the preterm infant. In T.M. Field, A.M. Sostek, S. Goldberg, & H.H. Shuman (Eds.), *Infants born at risk: Behavior and development.* New York: SP Medical and Scientific Books.

Thomas, A., & Chess, S. (1980). *The dynamics of psychological development.* New York: Bruner/Mazel.

Weatherston, D.J., Boger, R.P., Richter, R.A., & Bagchi, J. (1983). Volunteering for family strength. *Infant Mental Health Journal, 4* (4), 309–315.

Williams, J. (1981). *Parents of prematures resource directory.* Houston, TX: Parents of Prematures, Houston Organization for Parent Education.

CHAPTER 9
Program Design of Parent-Support Systems as a Function of Population Served: Some Comparisons

Earladeen Badger
University of Cincinnati

Barbara M. Goldman
New York, N.Y.

Profound changes have occurred in American society over the past 25 years. We have witnessed large increases in the proportion of women who work outside the home; growing numbers of children living in families headed by women; evolution of women's new attitudes toward their roles in society; increased mobility leading to the disappearance of the extended family; expansion and increasing specialization of the human-service occupations; and continuation of the long-term trends toward urbanization and suburbanization. Research tells us that in a climate of change, environmental stresses may have a negative impact on the family, which can affect the quality of child care provided (Bronfenbrenner, 1974). At a recent national conference on family-support systems, cosponsored by the Administration for Children, Youth, and Families and the Family Support Project of Yale University's Bush Center, an important fact emerged: An increasing proportion of America's families are finding that they need help in fulfilling their children's basic needs (Zigler, Weiss, & Kagan, 1983).

For decades, such institutions as government agencies and the school system served as buffers against the hard realities of life. And yet, the feelings of bewilderment, powerlessness, and alienation that engulf parents when they are forced to deal with bureaucracies, institutions, and professionals in order to receive needed services for their children have been well documented (Berger & Neuhaus, 1977; Keniston, 1977; Steiner, 1976).

197

During the 1970s, we began to disengage ourselves from the institutions that had disillusioned us, and we began to take independent action. Grass-root, self-help organizations began to replace institutional help as a response to needed services. Armed with evidence of the long-lasting effects of early education programs for preschool children of the poor (Lazar, Hubbell, Murray, Rosche, & Royce, 1977), advocates of birth-to-3 programs joined the self-help movement. With limited public dollars, parents became effective advocates for the continuation of Head Start and the Handicapped Children's Early Education Programs. Because the children served were young, parents naturally became co-participants in many programs.

Many of these parents became apt students of child development and effective imitators of the professional teacher's interactions with children. In fact, one of the positive effects of the early education models of the 1960s was that educators began to acknowledge the impact parents have in fostering the development of their children and began to treat the parents as partners (Badger, 1971; Gordon, 1969; Klaus & Gray, 1968; Levenstein & Sunley, 1968). This democratic treatment not only helped low-income parents to become effective teachers of their preschool children, but also served to improve their self-concepts and feelings of worth—in part restoring what had been taken away from them by "helping" institutions during the course of recent social history.

What has evolved, then, in early childhood education—notably in birth-to-3 programs—over the past 15 years is a progressive series of changes in authority and structure. In the beginning, we had Federal mandate and control. Programs were for the disenfranchised—the poor and the handicapped. As Federal dollars diminished, local agencies and communities had to search for new funding sources. The programs that survived often had a strong parent constituency and were able to politicize their needs at the local and state levels. And, as parents became more involved in all aspects of program design and delivery, interest and demand spread to include no-risk populations of parents, much as it did with Maria Montessori's program, which was developed in response to the educational needs of poor children in Italy and only later transported to the United States as a program for socially advantaged preschoolers. The strength of parent education/support programs today rests in their availability to all families.

The intent of this paper, then, is to discuss programs to meet the needs of all parents who are struggling to take care of themselves and their children during these turbulent times. The needs and abilities of these parents are diverse, and so multiple options must be available to them for education and support. For these parents, the process of change may be as important as the outcome (Naisbitt, 1982).

CHARACTERIZATION OF PARENT-SUPPORT PROGRAMS

To appreciate the growth and changes that have occurred in birth-to-3 programs during their infancy, we can examine program data collected by United Services for Effective Parenting (USEP), a network of more than 300 birth-to-3 programs that has evolved in Ohio over the last 10 years (Badger & Burns, 1982a). These data may well reflect a national picture.

In 1978, and again in 1981, we surveyed the characteristics, practices, and services of USEP birth-to-3 programs. Although the movement to provide educational programs beginning soon after birth is new in Ohio, it is one that appears to be growing fast. In 1978, 15,884 (or 3%) of Ohio children under 4 years of age were receiving services from 165 programs. By 1981, 50,650 (or 14%) of Ohio children were being served by 273 programs. More than two-thirds of these programs had operated for fewer than 10 years.

How can we interpret the unprecedented growth of birth-to-3 programs in Ohio, a state with no legal mandate to provide educational services to the preschool population? We can begin by characterizing USEP programs in terms of the populations they serve: enrichment programs for low-risk, low-SES parents; intervention programs for high-risk infants and their parents; and education/support programs for no-risk, middle-class families.

Briefly, the *enrichment programs* are designed to provide educational stimulation to children who are developmentally at risk for mild mental retardation as a result of the circumstances of poverty. Parents are generally coparticipants in these programs. Often, nutrition and health care are a vital part of the treatment plan. Depending on the resources of the family, educational services may be delivered at home or in a center. These programs include Head Start, Family Life Education, adolescent parent classes, and center-based or home-based day care for infants and toddlers whose welfare parents must work.

The *intervention programs* are designed to provide specific interventions that will prevent or ameliorate a handicapping condition present at birth or soon after. The program may be part of a comprehensive treatment approach for a child who is severely mentally retarded or has cerebral palsy; or it may be a specialized program for the hearing or visually impaired child, or for the low birth-weight, premature infant. Parents usually are actively involved in the intervention program. The programs most often are conducted in centers that are under the auspices of the departments of Developmental Disabilities, Mental Retardation, or Special Education, but they also include homebound programs for the very young child.

The *education/support programs* are designed to provide parents with information about child development and opportunities for shared experiences. This typically occurs in small classes or discussion groups. These programs function as self-help groups, operate on a modest budget, and usually employ a part-time staff person or volunteers. They include parent cooperative–play groups or nurseries, YWCA and Red Cross classes, and parent-support groups.

Because one-fourth of USEP programs use volunteers to deliver services, we might infer that parenting programs are among the growing number of self-help groups flourishing across the nation. And, in contrast to the recent past, when new programs were instituted predominantly for the poor and the handicapped, a new population of middle-class, no-risk families are expressing interest in joining programs where they can discuss options for dealing with their children's social, emotional, and physical growth.

As shown in Table 1, the growing interest among no-risk families in parenting-support programs has changed the complexion of parenting programs in Ohio. In terms of actual numbers of programs, all three categories of parent support grew from 1978 to 1981. However, the percentage of USEP programs targeted to no-risk, middle-class parents jumped from 21% in 1978 to 36% in 1981.

These data underline the importance of providing supportive programs to meet the needs of parents from *all* segments of our population—i.e., enrichment, intervention, and education/support programs. To explore the specific designs of these three types of parent-support systems, we can turn to three replicable educational models designed and delivered over the past 12 years by the Newborn Division of the Department of Pediatrics at the University of Cincinnati College of Medicine: (1) an enrichment program for new teenaged mothers, (2) an intervention pro-

Table 1.   Educational Program for the Birth-to-3 Population in Ohio*

		1978		1981	
Target Population	Type of Program	No. of Programs	Percent of Total	No. of Programs	Percent of Total
Socially high-risk parents	Enrichment	48	29%	68	25%
Medically high-risk infants	Intervention	78	47%	101	37%
No-risk families	Education/support	34	21%	98	36%
Not specified		5	3%	6	2%
Total: all programs		165	100%	273	100%

*Source: United services for effective parenting program and resource directory, Cincinnati, Ohio, 1981.

gram for premature infants and their parents, and (3) an education/ support program for no-risk, middle-class parents.

ENRICHMENT MODEL: THE INFANT STIMULATION/ MOTHER TRAINING PROGRAM

Late in 1972, health-care providers in the Cincinnati area focused on the scarcity of existing supportive services for new teenaged mothers and their infants. The Cincinnati Maternal and Infant Care Project brought together a multidisciplinary team of health-care professionals to design, implement, and evaluate an educational program for these mothers and their developmentally high-risk infants. The result of these efforts was the Infant Stimulation/Mother Training (IS/MT) Project, a research- and service-oriented pilot project initiated by medical staff from University Hospital (formerly Cincinnati General Hospital) and the Newborn Division of the University of Cincinnati College of Medicine.

University Hospital serves a large population of inner-city blacks and white Appalachians; 90% of its patients are medically indigent. When the IS/MT Project began, 16% of the approximately 3,000 babies delivered yearly at this hospital were born to mothers who were 16 years old or younger. The IS/MT Project represented an attempt to intervene in the lives of these teenagers beginning with the birth of their firstborn infants. Its underlying philosophy was that the parent is the primary teacher—i.e., whether an infant thrives is determined largely by the care-taking environment provided by the mother.

Design

For the 1973 pilot project (Badger, Elsass, & Sutherland, 1974), 48 mother-infant pairs were recruited from the postpartum unit of University Hospital on the 2nd or 3rd day after delivery. The rationale for choosing the lying-in period as the optimal time to interest young mothers in parenting programs, the recruitment strategies used and their success, and the incentives offered have been detailed previously (Badger, 1981a; 1981b).

The project design tested the relative effectiveness of two treatment protocols for high-risk mothers (16 years of age and younger): 1½-hour weekly mother-infant classes (held during the evening pediatric clinic) that began when infants were 4 to 5 weeks old and continued until they were 12 months old; and supportive monthly home visits by a nurse or social worker. To assess the developmental risk of infants of high-risk mothers and the impact of a group instruction approach on maternal behaviors, lower-risk mothers (aged 18 to 19 years) and their firstborn were included in the treatment design.

Several approaches were used to evaluate the effectiveness of the IS/MT Project (Badger, 1981b; Badger & Burns, 1980; Badger, Burns, & Rhoads, 1976). Infant development was assessed each month with three of the criterion-referenced Uzgiris-Hunt Infant Ordinal Scales of Psychological Development—Object Permanence, Development of Means, and Vocal Imitation (Uzgiris & Hunt, 1975). In addition, the norm-referenced Bayley Scales of Infant Development (Bayley, 1969) were administered at age 12 months by a certified Bayley tester who did not know the treatment assignment of the infants. Mother-infant interactions during classes were observed, recorded, and rated according to a categorized interaction scale (Badger, 1979). To assess how well mothers learned material presented during classes, a 25-item questionnaire on health, nutrition, and child development was given during the first class and again during the eighth. The evaluation also included a 3- and 5-year follow-up of members of the original pilot group who could be located, assessing both child performance and the mother's social circumstances (Badger, 1981b).

The pilot project subsequently was adapted to a service program for young mothers delivered at University Hospital (Badger, 1981b; Badger, Burns, & Rhoads, 1976). From 1974 through 1982, a new class of 15 high-risk mothers and their firstborn infants was recruited each month from the hospital's postpartum unit. Over the 9-year service program, more than 1,000 mothers and their infants were offered a series of 20 weekly classes that began when infants were 3 to 5 weeks old and continued until they were approximately 6 months old. Program goals, teaching strategies, and incentives were the same as in the pilot project.

Delivery

Because the teenaged mother's immaturity and social circumstances hamper her from acting as her infant's primary caretaker and place her child at developmental risk, the IS/MT model is designed to reinforce her primary caretaker role as well as her satisfaction in that role. It incorporates an infant-stimulation curriculum and a mother's training model that were developed and tested at the University of Illinois and at Parent and Child Centers in Illinois and Georgia (Badger, 1971, 1972; Karnes, Teska, Hodgins, & Badger 1970).

The curriculum for the mother-training classes and the specific infant skills taught and their developmental sequence have been described elsewhere in detail (Badger, 1977a, 1981c; Badger, Burns, & Rhoads, 1976). The curriculum focuses on the mother as well as the infant and includes instruction on infant development, female sexuality, birth control, nutrition, accident prevention, and discipline. The infant-stimulation curriculum is designed to meet the following training goals (Badger, Burns, & Rhoads, 1976):

1. To help mothers understand that their interactions with their babies will significantly affect their children's later development.
2. To encourage mothers to respond to their infants' vocalizing and to infant behavior that indicates stress.
3. To teach mothers to carefully observe their infants' play and to select those activities that evoke interest rather than boredom or stress.
4. To train mothers in infant development skills, teaching mothers how to choose appropriate materials to stimulate their children's growth.

In the IS/MT model, the group leader is both an instructor and a mother model (Badger, 1977a, 1977b; Badger, Burns, & Rhoads, 1976). In place of didactic instruction, she *demonstrates* appropriate maternal behavior and encourages the mothers to *repeat* the behavior she models. As mothers become more responsive to their infants, the class leader regularly *reinforces* and *extends* this behavior. When a mother appears indifferent or fails to respond appropriately to her infant's needs, the group leader may *confront* the individual to change inappropriate behavior or may call on other mothers for help, capitalizing on the adolescent's need for peer approval.

The class setting surrounds the adolescent mother with her true peers—other mothers of similar ages and backgrounds whose babies are at the same stage of development as her own. The positive *peer pressure* that develops as the teenaged mothers' camaraderie and mutual respect grow helps reinforce appropriate behavior with their children (Badger, 1977b). As mothers attend child-development classes, many natural opportunities exist for open discussion of family problems, sexual relationships, and personal goals and plans. This regular sharing of common problems promotes peer acceptance and support—powerful motivators of adolescent behavior.

Evaluation

At the conclusion of the IS/MT Pilot Project (Badger, 1981b) we were able to provide partial answers to the following questions:

1. *Are infants of socially disadvantage teenaged mothers (age 16 and under) in jeopardy?* Testing data at 12 months suggest that infants

of adolescent mothers begin to fall behind very early in life and are indeed in jeopardy, but this was not apparent in infants of high-risk mothers who attended weekly classes. The performance of these infants matched or surpassed that of the infants of lower-risk, more mature mothers.

2. *Can a mother-training program be used effectively with the teenage mother and her infant, considering the special problems of school continuation, peer pressure, and surrogate mothering of the infant?* The feasibility of training classes as a viable means of serving at-risk mothers and their infants seemed to be confirmed by the high rate of attendance and participation in the weekly classes. Young inner-city black mothers apparently are interested in learning good mothering techniques and are responsive to the idea at the time their babies are born. Some of the Appalachian mothers included in the study, however, were less able to attend classes regularly or to return to high school. Perhaps they were lacking in the kind of family support and stability that would allow them to make plans for themselves. The white mothers who remained in the study, on the other hand, were responsive to the services offered; and, although the test results of their infants were not included because of attrition, they benefited from the program.

3. *How did 15- to 16-year-old mothers differ from 18- to 19-year-old mothers as participants in mother-training classes?* At the time of recruitment, younger mothers more readily felt they could manage 1 evening a week than did older mothers. This was somewhat surprising, because the younger mothers would be returning to school during the day. The older mothers, on the other hand, had completed high school and, for the most part, indicated no immediate plans to seek employment outside the home. Generally speaking, the younger mothers appeared to be more interested in the classes and willing to invest the time to learn parenting skills than did the older mothers, who felt they already knew these things by reason of their age. The autonomy of the older mothers was further reinforced by their financial independence, for they qualified for a monthly welfare check or had the potential ability to get a job. Conversely, the younger mothers were obliged to remain at home under the supervision of their own mothers, and their only option toward independence was to complete their secondary educations. Most of the younger mothers planned to return to school, and this decision meant surrendering their baby to the maternal grandmother for primary care.

It appeared that the significantly accelerated motor development of the infants of high-risk mothers who attended classes over that of the infants of lower-risk mothers who also attended classes may be a result of observed differences in their physical and emotional responsiveness; high-risk mothers participated more readily in physical play with their infants and were generally spontaneous in these interactions; lower-risk mothers, though just as attentive to their infants, were more often self-conscious and inhibited in demonstrative play with their infants.

4. *Is birth or the perinatal period an optimal time for intervention in a poverty population whose children routinely experience developmental delays?* Project staff suspected that most of the high-risk mothers viewed their participation in the mothers' training classes as a means of more clearly establishing their role as mothers, perhaps in competition with their own mothers, who were assuming primary care of their infants as they returned to school. If this observation was true, it builds a strong case for reaching the teenaged mother during the perinatal stage of her infant's development. Ultimately she must assume primary responsibility for the child. To postpone the parenting role until she reaches the age of majority can be damaging, not only to the child's development—i.e., feelings of rejection—but also to the mother's own feelings of self-worth and to her later success as a mother.

5. *Is group instruction more effective than an individualized approach?* The initial resistance and suspicions of some of the mothers in the lower-risk group toward a class instructional approach, the child-related interest and involvement observed by the home visitors of the older mothers who were in the home-visit treatment group, and the comparable performance at 12 months of both groups of infants of 18- to 19-year-old mothers suggested that group or individual instruction may be equally viable interventions with older, more mature mothers. As noted previously, the treatment effect as measured by infant performance at 12 months of age occurred primarily in the comparisons of infants of mothers aged 16 years and younger; and as high-risk mothers in the home visit group were observed by project staff to be minimally involved with their infants, the group instructional approach seemed to be especially effective in helping the younger mothers attach to and respond appropriately to the developmental needs of their infants. The satisfactions a new mother experiences in her associations with a peer group of young mothers, the therapy provided through the sharing of common problems, the availability of positive adult teaching models, and the interest and concern extended toward her and her infant by attendant staff all serve to influence her growth as a person and as a mother in positive ways.

6. *What kind of mothers cannot be served with a mother-training program model?* Our experience indicated that only a few mothers had personal problems that were so longstanding and of such magnitude,

and whose resources were so limited, that they were unable to profit from a program of this kind. This was especially true among the white Appalachian mothers. Three of these mothers eventually lost custody of their infants.

7. What are the advantages of carrying out a mother-training program under the umbrella of a medical center? During the first year of life, an intervention program that includes comprehensive medical services and provides useful information in the areas of health, nutrition, and child development facilitates the maximum development of infants. Our observations and developmental testing of the 42 infants whom we were able to follow during the first year of life seemed to affirm that infants develop and thrive when (1) they are well nourished; (2) they develop a strong primary attachment to their mothers; (3) mothers consistently and appropriately respond to the physical and emotional needs of their infants; (4) mothers provide them with varied mouthing, visual, and manipulative experiences; and (5) preventive health services and crisis treatment are easily accessible. Overall, mothers who attended weekly classes seemed to have greater awareness of their babies' physical welfare and to rely more on a health facility when they sensed a problem. It may be of greater significance that no hospitalizations occurred among the infants in the class groups compared with the hospitalization of three infants in the home-visit groups.

From 1977 through 1979, we held follow-up telephone interviews with 261 of the mothers who had attended the service program of mother-infant classes and whose infants were 12 to 24 months of age. The results of the service program follow-up (Badger, 1981b; Badger & Burns, 1980) supported findings from the pilot project indicating that regular participation in IS/MT classes positively affected the ability of young mothers to realize educational and employment goals and to plan and limit family size.

The ease of recruitment of high-risk mothers during the lying-in period following delivery suggests that educational intervention during infancy may be an important new dimension of both behavorial pediatrics and early childhood education. Further, services are readily available from persons in several professional disciplines—doctors, nurses, social workers, nutritionists, psychologists—and these can be integrated into a single, coordinated effort. Changes in attitude were noted in the medical and nursing staff as regards the outcomes for the teenage mother and her infant. We began to hear about the "smart" babies in the mother-training classes. Attitudinal changes of this kind argue for the expansion of health-service-related programs that are distinguished by a human response to their delivery of care.

INTERVENTION MODEL: HOSPITAL-BASED SERVICES
FOR PREMATURE INFANTS AND THEIR PARENTS

The patients are tiny and their medical problems can be immense. For the infant born with heart or lung disease, life begins as an all-or-nothing struggle—a struggle that, until recently, the infant usually lost. Today, largely due to the advanced medical technology deployed in neonatal special-care nurseries, sick newborns who would have died a few years ago are being saved. Moreover, the outcome for these infants continues to improve (Kopp & Parmelee, 1979). When these infants are members of low SES families, however, the poverty environment increases the risk of long-term damage (Broman, Nichols, & Kennedy, 1975; Scarr-Salapatek & Williams, 1973; Werner, Bierman, & French, 1971; Birch & Gussow, 1970).

In 1977, the IS/MT Program joined the Handicapped Children's Early Education Programs (HCEEP) network, giving us the opportunity to introduce infant stimulation and parent education and support within the environment of a neonatal special-care nursery at Cincinnati General Hospital (now University Hospital) and pediatric follow-up clinics at Children's Hospital. The mother-training program developed for teenaged mothers and their firstborn was adapted to serve these premature, low-birth-weight infants and their socially disadvantaged parents during the infants' first year of life.

Design

Because IS/MT was one of the first HCEEP projects to focus on the efficacy of beginning educational intervention at birth with infants at risk for developmental delay (prematurity, low-birth-weight), we were mindful of the importance of providing a variety of service options. Our population included not only biologically at-risk infants, but also their socially at-risk parents, so we were interested in identifying factors associated with parental participation in early intervention services. If the infants appeared to be faring well at 12 months of age (corrected gestationally) as determined by both the Bayley and Uzgiris-Hunt Infant Scales (which was the case), one might appropriately ask which treatment events seemed to make a difference and are therefore recommended. The in-hospital educational intervention included (1) training nurses in infant stimulation and parent education/support techniques, (2) involving parents in the physical and emotional care of their sick infants, and (3) offering emotional support and information to parents during their infants' hospitalization through parent-support-group meetings.

Following the infants' discharge from the hospital, weekly supportive home visits and/or mother-infant classes offered guidance to parents in their interactions with infants as a supplement to the delivery of well-baby care and medical follow-up in the pediatric clinic at Children's Hospital.

Delivery

In-Hospital Services. In the process of changing the environment in the neonatal intensive care unit (NICU), nurses were introduced and trained to implement a series of infant stimulation techniques (i.e., *animate*— face-to-face contact, stroking, holding, rocking, talking; and *inanimate*—music boxes, visual targets, rattles, squeaky toys). The increased sensitivity and observational skills of the nurses to the individual needs of the infants resulted in the incorporation of new practices and procedures into the nursing protocol. This in turn was transmitted to parents through demonstration and instruction of appropriate behaviors.

The physician's assistant and project neonatologist began to conduct parent-support-group meetings 1 evening a week. These meetings provided an environment where parents could express their anxiety, anger, and concerns about their sick infants. Interactions among parents provided emotional support. The doctor and physician's assistant were available to provide medical information as the infants' condition and prognoses were discussed. The favorable response of parents resulted in the development of a 6-week curriculum and regular inclusion of NICU nursing staff. Topics for discussion included intrauterine development, process of adjustment to the birth of a premature infant, parent–infant bonding, parenting skills, medical complications of premature infants, delayed growth and development, and follow-up care.

Weekly Mother–Infant Classes. In order to meet the multiple needs of high-risk infants and their families, weekly mother-infant classes were offered and coordinated with the pediatric follow-up clinic visits. Each class session maintained a mother-centered as well as a child-centered focus. In the first part, with a minimum of staff guidance, mothers introduced problems that were child-specific or that related to family adjustment. In the ensuing discussions, the leader reinforced positive attitudes and suggested alternative behaviors; however, even more importantly, she encouraged mothers to provide their own vehicle for attitude change through interactions with each other. During the child-centered portion of the class session, we followed the mother teaching-learning format developed for adolescent mothers and their fullterm infants.

Home Visiting. An important adjunct to the weekly mother-infant classes was the home-visiting component. The stimulation program introduced in the class setting was strengthened and expanded in the home. On a one-to-one basis, the home visitor involved the mother in bringing the infant into contact with appropriate materials and objects, enacting stimulation activities to elicit appropriate motor, intellectual, and personal-social responses. Through the mother's informal contact with the home visitor, she acquired an understanding of the nature, needs, and normal development of babies. The individualized education program (IEP) was developed as the home visitor responded to the unique needs of each infant as well as to the emotional demands of the parent.

Depending upon the needs and interests of the mothers, they participated in either the class or home components. Those who participated in both profited from group as well as individualized instruction. We noted, however, that the majority of our mothers lacked control over their lives and were members of multiproblem families. Understandably, this often resulted in poor class attendance and negatively affected their participation in the home-visiting component.

Evaluation

Our successful intervention experience with teenaged mothers and their fullterm infants did not prepare us for the frustration and job stress associated with service to a socially and medically at-risk population of infants and their families.

Whereas fullterm infants of teenaged mothers are usually responsive and invite interaction with their mothers, premature infants are often sickly, difficult, and unresponsive after discharge from the hospital (Field, 1979; Als, Lester, & Brazelton, 1979). When a premature infant is paired with an immature, poorly motivated mother, s/he seems unable to involve the mother in positive ways. In turn, the mother's satisfactions are not forthcoming if her initial overtures to feed, console, or stimulate the infant do not meet with success. Strengthening the bond between mother and child can be a pleasurable experience when the interventionist has only to coach the immature mother to respond appropriately to the cues of her infant. When there are no consistent cues, however, and the baby is difficult and compares unfavorably (in the eyes of the mother) with other babies, Herculean efforts are required by the interventionist(s).

Because of the enormous personal and financial problems that characterized many of the 86 families who were invited to participate in the program during 1977 and 1979, daily communication among team members often supplemented weekly planning meetings. The limited resources of the families routinely involved staff in:

- delivering infant formula and diapers;
- supplying clothing and baby furniture;
- providing transportation to and from the hospital; and
- advocating adequate housing and financial assistance through the local welfare department and housing authority.

The energy required for day-to-day survival in many of the families also negatively affected parents' ability to:

- visit their sick infants in the nursery;
- keep scheduled medical appointments;
- participate in postnatal parent-infant classes; and
- be available emotionally during visits to their homes.

We also found *that parents generally did not welcome any structured type of program for 3 to 4 months after they took their infants home from the hospital.* It was almost as though they needed to prove to themselves that this was in fact *their* baby and they wanted time alone with him or her. Some, however, needed extensive social services— i.e., a better place to live, family counseling, the necessities of life. This was particularly true with single parents who had other preschoolers and little family support. There was a notable relationship between class attendance and number of children in the family: mothers with more children at home were less likely to attend classes. For those mothers who were not overwhelmed with the care of other children, there was expressed interest in attending parent-infant classes after a 3- to 4-month "settling in" period. They were ready to share their concerns about their babies' development with other mothers and were eager for class instruction.

The infant-assessment data we collected and analyzed seemed to provoke more questions than answers (Badger, Burns, & Deboer, 1982b). The gestationally corrected Bayley scores (mental and physical) on the 47 infants whom we were able to test at 12 months of age provided evidence that infant development was within the normal range. It is difficult, however, to know which of the following interventions contributed to the treatment effect: the training program for special-care nursing staff; the superior medical care that the infants received shortly after birth; the parent-support-group meetings that served to bring parent and infant together; the extensive supportive home visiting provided by the staff social worker, special educator, and/or paraprofessional teacher aides; or the mother-infant classes that were conducted as an adjunct to pediatric clinic visits.

In comparing 12-month Bayley motor scores of those infants weighing less than 1,800 grams at birth whose parents had a weekly support group available for them to attend during infant's hospitalization versus those who did not, it was apparent that participation in that service component seemed to have a measurable effect. Support-group infants scored significantly higher on the 12-month motor scales than infants whose parents did not attend the parent-support group (Badger, Burns, & Deboer, 1982b). Similarly, nurse–infant behavioral interactions with the same-birth-weight infants significantly improved over an 18-month period as a result of the nurses' training program (Spiker, Burns, & Elsass, 1981).

We would be remiss if we failed to acknowledge our disappointment in seeing project infants' Bayley mental scores decrease at the second year of testing, especially in the area of language development. This phenomenon has been reported by others working with the socially disadvantaged (Golden & Birns, 1976; Deutsch, 1973). It appears as though mentally depressed welfare mothers do not provide a rich language model for their toddlers to imitate.

Evaluation of the cost effectiveness of each treatment component as it relates to parent participation is an important consideration. In the pilot project, the prorated annual cost per family was $2,180. This is a significant amount of money at a time when human services are experiencing severe financial cutbacks. If these Federal spending cuts continue—and there is reason to believe that they will—prevention programs will be severely affected. Therefore, training programs that can demonstrate institutional change in the health-care system and that also improve patient care and family functioning ought to be recommended. Providing training to University Hospital nursery staff resulted in (1) a nursing protocol that positively influenced their behavioral interactions with infants, (2) parents' inclusion in the care and graded stimulation of infants, and (3) weekly parent-support-group meetings during infants' hospitalization. It is because of these positive outcomes, which can be accomplished with minimal cost to hospitals, that maternity and infant care nursing staff have become our primary focus in the HCEEP outreach training project.

What did we learn that we can recommend to others who will be serving similar populations of infants and parents? A review of IS/MT's comprehensive service program for premature, low-birth-weight infants and their low SES families, as it relates to changing the physical and social support systems, both within the medical center and the home environment suggests the following:

1. Training programs for neonatal special-care nursing staffs can improve nurses' behavioral interactions with infants. This may positively influence infant outcome, particularly with infants

weighing less than 1,800 grams at birth (Spiker, Burns, & Elsass, 1981).

2. Conducting parent-support-group meetings during infants' hospitalization allows and encourages parents to resolve their ambivalent feelings about their infants and also serves to involve them in their infants' physical and emotional care. These behaviors are important in the bonding process and are particularly important for parents of infants weighing less than 1,800 grams at birth (Minde et al., 1978).

3. Providing transportation for low SES parents to attend meetings, classes, and clinic visits is an important requisite for their participation in treatment events (Badger, Burns, & Rhoads, 1976).

4. Working with the hospital perinatal staff serves to coordinate many necessary team members who are critical for the optimal development of the infant—i.e., nutritionist, social worker, neonatologist, psychologist, speech pathologist (Badger, Burns, & Deboer, 1982b).

5. Offering flexibility in the scheduling of educational-intervention services allows parents the freedom to participate when they are ready. Recognize that most mothers, with the exception of those without family resources, need time alone with their baby for 3 to 4 months after the infant's discharge from the hospital (Bromwich, 1981).

6. Providing baby-sitting for older children, infant food and clothes, family counseling, and other necessary social services for low SES mothers is critical to improving family functioning and strengthening their relationship with their infants (Keniston, 1977).

7. Recognizing that serving medically and socially high-risk infants and their families exacts a toll on a committed staff; regular opportunities must be provided for their personal and professional development (Badger, Burns, & Deboer 1982b).

8. Matching infants and their families, depending on their needs and interests, with special focus follow-up programs is important when developmental delays persist during the second year of life (Badger, 1981b).

We recognize the many problems that negatively influenced parents' ability to utilize project services, but we do not minimize the importance of continued intervention efforts that will strengthen the early parent-child relationship. If tiny infants are to survive as a result of modern medicine, then equal emphasis must be placed on assuring their quality of life. Without extrafamilial support, a case can be made for saving the baby while losing the mother.

EDUCATION/SUPPORT MODEL: INFANT/TODDLER
LEARNING (ITL) PROGRAM

In response to the growing demand of no-risk, middle-class families for education/support programs following the birth of their first infant, we began in 1982 to design and implement a service program to meet their needs and interests. The amazing increase of USEP programs for the no-risk population—from 21% in 1978 to 36% in 1981 (see Table 1)—seemed to confirm that the future of birth-to-3 programs rested in their availability for all parents. Additional evidence augured well for the inclusion of this population. Changes in hospital delivery methods—encouraging bonding, father involvement, and parental interest in ongoing support—served to prime the pump. Coupled with a decade of research on the amazing repertoire of the newborn infant, there was good reason to believe that a programmatic fad of the '70s could become institutionalized during the '80s. If quality control was assured in these programs through accrediting program deliverers and developing a sound technology of early-childhood education, a convincing argument could then be made for the survival of birth-to-3 programs. And, as budget cuts for the poor and the handicapped programs began to occur in 1980, we were pressed to begin to enjoin the private and the public sectors.

Design

A curriculum first designed for and tested with socially disadvantaged children during their first 3 years of life (Hunt, 1975; Karnes, Teska, Hodgins, & Badger, 1970), was revised and adapted as a parent's guide. Entitled *Infant/Toddler: Introducing Your Child to the Joy of Learning* (Badger, 1981c), it presents a sequence of early-learning experiences with extended activities and materials recommended to help parents stimulate their child's intellectual capabilities. Reducing parental anxiety, fostering competence in children and confidence in parents, and creating a mutually joyous parent-child relationship are the ingredients. The resultant program—Infant/Toddler Learning (ITL)—is played out in monthly evening seminars (Mom, Dad, and Baby) that begin sometime during child's first 6 months of life and continue until s/he is approximately 3 years of age.

Unlike the enrichment program model for teenage mothers and their offspring and the intervention program model for premature infants and their socially disadvantaged parents, which were supported by public funds, enrollment in ITL exacts a fee for participation.

Delivery

Pilot Program. Beginning in Cincinnati in January 1982, parental interest in ITL program participation was explored by three methods. Prenatally, prospective parents were approached in childbirth education classes at Fort Hamilton-Hughes Hospital and at a local obstetrician's office during scheduled Saturday morning parenting seminars. Postnatally, mothers were approached at Jewish Hospital shortly after delivery. While all three methods were fruitful, the least effective was the postnatal approach. Of the 98 mothers approached at Jewish Hospital shortly after delivery who expressed interest, we learned the best indicator of those who would actually join was whether they had attended a prenatal class program. All of the 72 families who participated in the pilot program had attended one or more types of prenatal class instruction. It was subsequently determined that in 1 out of 7 deliveries, there is real motivation to participate in an educational program of this kind. These are almost exclusively first-time parents.

The profile of the average family who participated in the ITL pilot program was a 27-year-old mother and a 30-year-old father, both first-time parents, both involved in infant care-giving, both college educated, and 1 out of 2 mothers working full or part time.

Seventy-two families—of eight families per seminar group—completed a series of six monthly seminars, beginning when their infants were 2 to 4 months of age; the fee was $30. The seminars were always scheduled in the early evening in order to include fathers. Attendance was high; absences occurred only due to illness or the scheduling of vacations. Preliminary evaluation—completion of 14-item Program Questionnaire and feedback provided in class and telephone contact—recommended a balance between demonstration of specific infant-stimulation activities and opportunities for parents to share information about different methods of care-giving. And, when current research in infant development—temperamental characteristics, state behaviors and styles of parent–infant interaction—was expanded and applied by the instructor during classes, it was positively reinforcing to parents.

All of the parents were told that they could telephone their ITL instructor during times of stress. Some did, but most did not. The six families that exercised this option had fussy, difficult infants. The role of the instructor was *not* to give specific advice but rather to *listen* to the parent and *support* him/her in an appropriate course of action. As expected, the first 3 to 4 months were especially stressful for these parents. Happily, they did not call to resolve medical problems, which were more appropriately directed to the family pediatrician, but to talk, allay their anxiety, and to receive emotional support. Nonetheless, the professional training of the instructors—neonatal physician's assistant and master's degree in mental-health nursing—provided an excellent match for the infant-seminar series.

Service Program. When almost two-thirds of the families who completed the first 6-month pilot series of ITL Seminars accepted a more than 100% increase in participation fee (from $30 to $75 per 6-month seminar series) and elected to continue, we were ready to recruit new families. Whereas word of mouth among ITL families attracted one-fourth of new participants, two weekly seminars totaling 4 hours and offered quarterly through the University of Cincinnati's noncredit Department of Continuing Education accounts for more than one-half of ITL's new families. The course seminars, entitled "Infant/Toddler Learning: Parent as Teacher" are directed toward prospective and new parents. Between 30 and 35 persons will pay $15 to attend these two seminars whenever they are offered.

Of the 110 families currently enrolled in the ITL Program, 42 have participated for more than a year. Families are grouped according to the age of their child. There are 16 different groups, with children ranging from 3 to 32 months in age. Each class group may have a variance of 2 to 3 months in the age of the children. The groups function as mini-families in several ways. Parents become close friends with one another, organize play groups, and socialize together outside of class.

Evaluation

Systematic evaluation of the ITL curriculum impact on children and parents and the selection and training of successful program replications is in the formative stages of development. In the interim, we are able to report that curriculum development evolves through parents' completion of a program questionnaire at the end of each 6-month series of seminars and by repeated program replication and sharing among trained instructors in Cincinnati, Dayton, Columbus, Toledo, and Akron, Ohio, and in Grand Rapids, Michigan. An ITL Teacher's Guide for 30 monthly seminars is in the process of being tested and revised in the areas of (1) format of classes, (2) suggested activities and educational materials, and (3) child- and parent-centered focal concerns. ITL program replicators have attended monthly meetings over a period of 12 months to exchange information and to strengthen their expertise as teachers. The latter has been accomplished through the viewing of Cincinnati's videotapes of ITL family seminars in action.

Parents' evaluation of the ITL Program has repeatedly confirmed that their primary interest is in discovering how to increase their child's learning opportunities. Secondarily, they are eager to meet like parents in order to discuss different methods of care-giving.

Towards these ends, ITL instructors:

1. reinforce their best efforts as primary teachers of their child;
2. provide learning activities that match their child's interests and abilities;
3. discourage competition by emphasizing the unique learning style and personality of each child; and
4. provide opportunities for sharing at the beginning and end of each seminar.

What we do *not* do is give advice to parents about how to raise their child. There is enough of that in the many child-rearing guides that are available over the counter. When a parent has deep-seated problems that interfere with the teaching-learning format of the ITL Program, they are referred to an affiliated USEP agency that can better meet their needs for personal counseling. Program fidelity is assured when all parents realize that the ITL Program is first and foremost an individualized approach to translating the parents' guide *Infant/Toddler: Introducing Your Child to the Joy of Learning* into action.

Although child progress is not currently evaluated in the ITL Program, the format and structure of family seminars, play activities, involvement of parents as teachers, and peer-contact support achievement of the following child-oriented goals:

1. healthy and realistic self-concept;
2. appropriate and effective interpersonal skills;
3. positive attitudes toward learning;
4. task commitment;
5. exploratory behavior and risk taking;
6. creative and productive thinking, and
7. higher-level thinking processes.

Achievement of the preceding goals with parents who need only minimal assistance in orchestrating their child's best performance is at present clearly visible in videotapes of the seminars in action. However, in the absence of a control group, we are unable—nor is it our intention—to document that ITL children are superior in any way to those children who are not in the program.

RECOMMENDED PRACTICES

During the past decade there has been an unprecedented proliferation of parenting programs across the limited states. While the initial focus of these programs was on improving the circumstances of disenfranchised populations—socially and biologically high-risk infants and their parents—it has recently become a cause celebre among all parents. This movement, documented by USEP in Ohio in the dramatic increase of education/support-type programs for no-risk families over a 3-year period (1978–1981), suggests that program options will grow both in number and quality to meet the demands of all parents. Today's middle-class parents want access to family-oriented educational and support programs.

The overview of three different program models presented in this chapter highlights some of the obvious differences in the design, delivery and evaluation of parent-support systems as a function of the needs of the population served. These differences are outlined in Table 2 and discussed within the context of our 12-year experience in providing a spectrum of services to three disparate populations.

Program Design

The time of introduction differs according to population served. Enrichment (teenaged parent) and intervention (premature, low-birth-weight infant) programs are best introduced postnatally, whereas education/ support (no-risk family) programs are welcomed during the prenatal period. Specifically, we found that teenaged mothers are responsive to extrafamilial support systems within 3 to 5 weeks after delivery. Parents of premature infants, on the other hand, while interested in attending parent-support groups during their infant's hospitalization, chose not to formally participate in any parent–child support system until their child was between 3 to 4 months of age. And mature no-risk parents who are firmly attached to their infant in utero seem eager to enroll in education/support programs during the prenatal period.

The recruitment process is closely aligned with the time of introduction. A sensitive period for recruiting and involving teenage mothers is shortly after delivery of their firstborn infant. With parents of premature infants, we found that a telephone number that can be used for individualized help after the infant's discharge from the hospital might be a welcome bridge to formal program participation of parent and child during the second half of the child's first year of life. Recruitment of no-risk parents—mother and father—for inclusion in formalized parent-

Table 2. Parent Support Systems

	Enrichment	Intervention	Education/Support
Design	*Target programs to low SES parents (e.g., single, teenaged mothers) *Recruit parents and introduce program postnatally, within 3–5 weeks after delivery *Offer 6 months of weekly parent-infant classes as supplement to delivery of well-baby care	*Target program to high-risk (premature/SGA/low-birth-weight) infants and their parents *Recruit parents and introduce program postnatally, when infant is 3–4 months old *Offer flexible, short-term program options—e.g., biweekly or monthly parent–child classes tied to follow-up clinic visits	*Target program to mature, no-risk parents *Recruit parents and introduce program prenatally *Offer short-term educational classes prenatally (childbirth and child development) and both short- and long-term programs when infant is 3–6 months old
Delivery	*Employ staff sensitive to multiple needs of socially disadvantaged families *Use curriculum that is both infant-centered (child development) and parent-centered (psychosexual development, vocational training)	*Employ team approach (nurses, special educator, occupational and physical therapist) to implement individualized program for parent-infant dyads *Use comprehensive treatment approach, drawing from and coordinating several professional disciplines to develop individualized educational program	*Employ experienced instructors who have broad range of information from which to draw *Use child-development curriculum that is a rich blend of well-defined theory and practice

Evaluation	*Use a direct teaching approach, creating parental anxiety to promote rapid change in attitudes and behaviors	*Use a nondirective teaching approach, responding supportively to the individual cues provided by each parent-infant dyad	*Use an indirect teaching approach, allaying parental anxiety and supporting parents in their care-giving roles
	*Collect and analyze data that measure program accountability in areas of recruitment, parent participation, and satisfaction: Are you doing what you set out to do?		
	*Measure infant development, parent-infant interaction, and parent's involvement in self-improvement plan—e.g., school, employment	*Measure infant development, parent-infant interaction, and parent's ability to cope in care-giving role	*Measure parent-infant interaction and parent's written evaluation of program
	*Consider serendipitous gains—ease of recruitment, model replications, and advocacy for teenaged parenting programs	*Consider serendipitous gains—continuation of certain service components—e.g., change in nursing protocol to include infant stimulation practices, and parent support groups in intensive-care nursery	*Consider serendipitous gains—ease of recruitment, model replications, and advocacy for primary prevention programs

support systems occurs prenatally during (1) childbirth instruction (Lamaze, Husband-Coached Childbirth), (2) obstetrical visits, and (3) continuing education courses and seminars.

The *duration* of the program should be established at the onset. While the needs of teenaged mothers appear to be enormous, a 6-month period of postpartum weekly classes was sufficient to influence attitudinal and behavioral changes and to connect mothers with ancillary services and programs from which they would benefit. Parents of biologically high-risk infants may want and need to exercise the option of participating in a variety of programs. For example, a short-term, biweekly, or monthly mother-child class program carried out in conjunction with a medical follow-up clinic may serve as a springboard for supplemental involvement in a baby gym, sensorimotor integration, or multiphasic therapy program for the child. Depending on the handicapping condition of the child and the family dynamics, long-term support systems of various types may be necessary. Mature, no-risk parents seem to prefer short-term childbirth and child development courses prenatally, but are ready to commit themselves to both short-term (baby gym and swim) and long-term (monthly ITL family seminars) educational programs when their child is 3 to 6 months old.

Program Delivery

The *staffing* pattern requires mature, knowledgeable, caring, and energetic people for all forms of parent-support systems. In addition, those professionals working in enrichment programs must be particularly sensitive to the special needs of socially disadvantage parents and recognize the importance of including ancillary supportive social services. Hospital-based nursery personnel, special educators, and occupational and physical therapists all might be involved in the delivery of support systems for special infants and their parents. And no-risk parents who are searching for information and support need to be matched with professionals who have a broad range of information and experience from which to draw.

The *curriculum* should be tailored to the expressed needs of the parents in order to be relevant and effective. While teenaged mothers need to understand child development in order to interact appropriately with their infants, they are also searching for ways to learn more-adult behaviors in the areas of sexuality, schooling, and employment. The curriculum should, therefore include clarification of and commitment to desired values in these three areas. Parents with biologically high-risk infants will express more diversity in their needs, and individualized educational programs may be necessary. This requires a team approach involving a variety of professional disciplines and a coordinator who orchestrates the curriculum approach. No-risk parents, eager to access current information and practices, will respond best to a no-nonsense approach, with a curriculum that is well defined and executed.

The *teaching goals and techniques* vary in response to the maturity and adjustment of the parents. With the single, teenaged mother, the instructor will employ a more direct teaching style—demonstrating parenting techniques, encouraging imitation, confronting a mother (when necessary), and using group process and pressure to promote change in attitudes and behaviors. With a parent of a biologically high-risk infant, the instructor will employ a nondirective approach. Sensitivity to the cues provided by the parents regarding their needs, concerns, and anxieties will determine direction of individualized approach and referral and involvement with ancillary treatment and support systems. With mature, no-risk parents, the instructor is well advised to employ an indirect teaching approach. Falling into the pitfall of "giving advice" can occur as a substitute for the delivery of accurate information on child development, as well as the support of the parent's right and responsibility to formulate his/her own methods of care-giving.

Program Evaluation

The formative evaluation of program design and implementation measures whether you did what you set out to do; the summative evaluation measures program impact on the subjects involved.

The *formative* evaluation process should occur at regular time intervals (weekly, monthly) for all types of program models. Changes, additions and/or deletions related to program design and delivery should be based on the ongoing collection and analysis of both quantitive and qualitative data. Failure to carry out this kind of evaluative process typically results in parent-support systems that do not evolve as exemplary program models. It is obvious from the presentation of the three different program models in this chapter that the *intervention* model—hospital-based services for premature infants and their parents—was the most difficult to deliver, to track, and to evaluate because of the many different service components. We learned from this experience that many service components do not make a program.

The *summative* evaluation process occurs typically after the completion of a well-designed program. Outcome measures may relate to differences between an experimental and control group, as in the IS/MT model for teenage mothers, and may be child, parent, or family oriented. What you measure is what you set out to prove. The scourge of evaluating parent-support systems, however, is the inherent difficulty of combining research and service in well-designed studies. It may seem that as you are making changes as a result of your formative evaluation that you are contaminating and/or confounding the data from your summative evaluations, as in the example of our intervention model for premature infants and their parents. The realities involved in summative evaluations of parent-support systems are that experimentally controlled program models such as IS/MT are expensive and difficult to do well, and that the state of the art is such that program models such as ITL evolve as an expression of a new movement and as successful adaptations of prior testing and evaluation.

Some serendipitous evaluations of successful program models include the following:

1. *Successful programs never have to worry about program referrals or recruiting.* Parents who are satisfied tell their friends. This phenomenom occurred with both the IS/MT and ITL Program models.
2. *Programs that are well designed and documented result in successful replications by others.* Practicum experiences and training workshops for replication of both the IS/MT and ITL Program models have spawned new programs in more than 30 states during the past 10 years.
3. *Social change occurs through individuals as well as through institutions.* A collective consciousness is present in those who have designed and delivered programs and those who have participated in them. Parent-support systems now are part of a national movement that translates the old adage, "an ounce of prevention is worth a pound of cure," into action.

REFERENCES

Als, H., Lester, B.M., & Brazelton, T.B. (1979). Dynamics of the behavioral organization of the premature infant: A theoretical perspective. In T.M. Field (Ed.), *Infants born at risk*. Jamaica, NY: Spectrum.

Badger, E. (1971). A mothers' training program—The road to a purposeful existence. *Children, 18*(5), 168–173.

Badger, E. (1972). A mothers' training program: A sequel article. *Children Today, 1*(3), 7–11.

Badger, E. (1977a). *Postnatal classes for high-risk mother-infant pairs*. Cincinnati: University of Cincinnati College of Medicine.

Badger, E. (1977b). The infant stimulation/mother training project. In B. Caldwell, & D. Stedman (Eds.), *Infant education: A guide for helping handicapped children in the first three years* (pp. 45–62). New York: Walker.

Badger, E. (1979). Mildly to moderately handicapped infants: How do you assess the progress of both mother and infant? In T. Black (Ed.), *Perspectives on measurement* (pp. 39–46). Chapel Hill, NC: Technical Assistance Development System.

Badger, E. (1981a). Recruitment and attendance of high-risk adolescent mothers for training in parenting. *Journal of Adolescence, 4,* 219–229.

Badger, E. (1981b). Effects of parent education program on teenage mothers and their offspring. In K.G. Scott, T. Field, & E.G. Robertson (Eds.), *Teenage parents and their offspring* (pp. 283–310). New York: Grune & Stratton.

Badger, E. (1981c). *Infant/Toddler: Introducing your child to the joy of learning.* Paoli, PA: Instructo/McGraw Hill.

Badger, E., Burns, D., & Rhoads, B. (1976). Education for adolescent mothers in a hospital setting. *American Journal of Public Health, 66,* 469–472.

Badger, E., & Burns, D. (1980). Impact of a parent education program on the personal development of teenage mothers. *Journal of Pediatric Psychology, 5,* 415–422.

Badger, E., & Burns, D. (1982a). A model for coalescing birth-to-three programs. In L. Bond & J. Joffe (Eds.), *Facilitating infant and early childhood development.* Hanover, NH: University of New England.

Badger, E., Burns, D., & Deboer, M. (1982b). An early demonstration of educational intervention beginning at birth. *Journal of the Division for Early Childhood, 5,* 19–30.

Badger, E., Elsass, S., & Sutherland, J.M. (1974). *Mother training as a means of accelerating childhood development in a high-risk population.* Paper presented at the meeting of the Society for Pediatric Research, Washington, DC.

Bayley, N. (1969). *Bayley scales of infant development.* New York: Psychological Corporation.

Berger, P., & Neuhaus, R. (1977). *To empower people: The role of mediating structures in public policy.* Washington, DC: American Enterprise Institute.

Birch, H.G., & Gussow, J.D. (1970). *Disadvantaged children: Health, nutrition and school failure.* New York: Harcourt, Brace and World.

Broman, S.H., Nichols, P.L., & Kennedy, W.A. (1975). *Preschool IQ.* Hillsdale, NJ: Erlbaum.

Bromwich, R. (1981). *Working with parents and infants: An interactional approach.* Baltimore: University Park Press.

Bronfenbrenner, U. (1974). *Is early interaction effective? A report on longitudinal evaluations of preschool programs.* Washington, DC: Department of Health, Education and Welfare.

Deutsch, C.P. (1973). Social class and child development. In B.M. Caldwell & H.N. Riccuiti (Eds.), *Review of child development research* (Vol. 3). Chicago: University of Chicago Press.

Field, T.M. (1979). Interaction patterns of preterm and term infants. In T.M. Field (Ed.), *Infants born at risk* (pp. 333–356). Jamaica, NY: Spectrum.

Golden, M., & Birns, B. (1976). Social class and infant intelligence. In M. Lewis (Ed.), *Origins of intelligence* (pp. 299–351). New York: Plenum.

Gordon, I. (1969). *Early childhood stimulation through parent education* (Final report of the Children's Bureau for Department of Human Resources). Gainsville: University of Florida.

Hunt, J.M. (1975). Variations in the mean ages of achieving object permanence under diverse conditions of rearing. In B. Friedlander, M. Sterritt, & G. Kirk (Eds.),

Exceptional infant 3: Assessment and intervention (pp. 247–262). New York: Brunner/Mazel.

Karnes, M.B., Teska, J.A., Hodgins, A.S., & Badger, E. (1970). Educational intervention at home by mothers of disadvantaged infants. *Child Development, 41,* 925–935.

Keniston, K. (1977). *All our children: The American family under pressure.* New York: Harcourt, Brace Jovanovich.

Klaus, R., & Gray, S. (1968). The early training project for disadvantaged children: A report after five years. *Monographs of the Society for Research on Child Development* (33), No. 120.

Kopp, C.B., & Parmelee, A.H. (1979). Prenatal and perinatal influences on infant development. In J.D. Osofsky (Ed.), *Handbook of infant development.* New York: Wiley.

Lazar, I., Hubbell, R., Murray, H., Rosche, M., & Royce, J. (1977). *Summary report: The persistence of preschool effects* (To the Administration on Children, Youth and Families). Washington, DC: Department of Health, Education and Welfare.

Levenstein, P., & Sunley, R. (1968). Stimulation of verbal interaction between disadvantaged mothers and children. *American Journal of Orthopsychiatry, 138,* 116–121.

Minde, K., Trehub, S., Corter, C., Boukydis, Z., Celhoffer, L., Marton, P. (1978). Mother-child relationships in the premature nursery: An observational study. *Pediatrics, 61*(3), 373–379.

Naisbitt, J. (1982). *Megatrends.* New York: Warner.

Scarr-Salapatek, S., & Williams, M.L. (1973). The effects of early stimulation on low-birthweight infants. *Child Development, 44,* 94–101.

Spiker, D., Burns, D., & Elsass, S. (1981). *Nurse–infant interaction: Before and after training.* Unpublished manuscript, University of Cincinnati College of Medicine.

Steiner, G. (1976). *The children's cause.* Washington, DC: Brookings Institute.

Uzgiris, I., Hunt, J.M. (1975). *Assessment in infancy: Ordinal scales of psychological development.* Urbana: University of Illinois Press.

Werner, E.E., Bierman, J.M., & French, F.W. (1971). *The children of Kauai.* Honolulu: University Press of Hawaii.

Zigler, E., Weiss, H., & Kagan, S. (1983). *Programs to strengthen families: A resource guide.* New Haven, CT: Yale Bush Center in Child Development and Social Policy Family Support Project.

CHAPTER 10
A Preventive Intervention for Couples Becoming Parents

Carolyn Pape Cowan
Philip A. Cowan
University of California, Berkeley

This chapter describes a preventive intervention that focuses on couple relationships during the period when partners are becoming parents for the first time. Developed at the University of California, Berkeley, the intervention is a 6-month-long couples' group that extends from pregnancy through 3 months postpartum and is co-led by male-female teams of trained mental health professionals. In this case, the leaders are married couples.

The intervention was conducted as part of the Becoming a Family Project, a longitudinal study of couple relationships during family formation. The theoretical model guiding the study led us to focus on an analysis of the family from the perspective of five domains which we believe combine to determine couple relationship quality:

1. each individual family member, including self-esteem and adaptation
2. the marital relationship, including partners' mutual role arrangements and patterns of communication
3. each parent–child relationship
4. intergenerational relationships with each family of origin
5. the balance between couples' life stress and social support, including work and friendship networks

This research is supported by NIMH grant R01 MH-31109. The authors gratefully acknowledge the contributions of other members of the research team: Ellen V. Garrett & William S. Coysh and Harriet Curtis-Boles & Abner J. Boles, the other leaders of the intervention groups; Gertrude Heming, data analysis, and Dena Cowan, data preparation. Thanks also to Dan Wile for his incisive comments on an earlier draft of this chapter, and to Emily Hancock, whose consultation with the first author was most supportive and helpful.

In the longitudinal study, we assessed each of these aspects of couple life in late pregnancy and again at 6 and 18 months postpartum, examining the impact of each on men, women, and marriage.

Though becoming a parent is anticipated by many with celebration and joy, this dramatic change in adult life is increasingly being described as a time of stress and potential crisis. The picture of a major life transition as disequilibrating fits well with the finding that life changes can be stressful, even if the events are anticipated and evaluated as positive (Dohrenwend & Dohrenwend, 1974; Holmes & Rahe, 1967). But how individuals or couples can be helped to manage the two-pronged aspects of crisis—opportunity and danger—is not yet clear.

Before describing the study in more detail, we summarize prior research on the transition to parenthood and on interventions for expectant or new parents; we use the findings to make a case for an intervention directed toward mothers, fathers, and the marital relationship.

ASPECTS OF COUPLE RELATIONSHIPS THAT CHANGE WITH PARENTHOOD

Sociologists have been studying the transition to parenthood since LeMasters's (1957) rather startling evidence that 83% of couples who had recently become parents reported experiencing a moderate or extreme crisis during the first year of parenthood. The fact that most of these couples also stated that they had recovered has not been cited as often as LeMasters's more alarming findings. His main conclusion was that new parents were "not sufficiently prepared for the reality of parenthood" and that interventions might help them cope with the unexpected strains of becoming a family.

A controversy developed in the sociological literature about whether the transition to parenthood could legitimately be considered a crisis (cf. Hobbs, 1965; Hobbs & Cole, 1976; Russell, 1974). Unfortunately, the definition of crisis in these studies was reduced to arbitrary cutoff scores on a questionnaire asking parents whether they had experienced a designated set of "bothersome events." Finding few parents falling into his "crisis" category, Hobbs argued that the case for crisis had been overstated (Hobbs, 1965; Hobbs & Cole, 1977). At the same time, ample evidence from many sources in the psychological and psychiatric literature demonstrates that this major life transition brings potentially disequilibrating change in key aspects of parents' lives. That evidence can be summarized very briefly under the domains that we have suggested combine to affect marital quality. Taken together, investigations of the transition to parenthood show that partners experience shifts in their sense of themselves, their role arrangements, their communication as partners, their relationships with their families of origin, and their life stress and social support outside the couple relationship.

Women especially seem to experience lowered self-esteem when they become mothers (Rossi, 1968), and mothers of children under 5 have been found to be at greater risk for depression (Brown, Bhrolchain, & Harris, 1975). Recent data suggest that a substantial proportion of new fathers may experience symptoms of depression in the weeks and months following their first child's birth (Zaslow et al., 1981).

When partners become parents, their established arrangements for household tasks tend to shift to a more traditional division of labor, with women doing more of the household tasks than men (Hoffman, 1978) and more of the child-related tasks than either women or men had expected (Cowan & Cowan, 1981).

Several studies of couple communication in partners becoming parents are suggestive of increased difficulty for spouses. Declines have been reported in *amount* of communication (Meyerowitz & Feldman, 1966), with a suggestion that *quality* of communication decreases as well (Raush, Barry, Hertel, & Swain, 1974).

Until recently, accounts of change in the relationship between grandparents and their children around the transition to parenthood were largely anecdotal. Tinsley and Parke (1984) show how the entrance of a grandchild into the family sets in motion a chain of circular reactions throughout the family system. Our own interviews suggest that the birth of a first child leads most parents to think about relationships with their own parents in new ways. A few men and women renewed contact after months or years of a more distant relationship; others described being let in on family discussions formerly saved for "the grown-ups" in the family.

Life stressors outside the immediate family often shift as partners become parents. Men and women move to new communities, change or lose jobs, get married, become ill, lose family members through death, and so on (Cowan & Cowan, 1981). It has been demonstrated that these kinds of life changes have a potential for influencing the physical and psychological well-being of adults (Dohrenwend & Dohrenwend, 1974; Horowitz, Schaefer, Hiroto, Wilner, & Levin, 1977) and that adults experiencing major life transitions tend not to seek help from others (M. Lieberman, 1981a).

It would appear that the absolute amount of life stress is not the crisis maker, but rather that the *balance* between life stress and available support affects both individual and family functioning. It seems reasonable to suggest that ongoing pre- or postbirth stress that is not buffered by adequate support could have cumulative negative effects on parents and their young children. Nuckolls and her colleagues, for example, have shown that when life stress is high and social support low for expectant mothers—including support from their husbands—they are at increased risk for pregnancy and birth difficulties (Nuckolls, Cassel, & Kaplan, 1972). Crockenberg (1981) reported that mothers' social support assessed at 3 months postpartum was a good predictor of infant secure attachment at 12 months—especially for mothers with irritable babies. Data from these studies suggest that circular patterns are formed when stress is experienced by a parent, a child, or a couple; regardless of where the stress begins, it can be amplified in interactions with other family members.

Especially because so many couples are forming new families far from their families of origin, many without the naturally occurring supports of earlier times, there may be a potential for increased strain on the marriages of partners becoming parents. Although we would argue that having a baby may not *cause* a marital crisis, the changes that accompany first-time parenthood for contemporary partners may contribute to individual and marital stress by providing new challenges *to the couple relationship.* Above and beyond their experience of the transition itself, a couple's ability to confront change and cope with unexpected stress may rest on the state of the marriage (cf. Belsky, 1979). Recent findings from a national survey demonstrate that the time gap between family formation and family dissolution may be narrowing (Bumpass & Rindfuss, 1979), suggesting that contemporary families may be at greater risk for distress during family formation than earlier cohorts.

The Centrality of the Couple Relationship

Although the findings in each of the studies cited suggest that change in one partner affects the relationship between the spouses, the couple relationship has rarely been studied directly. Cross-sectional studies have shown that marital satisfaction begins declining for both men and women early in the marital life cycle. Although the decline in satisfaction is statistically associated with the onset of child-rearing (Glenn & Weaver, 1978; Spanier & Lewis, 1980), we really have no good evidence for a causal connection because, until recently, most studies of the transition to parenthood have been cross-sectional or retrospective. Researchers have focused on one—or at most two—aspects of partner or couple life, when, as we have seen, change appears to occur in many dimensions of parents' lives simultaneously. The possibility that these aspects of couples' lives interact and amplify each other has not yet been explored.

Finally, the transition to parenthood has been looked at almost exclusively from the woman's point of view, lending support to the already popular notion that it is women who do the changing when a couple becomes a family. Even with some recent attention to the study of new fathers (cf. Lamb, 1981; Parke, 1979; Zaslow et al., 1981), the relationship *between* the partners has largely been ignored. Yet, incidental findings in three recent longitudinal studies show that the quality of the marriage is the best predictor and correlate of both maternal and paternal adjustment to birth and parenthood (Grossman, Eichler, Winickoff, et al., 1980; Shereshefsky & Yarrow, 1973; Wenner et al., 1969). Only Grossman and her colleagues attempt to examine the impact of the transition on the child's development. Transition, then, has not been treated as an issue for the whole family system, with examinations of each individual and relationship within it.

EXISTING SERVICES FOR EXPECTANT PARENTS

Writers in the health and mental-health disciplines have suggested that preventive programs or services designed to buffer individual or family stress may prevent dysfunction in those who are facing increased strain (cf. Caplan, 1961, 1964). Although empirical studies of the transition to parenthood have emphasized the potential for change, stress, and even crisis for couples becoming parents, the mental-health community has not followed Caplan's urging to develop and evaluate preventive services that might buffer stress or limit what appear to be well-documented declines in new parents' self or marital satisfaction (Grossman, Eichler, & Winickoff et al., 1980; Rapoport, Rapoport, & Streilitz, 1977; Rossi, 1968; Shereshefsky & Yarrow, 1973). Several interventions for parents of infants *at risk* are reported in this volume—teenage mothers are discussed by Crockenberg (Chapter 1) and parents of premature infants by Cherniss (Chapter 8). But services for parents whose children are not at special risk have been confined to childbirth preparation, baby care and development, and parent-support groups. Our focus here is on the potential stresses of making the transition from couple to family for parents with no prior identified risk.

Just as studies of family formation pay primary attention to the experience of mothers, services for expectant or new parents have been directed almost entirely to women. Most have been developed by health-care professionals and paraprofessionals concerned about the health of mothers and infants. The focus of these programs spans a wide range, from exercise classes and childbirth preparation to books and groups on baby care and child development. Most classes and support groups are offered explicitly to women, or are held at times when father would find it difficult to attend.

Preparation for childbirth. Childbirth preparation classes have included fathers; partners are trained to work together to lessen the pain and anxiety of labor and delivery. Although both parents are often involved, these programs do not usually focus on marital issues raised by the changes of pregnancy and actual parenthood. Thus, after weeks of effort devoted to managing the day of labor and delivery, each "pre-pared" couple sets off to make the adjustments of the next 20 years virtually on their own.

There is some evidence that fathers' involvement in prepared childbirth enhances men's and women's feelings of competence and satisfaction with the birth process and with parenthood in the immediate postpartum period (Entwisle & Doering, 1981). Women with childbirth preparation tended to have shorter labors, less medication during delivery, and more positive feelings about the birth experience than women without such preparation. Entwisle and Doering have proposed that the effec-tiveness of preparation "cannot be attributed to reducing pain directly," but that preparation "may shield persons from stress, suggest[ing] that active control is the major benefit conferred by preparation" (1981, pp. 249, 250). Because almost all of the preparation takes place in groups that include the father, we don't really know whether the positive effects of childbirth preparation are attributable to reduced stress, to the effects of general social support, or to other couple-relationship factors.

Groups for parents. Though child-care classes and parent-support groups continue to grow in popularity in the United States, there are few systematic evaluations of their effectiveness. Two studies found few significant differences in adjustment to parenthood between group participants and comparable parents without an intervention. A third study designed explicitly for fathers had no evaluation component. A fourth study of 19 couples who were parents of 4- to 12-month-olds assessed a training program for encouraging competence in the parent-infant dyad.

1. Riebstein (in M. Lieberman, 1981b) assessed the impact of mothers' self-help groups on women's adjustment to parenthood. She found no differences in maternal adjustment when women who participated in support groups were compared with controls. Riebstein explained that mothers' explorations of negative reactions to new motherhood in the leaderless groups was associated with *increased* feelings of role strain and dissatisfaction. In addition, women who felt they could not discuss marital issues with their husbands found the adjustment to parenthood more difficult, whether or not they attended a self-help group. It seems possible that discussions in the leaderless self-help groups may have led some women to become more aware of their distress about being unable to discuss marital concerns with their partners, and their distress may have contributed to increased role strain.

2. Wandersman (1983) examined the impact of a number of parent-infant support groups in the United States. Despite the fact that par-ticipants in a number of groups felt that they had been helped, Wan-

dersman found few objective effects of participation on adjustment or family functioning. Combining results of studies of prebirth and postbirth parent groups, some self-help groups and some with trained leaders, Wandersman concluded that systematic evaluation of parent groups has been lacking. She suggests that "our expectations of positive benefits of parent-infant support groups need to be revised to fit our more sophisticated understanding of the concept of support and its relationships."

3. Bittman and Zalk (1978) described groups for new fathers in which men explored their roles as parents. Although the writers were enthusiastic about the intervention, there was no evaluation component in the study. Thus, we do not know whether men who participated in a fathers' group found less strain and more satisfaction with themselves or their marriages after the intervention, or whether men's sharing of negative experiences may have increased role strain or dissatisfaction as it did for Riebstein's women (cited in M.A. Lieberman, 1981). Bittman and Zalk having had no control group without an intervention, we cannot assess the *comparative* benefits of their intervention groups for fathers.

4. Dickie and Gerber (1980) designed a parent-training program to increase competence in parent-infant dyads. The researchers hoped that training parents to be more responsive to their infants' cues would increase both parent and infant responsiveness. Observers blind to which parents were trained and which were controls, rated videotapes of parent-child interaction at home. Ratings showed that contingent responsiveness was greater in the trained parent-infant dyads. The researchers comment on an interesting reciprocal relationship between increases in trained fathers' interactions and decreases in their wives' interactions with the babies. As Dickie and Gerber point out, these findings illustrate the necessity of studying all family members when assessing parental competence. Although the researchers had hoped that the intervention would increase mothers' and fathers' own feelings of competence, their self-reports did not reveal differences between intervention participants and controls.

The sparse data from existing programs for new and expectant parents have produced more questions than answers. In order to understand the impact of interventions for parents, there is a need for more systematic evaluation studies of both positive and negative effects for parents and for their children. It is important that the criteria for testing effectiveness be conceptually related to the goals of the interventions and that assessment measures become more consistent across studies. The existing data suggest that the effects of self-help groups are equivocal at best; while parents often *say* that interventions have been helpful, few attempts to demonstrate effects on the participants have been successful.

Mental Health Professionals as Counselors

In addition to our own work (Cowan, Cowan, Coie, & Coie, 1978; C. Cowan, 1983), we know of only two interventions for expectant or new parents that (a) provided trained mental-health professionals as individual or group counselors and (b) included an evaluation component in the study. The first was directed to pregnant women, the second to expectant couples.

1. As part of their investigation of the psychological aspects of pregnancy and adaptation to parenthood, Shereshefsky and Yarrow (1973) offered several subsamples of expectant mothers' individual counseling prior to childbirth. Their findings suggested that one counseling method was associated with women's positive experience of giving birth, although it did not seem to affect mothers' early adaptation to parenthood.

Anticipatory guidance consisted of regular individual counseling sessions with a mental-health professional; counselors helped expectant mothers focus on "psychological preparation for the stresses of pregnancy, delivery, and parenthood" as they completed the third trimester of pregnancy and approached birth (Shereshefsky & Yarrow, 1973, p. 156). When all mothers in the study were assessed 6 months after birth, women who had been in the subsample with anticipatory guidance counseling had maintained stable levels of marital satisfaction since pregnancy; women in two other counseling subsamples and those in the no-counseling comparison group showed declining marital satisfaction over the same period. The authors reported that the quality of the marital relationships of both counseled *and* comparison mothers was the most significant predictor of women's adaptation to parenthood. This corresponds to Grossman and her colleagues' findings for mothers *and* fathers (Grossman et al., 1980), although in neither study were the marriages studied in depth. Although fathers' experiences of the transition were not investigated in depth, these findings leave gaps in our understanding of how "marital quality" or the counseling intervention may have contributed to maternal adaptation.

2. A second intervention staffed by mental-health professionals was developed for couples in West London by Clulow, a mental-health professional, and several associates who were health visitors in the British medical system (1982). Reporting on groups that were offered to expectant couples with the aim of strengthening the couples' relationships during the transition to parenthood, Clulow described mixed results. Although some participants completed the series of six once-a-month meetings and reported that the discussions had helped their adjustment to parenthood, no effects on the marriage were visible to the couples' group leaders. Yet when the health visitors came to parents'

homes to answer questions about the baby's health, many heard parents' hints or reports of marital tension. Because the couples' groups were not consistently well attended—especially after birth—and because participants tended not to focus on marital difficulties in the group discussions, Clulow seemed discouraged about the potential for a couples' group to affect the marriage positively at this stage of life; he recommended to groups of health visitors that more effort be placed on consulting.

One of the difficulties of interpreting the effects of the British couples' groups lies in the fact that no prebirth measures were completed by the expectant parents. There was therefore no basis on which to evaluate change from before birth with the postintervention questionnaire.

We have, then, a number of indications that the marital relationship may be a key to men's and women's adaptation to new parenthood and that interventions with parents or couples before or during the transition may have positive effects on the participants. But the impact of interventions on the marital relationship has not yet been systematically assessed. Our study was designed to test these hypotheses more directly.

THE BECOMING A FAMILY PROJECT

We began our pilot work on the Becoming a Family Project based on both professional and personal concerns about the distress we were seeing in couples and families long after the period of family formation. We designed an intervention focused on the marriages of new parents in the form of small groups for couples becoming first-time parents (Cowan et al., 1978). In each group there were four expectant couples and one trained leader couple. We believed that:

(a) A group might provide the kind of ongoing support that many couples lack as they create new families far from parents and kin.

(b) Groups composed of couples going through similar life experiences might normalize common strains and adjustments; by hearing that "we're all in the same boat," partners might come to feel that they were "not crazy" and that the stress they were experiencing was expectable for this stage of adult life (cf. M.A. Lieberman, 1981a).

(c) Offering groups for both men and women would demonstrate our belief that family-making can be a joint endeavor—not just during labor and delivery, but in the months before and after as well.

(d) In order to explore partners' anticipation of change, their ongoing experience, and their satisfaction with the realities of couple and family life once the babies were born, we needed regular meetings before, during, and after partners were becoming parents. The babies became part of the group as soon as they were born.

(e) The changes this transition brings for men and women can have a powerful impact on the couples' relationships. We designed our study questionnaires and the couples groups to focus on this usually neglected aspect of the transition to parenthood.

Participants in the Study

Ninety-six couples were recruited from private and clinic gynecology–obstetric practices and from community-wide newsletters in the larger San Francisco Bay area; 72 were expecting a first child and 24 couples, sought from the same sources, had not yet decided whether to become parents. All were invited to participate in a study of couple relationships during family formation. Participants live in 27 different towns and cities. When they entered the study, they ranged in age from 21 to 49 years and had been in their current relationships from 8 months to 12 years, with a mean length of relationship of 4 years. The mean age of expectant mothers was 28.9 years; of expectant fathers, 30.2 years. The partners not having a baby were, on the average, 1 year younger than the expectant parents. One-third of the participants were black, Asian-American, or Hispanic and two-thirds were Caucasian. Their educational backgrounds spanned a wide range from high school to postgraduate degrees, with a variety of jobs and family income from working class to upper-middle class.

Study Design

From all of the expectant couples, one-third were randomly selected and offered an opportunity to participate in small couples' groups with one of the three trained couples as coleaders. Of these, 85% accepted the invitation. New couples were randomly invited until there were 24 couples to fill six groups. Each group, led by one of three staff couples, met weekly for 6 months—25 meetings in all—throughout the last 3 months of pregnancy and the first 3 months of new parenthood.

Partners were interviewed and filled out a battery of questionnaires in late pregnancy and again at 6 and 18 months postpartum. The questionnaires, designed to assess individual and marital satisfaction and adaptation, focused on partners' sense of self, mutual role arrangements, couple communication, relationships with parents, life stress, and social support. Several of these measures are described briefly here. Each group participant completed the pretest questionnaires individually, at home, prior to the beginning of the couples' group meetings.

A second subsample of 24 expectant couples was interviewed and assessed at the same times, but did not participate in a couples' group. A third subsample of 24 expectant couples was followed over the same

period; they were interviewed but not assessed in late pregnancy as
our pilot work had indicated that the assessments themselves were
having an impact on the partners' experience of the transition. The final
sample of 24 couples were those *not* having a baby; they too completed
questionnaires and interviews with a staff couple and were followed
at comparable intervals. Each couple in the study was followed by the
same staff couple throughout the study.

The data presented here summarize the effects of the intervention
by comparing 23 couples who participated in one of the intervention
groups and 24 couples with no intervention, assessed from pregnancy
to 18 months after birth. We do not examine the effects of responding
to questionnaires and interviews prior to birth and do not compare the
new parents and childless couples in this chapter. The findings are
presented to answer the question: Can a 6-month-long intervention
aimed at the marriages of partners becoming parents help spouses achieve
more satisfaction and less stress—as individuals and couples—during
their transition to first-time parenthood?

The Intervention

The Group Leaders. The three staff couples, all married, co-led the
intervention groups and followed couples in every study condition
throughout the longitudinal study. Two of the couples were trained by
the authors, the coinvestigators of the longitudinal study. Five of the
six spouses were clinical psychologists at the pre- or postdoctoral level;
the sixth was a businesswoman. The initial 4-month training period
preceded the recruitment of study participants. Staff spouses completed
the study questionnaires, focusing on our own marriages and meeting
weekly as a group over a 4-month period. Discussion in the training
group followed the semistructured format designed for the intervention
groups with expectant couples. Monitoring the way we guaged our own
feelings about self-disclosure, staff couples explored aspects of individual
and couple life as they were evoked by the questionnaires and by day-
to-day events.

From our random selection of expectant couples in the larger study,
we formed and conducted six intervention groups over a 2-year period.
Group supervision of the clinical work in the intervention groups continued on a weekly and then bimonthly basis throughout the first and
second years of the study, with all staff couples discussing the progress
of each intervention group.

Group Structure. The couples' groups were 2½ hours long and were
usually held in evenings or on weekends to be compatible with participants' work schedules. Group members' responses to the study ques-

tionnaires served as a focus for the more structured part of each meeting. In completing the study questionnaires at home, each partner had already begun to think about each focused topic. A few were less revealing about their ideas and feelings at first, but over the 6 months of talking together, everyone shared some personal hopes, expectations, joys, and worrisome thoughts. Participants discussed how, for example, their perceptions and feelings about themselves, their division of family tasks, and their style of handling conflict, showing caring, or working on a problem affected them as individuals and as couples.

The unstructured part of each meeting was left open for couples to discuss any questions or concerns they had. We found that even though most were attending childbirth-preparation classes, men and women often expressed concern about being adequately prepared for giving birth as their due date approached. Would they be able to handle unexpected birth complications or visits with parents and in-laws when they brought their babies home? Others commiserated about employers who suddenly seemed less eager about maternity leaves than their written policies dictated. Both men and women described racing nervously toward work or school project deadlines and the baby's due date. Many wondered out loud if they would still feel close as a couple after the baby came.

Group Process. After several months of anticipation in group discussions, couples began to give birth. As each baby was born, he or she was welcomed into the group. Some couples did not miss a meeting in their eagerness to introduce their newborn and tell about the birth. Some "old hands" who'd been parents for weeks spontaneously brought dinners for the newest ones; this, they said, had been their greatest need.

Our group discussions began to mirror the couples' lives at home. A mother would cry over her dilemma about returning to work and her baby would begin sobbing with her. A father would become absorbed in feeding or diapering his daughter and we would all share his difficulty in following the discussion. Many expressed surprise at how easily their individual needs and their relationship as a couple were relegated to "the back burner" as they tried to cope with the extraordinary demands of a newborn and the rest of life. "It's so difficult to finish a 'grown-up' conversation," some said, "that it seems futile to begin talking at all." The leaders acknowledged that this difficulty is shared by all parents of young children and tried to help parents use the group setting to at least begin their conversations.

Parents often asked us our opinions about handling newborns, but we did not usually pose as "experts" on child-rearing. In fact, most new parents were already exposed to many authorities, each certain of his or her opinion. One of the major problems for new parents is that when they find the advice of different experts contradictory, they are so exhausted that they neglect to consider what *they* know about their own and their baby's needs. As group leaders, we saw our role as one of helping couples keep their balance while doing a three-ring juggling act: (a) looking after their baby, of course; (b) keeping track of each parent's individual needs and concerns; and (c) paying attention to what was happening to the relationship between them. Our goal was to help each couple find their own style of being parents and staying partners while attending to their particular family's needs.

On nights when all four babies were being fed simultaneously, it was painfully evident that new parents need looking after too. When partners worried about the lack of attention they were giving their marriage, we encouraged them to find ways of spending some time together. We helped some spouses talk during the group and worked with others to negotiate more private time together during the week.

When a couple used the protection of the group to work on a problem they couldn't resolve by themselves, we helped each spouse to describe his or her view of the situation. As Wile (1981) has suggested, based on his work with couples in distress, ignoring or bypassing feelings considered unacceptable often creates difficulty for the partner or the couple. Even when one could not or would not *act* on a feeling like "wanting to run away," admitting it to oneself and discussing it with one's partner or other group members often decreased feelings of isolation and worry. In several cases, we saw a couple through a major life crisis during the 6 months of a group. These events were often frightening to others in the group, but seeing serious problems faced rather than ignored boosted their confidence that couples could cope with very stressful situations.

By the time the groups ended, most parents felt close to some of the others with whom they'd "survived" the first months of becoming a family. Many commented that they did not have other *couples* with whom they could talk in this way; few of their friends seemed able to sustain interest in their pressuring concerns about how to handle a colicky baby or an exhausted spouse, or when to leave a newborn in someone else's care. And few would share concerns about the marriage as they had in our groups. While the rest of the world showed great interest in the newest member of the family, the groups provided a place for parents to keep track of themselves as individuals and as couples.

THE EFFECTS OF THE INTERVENTION

There were many subtle signs of the impact of the groups on some parents. Almost all intervention participants said that the couples' group had been helpful to their adjustment to becoming parents. Many members promised to see each other after the group was over. In fact, some families from the groups in our pilot study (Cowan et al., 1978) have remained friends over a 10-year period. A few couples developed shared child-care arrangements in their homes. One mother opened her own child-care center and cared for the toddler of another participating couple. That mother later became a consultant to a child-care center used by a third family in her original couples' group. In several different groups, important family occasions, including baby's christenings, children's birthdays, and one couple's marriage were celebrated by the entire group, including the leaders.

At the end of the 6-month intervention, participants in two couples' groups decided to go on without our leaders. One group continued to meet for 4 months, another for almost a year. In both cases the groups stopped meeting regularly when one of the couples began to discuss serious marital difficulties. At our 18-month postpartum follow-up with each couple, some couples reported that without experienced leaders, it had been difficult for the group to know how to encourage the safe exploration of others' marital problems.

The participants' evaluations and our qualitative observations suggest that couples' groups can help partners anticipate change and discuss differences—between spouses or between expectation and reality. With leaders who are trained to work with marital issues, a couples' group can provide a safe setting in which new parents can explore both small and complex marital problems as they develop. Couples often commented that they were relieved to discover that they were not alone—in their experience of confusion or strain or in their need to make new adjustments as individuals and couples.

We have been discussing our more qualitative observations of the group's impact on new parents. We turn now to the quantitative data on the effects of the intervention—from parents' self-reports over time of many aspects of their lives. The data we are reporting here come primarily from three-way analyses of variance and covariance (gender × time × condition). Because the men and women were partners, we treated their responses as related measures. Time was also a within-subject variable, with scores obtained in late pregnancy and at 6 and 18 months postpartum. The comparison between 46 group participants and 48 men and women who did not participate in a group constitutes the third dimension of the analyses. Most differences reported here were statistically significant with a probability of .05 or less. Given the relatively small number of couples, we discuss several interesting trends that do not reach this commonly-accepted significance criterion.

After Birth Follow-Ups

In some aspects of family life, we found no remarkable differences between couples in the intervention groups and those in the comparison sample. Six months after birth, for example, parents in both subsamples showed an increased sense of self as parents, especially women, while their sense of self as partner or lover declined sharply. Spouses in both samples reported that they were sharing household tasks less equally than they had before the baby was born. While the overall "load" carried by each spouse did not change significantly, the division of labor became more gender-stereotyped: mothers were doing more of the housework than they had done prior to birth and more baby-related chores than either partner had *predicted* during pregnancy. Fathers tended to be bringing in more of the family income and taking care of many away-from-home errands. Ninety-two percent of the study participants reported more conflict and disagreement in their marriage than they had during pregnancy. Family division of labor was the issue that couples rated most likely to lead to conflict, suggesting a link between decreased task sharing and increased marital conflict.

Despite all these fluctuations in life inside the immediate family, parents from both subsamples showed stable scores on a scale of life stress events (Horowitz et al., 1977) from pregnancy to 6 months after birth and increased positive social support, indicating availability of and satisfaction with friends, co-workers, and family (Curtis-Boles, 1979).

By 18 months after birth, partners' division of household and family tasks seemed to have stabilized in both subsamples of new parents; conflict and disagreement between partners continued to increase; general life stress remained stable; and social support began to decrease for both fathers and mothers. Thus, for couples with and without the intervention, the transition from pregnancy to 18 months after giving birth was a period characterized by many changes that might be considered negative for individual parents and for the couple relationship.

But beyond these general trends for all new parent couples, we found a number of significant differences between group participants and parents in the comparison sample:

1. *Sense of self.* On a measure we call *The Pie* partners described the main aspects of themselves. Given a circle 4" in diameter, each listed the main roles in his or her life right now, and divided *The Pie* into those aspects of self, based not on how much time is spent, but on how large each aspect of self feels. Over the transition to parenthood, mothers who had been in a couples' group showed a smaller decline in their descriptions of themselves as partners or lovers than mothers

without the intervention. Although both groups of mothers showed similar changes in their involvement in work or study when the babies were 6 months old, mothers who had been in the intervention showed a return to their prebaby worker or student self, while mothers without the intervention showed *Pie* pieces for work or study that were half the size of their prebaby self. Interestingly, neither subsample of mothers changed in *satisfaction* with self—as measured with *The Pie* or with the *Adjective Checklist* index of self-esteem (Gough & Heilbrun, 1980).

2. *Partners' mutual role arrangements* were measured on a 36-item *Who Does What?* scale (Cowan et al., 1978) on which each partner described his/her mutual division of household, decision-making, and child-related tasks. *Role Satisfaction* was inferred from discrepancies between "how it is" and "how I'd like it to be" on this measure. When the babies were 6 months old, partners' style of sharing baby care did not differ in the two samples, but fathers who had been in a couples' group were *less satisfied* with their involvement in the care of their babies than were fathers without the intervention. Ideal ratings indicated that fathers who had been in a couples group wanted to be doing more household and child-care tasks than they were.

By contrast, group mothers were *more satisfied* with the couple's division of housework and family tasks than mothers without the intervention, despite a similar range of division of labor style in both groups. It seems that participating in a couples' group had different effects on men's and women's feelings about the fathers' involvement in the family. Our discussions with parents in the groups made it clear that men wanted to be involved with their babies while continuing their outside-the-family work. Over the 6 months of continuing discussions, fathers became acutely aware of what is involved in the day-to-day care of a household with a baby and of the strain of being involved in the family and keeping pace with the demands of work. Many felt quite frustrated about reconciling these two central aspects of their lives in the first year of new parenthood.

While most mothers also felt these work and family pulls, those from the couples' groups may have been more satisfied with their husbands' involvement because their partners had regularly shared their concerns about running the household, raising their child, and what was happening to their relationship as a couple.

Satisfaction in group mothers may have provided a balance for dissatisfaction in their partners in the early days of new parenthood. Parents from the couples groups had more similar perceptions of their division of baby care than spouses without the intervention; by 18 months after birth, couples from the intervention groups were moving toward sharing the care of their baby more than the comparison couples. By the time the babies were 18 months old, fathers who had been in the couples' groups were more satisfied with their role in the care of their child than no-intervention fathers. Overall, satisfaction with "who does what?" remained stable for men who had been in the intervention groups, whereas fathers without the intervention showed a decline.

3. *Couple Communication.* Parents from both samples showed increases in marital conflict and disagreement throughout the transition to parenthood period. Though overall amount of conflict was not significantly different in the two subsamples of parents, couples who had been in the intervention reported more conflict about two issues: the division of labor and the quality of time they spent together as a couple. The group discussions may have contributed to more arguments about these aspects of life; it is also possible that group partners maintained the perspective provided by the weekly groups even after the intervention ended. When aspects of life were not satisfying to both partners, they may have continued to talk with each other in attempts to work them out to both partners' satisfaction.

There were no differences in the two subsamples in reports of positive change in the sexual relationship from before to after birth, but couples from the intervention sample reported fewer negative changes in their sexual relationship than partners without the intervention. This aspect of couple communication becomes very salient during the period of having a baby. The experience of sharing this critical life change as it was happening seemed to make it possible for many spouses to exchange information about a usually private aspect of married life. The finding of less negative change in intervention couples is consistent with our impression that when group members shared their experiences of unexpected changes in their sexual relationship, many partners became less worried and more hopeful about positive change.

4. *Marital Satisfaction.* Because there has been a great deal of evidence about diminishing satisfaction with marriage in new parents, we were most interested in examining any effects of the intervention on partners' feelings about the overall couple relationship, measured in our study with the Short Marital Adjustment Test (Locke & Wallace, 1959). Most researchers who have examined marital satisfaction from before to after birth report moderate but significant declines (Awalt, 1981; Belsky, Spanier, & Rovine, 1983; Blum, 1983; Grossman et al., 1980). In our study, the marital satisfaction of partners without the intervention dropped from pregnancy to 6 months after birth and dropped again, more sharply, from 6 to 18 months postpartum. Marital satisfaction declined initially for intervention group participants too, although their decline was less severe. But from 6 to 18 months postpartum, parents from the intervention groups maintained their level of marital satisfaction,

while no-intervention spouses continued their dissatisfaction spiral. Intervention participants' later stable scores on marital satisfaction were maintained despite the fact that couple conflict had increased and social support decreased.

5. *Marital stability.* A small but critical trend is also worth noting at this point in our study. It is based on information from all 96 couples in the study—72 becoming parents and followed to 18 months after birth; and 24 couples not having a baby, followed for a comparable period. Ten of the original 96 couples have separated or divorced. Four were in the initial sample of 24 couples who had not decided about having a baby—16%. The other six separated or divorced couples were partners who became parents but had no intervention group—12.5%. The marriages of all of the participants in the couples' groups were intact when the babies were 18 months old.

We are now in the process of following the families as the children reach 3½ years of age. In addition to examining the effects of marital quality on early child development, we will, of course, be asking whether the intervention effects held up over time for the parents or for their children.

EVALUATING THE RESULTS OF THE INTERVENTION

We have yet to examine many of the measures created for the larger study. Nevertheless, there are indications that working with both partners during the transition to parenthood may have positive effects on partners' feelings about the marriage. From a combination of participants' evaluations, from the quantitative data, and from our observations in the couples' groups, we can begin to speculate about how the couples' groups produce the effects they do.

What's "Preventive" about This Preventive Intervention?

It is clear that the groups did not prevent new parents from facing the typical changes and strains of new parenthood. Anticipating a particular change or a disagreement about how to handle their baby did not prevent partners from having tense middle-of-the-night discussions about what to do when their baby cried in those first confusing weeks after birth. But because extensive discussion had occurred in the groups prior to birth, spousal disagreements did not come as a shock to most parents in a couples' group. They tended to remember that others in the group had had different opinions on a number of issues. Rather than conclude that one spouse or the other was wrong, group members tended to bring their differences back to the group for renewed consideration.

The group did not seem to affect basic aspects of parents' behavior. Fathers in the couples' groups did not become more or less involved in housework or child care than fathers without the intervention. But by 18 months after birth, both men and women who had been in a intervention group were more satisfied with their role arrangements than parents without the intervention, even though group fathers had been the least satisfied 1 year earlier. One possible interpretation of these findings is that the groups function merely as a palliative to help parents feel more satisfied. Another possibility is that experiences in the group changed men's and women's expectations about their lives as parents and partners and that their expectations played an important role in how they felt about their family relationships (cf. Belsky, 1984; Garrett, 1983; Parke, 1979).

LeMasters (1957) had noted that the parents in his study seemed to be surprised by the discrepancy between their expectations and the reality of life as a family. The fact that marital satisfaction in intervention couples stopped going down may be attributable to the ways in which they thought about those changes. Because group parents knew that they were not the only ones having to adjust their individual and marital perspectives, the usual links between increasing role strain, marital disagreement, and satisfaction with marriage may have been temporarily unhooked. The opportunity to share these disconcerting aspects of family life with other new parents and with mental-health professionals who expected parents to experience some disenchantment, may have allowed parents in the groups to view their stresses as common to this time of life rather than as a commentary on their adequacy as a couple.

Another possible interpretation of the results draws on principles from cognitive theories of stress and emotion. According to Lazarus (e.g., 1984), the experience of stress is mediated by an individual's cognitive appraisal of events. In this view, a change in men's and women's perceptions of their experience as new parents could affect their experience of stress and their ability to cope adaptively. If the intervention helped normalize the strains of the transition, it may have encouraged parents to feel that they were not unique in finding the transition stressful and that they could have some control over what happened next. In postbirth interviews with all couples in the study, we noticed a pattern that seemed to differentiate intervention-group couples from those who had not participated in a group. Partners who had been group participants often recounted difficulties or dilemmas they were still grappling with: "We haven't solved all the 'who does what?' issues yet," one mother said, "but we're working on it." Many parents who had not been in a couples' group tended to report changes that seemed to be happening to them: "We're just not spending as much time together as we used to; and when we do, we find ourselves bickering a lot," a father reported in answer to a question about change in their life as a couple. It may be that partners in the couples' groups tended to maintain the group orientation to problems or disenchantment: when some aspect of life was not going as planned or desired, partners could think about it with their spouse or a friend and attempt to figure out how they might make different arrangements or take a new approach to the problem. In future analyses of our problem-solving and communication data, we will examine whether group participants felt themselves more able to talk about feelings and work out problems than partners without the intervention.

Cognitive and social learning theories suggest that passivity, helplessness, and hopelessness are breeding grounds for depression (Beck, 1972; Muñoz, 1976). Research has shown that low self-esteem and marital dissatisfaction are closely connected with depression (Weissman & Klerman, 1977), especially in parents of young children (Brown et al., 1975; V. Lieberman, 1982). Even though it was clear that both samples of parents experienced similar joys and strains, it may be that the intervention groups influenced participants' appraisals of their ability to affect their lives. This, in turn, could have created real effects on their experience of the transition. The fact that all of the couples from the intervention sample were still together suggests that there may be a connection between group participation and a feeling of being able to do something about marital tensions.

What's "Supportive" About This Social Support?

As we describe our work at professional meetings and community agencies, we find that listeners are quick to refer to our couples' groups as "support groups." We feel that the concept of support does not provide an adequate explanation of what the couples' groups do and how they do it. First, investigators are beginning to conclude that social support is not a homogeneous concept (Depner & Wethington, 1983; Lehmann, Shinn, Allen, & Simko, 1983; Wandersman, 1983). In addition to the material support that was occasionally provided for some group members by others, the Becoming a Family groups provided emotional support, information, and opportunities for learning and trying out new skills as parents and partners. Of equal or even greater importance, the groups provided a setting in which men and women were exposed to a wide range of feelings and experiences common to partners becoming parents. This made it less likely that any one of them would feel entirely isolated at this often confusing time of life.

Sharing feelings and information often extended to usually private aspects of couple life. One couple might hesitantly mention the awkwardness of making love late in pregnancy—of attempting to arrange bodies that no longer fit together easily. A father might reveal his initial feelings of terror until he was able to calm his screaming newborn when left alone with her for the first time. Much rueful laughter would follow, accompanied by squeals of "you too?" from others in the group. These shared moments clearly relieved tensions for some couples and answered questions for others. This sharing of personal moments was common in our groups as participants became comfortable and began to feel safe sharing their feelings with one another. It may be that these private details of couple life were more easily discussed in our groups because the group leaders were themselves married couples; we shared some of our own couple and family experiences when they were relevant to issues being discussed in the groups. While the British couples' groups also had coleaders, only one of the leaders was male. And because the British groups met only once a month, participants may have found it difficult to develop the closeness and trust necessary for sharing the more intimate aspects of married life.

Perhaps the most important difference between the American and British groups is suggested in Clulow's description of what happened when participants' marital tensions were broached in the group: when spouses mentioned differences or difficulties they faced once they became parents, the British group leaders also avoided discussing them (Clulow, 1982, p. 63). Thus, despite the very sophisticated conceptualization of the intervention, its effects were not immediately apparent. Perhaps, though, Clulow was premature in discounting the possibility that the groups could be effective. We found that if our coleaders could tolerate the discomfort of other group members, most distressed spouses seemed quite willing and even relieved to pursue a discussion of their difficulty. In addition to relieving some of the tension in the couple with the problem, the discussions often opened avenues for the couple in question and others to share earlier strategies for dealing with similar problem situations. Most important, the discussions served to demonstrate how common it is for partners to have different views of a pressing problem and to reinforce the notion that a satisfying resolution of a problem is closely connected with how partners go about working on it.

Short-Term and Long-Term Effects

Although the couples' groups offered emotional support and a place to try new ideas, they may also have served as temporary disequilibrators to some people. Despite the fact that group participants were outspoken about the groups' helpfulness, the data from our 6-month postpartum follow-ups suggest that participation in a couples' group may actually *contribute* to dissatisfaction and distress initially. Most measurable positive effects appeared more than a year after the groups ended.

From very different theoretical vantage points, Werner (1948) and Erikson (1968) propose that conflict, disequilibration, and temporary disorganization are *necessary* for individuals to proceed from one developmental stage to another. It may be that the positive effects of the intervention follow a period of disorganization, dissatisfaction, and some trial and error on the part of group parents. Getting feelings about unexpected change or dissatisfaction out into the open máy feel both disequilibrating and discouraging at first. As Lieberman (1981b) showed with new mothers' groups, discussing the negative aspects of new motherhood did not lower stress or role strain—at least not immediately after the intervention. Fathers in our groups reported more dissatisfaction with role arrangements, but they later showed more satisfaction and their couple relationship remained stable for a year after the intervention ended. In fact, they became even more satisfied with their role as parent in the long run than fathers who had no intervention.

Couples in the intervention groups not only showed more stability of marital satisfaction but also greater predictability/consistency over time, long after the groups had ended. The greater stability of group participants' marriages may represent their positive feelings about being able to work out their mutually demanding roles as a couple, as they began to do in the intervention groups. Because partners who were in the intervention groups shared their dreams and ideas about building a family regularly for 6 months, perhaps they questioned *the marriage* less and felt able to work on specific aspects of life in which they wanted to make adjustments.

The effects of the intervention were clearer at 18 months after the birth of the child than they had been at 6 months postpartum. This delay in the effects of the intervention may be one reason why intervention studies with a one-time "outcome" measure—often quite soon after the intervention ends—find so few visible effects. This pattern, too, suggests the hypothesis that the group facilitated the positive developmental properties of disequilibration. Like any major developmental change, integrating the effects into day-to-day lives takes time.

The Couple Focus

In most research on social support during the transition to parenthood, the wife is seen as needing support and the husband is seen as a potential provider. We believe the structure of the Becoming a Family groups conveyed a different message. Because the coleaders were male–female teams—in this case, married couples—each group provided a model of two spouses concerned about issues traditionally stereotyped as women's or men's. Questions about job pressures and crying babies were tackled by men *and* women. Discussions about individual *and* family development occupied the attention of fathers and mothers.

We have heard researchers and clinicians suggest that it is difficult to get men involved in a consideration of family issues. Though some men in our study were skeptical at first, most became active and responsive participants in our study. Especially in the couples' groups, men functioned as ongoing models for each other. As some fathers became involved in discussion and active care-taking of their newborns, others followed. They shared concerns about keeping their marriages vital. They diapered, fed, and soothed their infants, defying the stereotype of the uninvolved father. The structure and process of the group reinforced the attitude that regardless of inequalities of actual time spent with the baby (cf. Coysh, 1984), fathers and mothers were involved in a joint endeavor.

In a dissertation focusing on the problem-solving styles of some of the couples in our study, Jessica Ball found that a feeling of shared perspectives, or being "on the same side of the net," was associated with problem-solving satisfaction and satisfaction with the marriage as a whole (Ball, 1984). The perception of being on the same side appeared to be far more important to partners than whether they had found a solution to a particular problem. The opportunity for husbands and wives to explore marital issues together in the groups may have helped stop the decline in marital satisfaction. From parents' comments in our interviews and couples' groups, it seems clear to us that the feeling of working side by side and of being understood or appreciated is the essential validation and support needed by most husbands and wives during a demanding time in their lives.

Two qualifications must be made in discussing the results of this study. While the participants represented a range of the population of first-time parents in this geographical area, they are clustered in the lower- to upper-middle socioeconomic categories and do not include parents under the age of 20. Most significantly, the couples described here are those who agreed to become involved in a good deal of introspection about a very personal life change. Although the group participants were a random subset of the study sample, we have not assessed a random selection of American couples having a first child.

Important individual and marital differences exist *within* the group and no-group samples. Not all group participants felt understood by their partners—nor did all maintain their level of marital satisfaction. Conversely, many individuals and couples without an intervention group were doing very well at both 6- and 18-month postpartum follow-ups.

In future analyses of the whole sample, we will search for characteristics of the parents who found the groups helpful and of those who did not. We will be especially interested in partners and couples who coped well without a special intervention.

In summary, we have preliminary evidence that participation in a couples' group with trained mental-health professionals as leaders has a positive effect on both individual and couple functioning 1½ years after the birth of a first child. Even though sense of self and role arrangements shifted graphically for men and women early in the transition and marital conflict and disagreement increased throughout, participation in a couples' group seemed to buffer what has come to be viewed in the literature as the "normal" decline in marital satisfaction during the transition to parenthood. The intervention helped women retain their sense of themselves as partners and return to their prechildbirth levels of work or study; fathers were disappointed in their involvement with their babies at first, but became more satisfied a year later. By enabling both partners to keep their dreams of family life in sight as they worked together to master the differences during this major adult transition, the couples' groups buffered early declines in marital satisfaction and kept more families intact.

REFERENCES

Awalt, S.J. (1981). *Transition to parenthood: Predictors of individual and marital stability and change.* Unpublished doctoral dissertation, Department of Social Welfare, University of California, Berkeley.

Ball, F.L.J. (1984). *Understanding and satisfaction in marital problems solving: A hermeneutic inquiry.* Unpublished doctoral dissertation, Department of Psychology, University of California, Berkeley.

Beck, A.T. (1972). *Depression: Causes and treatment.* Philadelphia: University of Pennsylvania Press.

Belsky, J. (1979). The interrelation of parental and spousal behavior during infancy in traditional nuclear families: An exploratory analysis. *Journal of Marriage and the Family, 41,* 62–68.

Belsky, J. (1984, May). *The development of marriage and fathering across transitions.* Paper presented at the National Institute of Health: Men's Transitions to Parenthood Conference, Bethesda, MD.

Belsky, J., Spanier, G.B., & Rovine, M. (1983). Stability and change in marriage across the transition to parenthood. *Journal of Marriage and the Family, 45,* 567–577.

Bittman, S., & Zalk, S.R. (1978). *Expectant fathers.* New York: Hawthorn.

Blum, M.E. (1983). A longitudinal study of transition to parenthood in primiparous couples. Paper presented at the American Psychological Association, Anaheim, CA.

Brown, G., Bhrolchain, M., & Harris, T. (1975). Social class and psychiatric disturbance among women in an urban population. *Sociology, 9,* 225–54.

Bumpass, L., & Rindfuss, R.R. (1979). Children's experience of marital disruption. *American Journal of Sociology, 85,* 49–65.

Caplan, G. (1961). *Prevention of mental disorders in children.* New York: Basic Books.

Caplan, G. (1964). *Principles of preventive psychiatry.* New York: Basic Books.

Clulow, C.F. (1982). *To have and to hold: Marriage, the first baby and preparing couples for parenthood.* Aberdeen, Scotland: Aberdeen University Press.

Cowan, C.P. (1983, August). *A preventive clinical intervention aimed at the marriages of new parents.* Paper presented at the annual meeting of the American Psychological Association, Anaheim, CA.

Cowan, C.P., & Cowan, P.A. (1981, August). *Conflicts for partners becoming parents: Implications for couple relationships.* Paper presented at the annual meeting of the American Psychological Association, Los Angeles.

Cowan, P.A., & Cowan, C. P. (1983, April). *Quality of couple relationships and parenting stress in beginning families.* Paper presented at the biennial meeting of the Society for Research in Child Development, Detroit.

Cowan, C.P., Cowan, P.A., Coie, L., & Coie, J.D. (1978). Becoming a family: The impact of a first child's birth on the couple's relationship. In W.B. Miller & L.F. Newman (Eds.), *The first child and family formation.* Chapel Hill, NC: Carolina Population Center.

Coysh, W.S. (1984). *Men's role in caring for their children: Predictive and concurrent correlates of father involvement.* Unpublished doctoral dissertation, University of California, Berkeley.

Crockenberg, S. (1981). Infant irritability, mother responsiveness, and social support influences on the security of infant-mother attachment. *Child Development, 52,* 857–865.

Curtis-Boles, H. (1979). *Important people in your life.* Unpublished questionnaire, developed for the Becoming a Family Project, University of California, Berkeley.

Depner, C., & Wethington, E. (1983, August). *Methodological issues in the study of social support.* Paper presented at the annual meeting of the American Psychological Association, Anaheim, CA.

Dickie, J.R., & Gerber, S.C. (1980). Training in social competence: The effect on mothers, fathers, and infants. *Child Development, 51,* 1248–1251.

Dohrenwend, B.S., & Dohrenwend, B.F. (Eds.). (1974). *Stressful life events: Their nature and effects.* New York: Wiley.

Entwisle, D., & Doering, S. (1981). *The first birth: A family turning point.* Baltimore: Johns Hopkins University Press.

Erikson, E. (1968). *Identity, youth and crisis.* New York: Norton.

Garrett, E.T. (1983, August). *Women's experiences of early parenthood: Expectations vs. reality.* Paper presented at the annual meeting of the American Psychological Association, Anaheim, CA.

Glenn, N.D., & Weaver, C.N. (1978). A multivariate multisurvey study of marital happiness. *Journal of Marriage and the Family, 40,* 269–282.

Gough, H.G., & Heilbrun, A.B., Jr. (1965/1980). *The Adjective Checklist Manual.* Palo Alto, CA: Consulting Psychologists Press.

Grossman, F., Eichler, L., & Winickoff, S., et al., (1980). *Pregnancy, birth, and parenthood.* San Francisco: Jossey-Bass.

Hobbs, D.F., Jr. (1965). Parenthood as crisis: A third study. *Journal of Marriage and the Family, 27*, 367–372.

Hobbs, D., & Cole, S. (1976). Transition to parenthood: A decade replication. *Journal of Marriage and the Family, 38*, 723–731.

Hoffman, L.W. (1978). Effects of a first child on women's social role development. In W. Miller & L. Newman (Eds.), *The first child and family formation*. Chapel Hill, NC: Carolina Population Center.

Holmes, T.H., & Rahe, R.H. (1967). The social readjustment rating scale. *Journal of Psychosomatic Research, 11*, 213–218.

Horowitz, M., Schaefer, C., Hiroto, D., Wilner, N., & Levin, B. (1977). Life event questionnaire for measuring presumptive stress. *Psychosomatic Medicine, 39*, 413–431.

Lamb, M.E. (1981). *The role of the father in child development* (2nd ed.). New York: Wiley.

Lazarus, R.S. (1984). On the primacy of cognition. *American Psychologist, 39*, 124–129.

Lehmann, S., Shinn, M., Allen, J, & Simko, P. (1983, August). *Measuring social supports.* Paper presented at the annual meeting of the American Psychological Association, Anaheim, CA.

LeMasters, E.E. (1957). Parenthood as crisis. *Marriage and Family Living, 19*, 352–355.

Lieberman, M.A. (1981a). Comparative analysis of change mechanism in groups. In Blumberg, Kent, & Davies (Eds.), *Small groups*. London: Wiley.

Lieberman, M.A. (1981b). The effects of social support on responses to stress. In L. Goldberger & S. Breznitz (Eds.), *Handbook of stress*. New York: Free Press.

Lieberman, V. (1982). *Sex-role organization and sex differences in depression: A study of heterosexual couples*. Unpublished doctoral dissertation, University of California, Berkeley.

Locke, H., & Wallace, K. (1959). Short marital adjustment and prediction tests: Their reliability and validity. *Marriage and Family Living, 21*, 251–255.

Meyerowitz, J.H., & Feldman, H. (1966). Transition to parenthood. *Psychiatric Research Reports, 4*, 78–84.

Muñoz, R.F. (1976). The primary prevention of psychological problems: A review of the literature. *Community Mental Health Review, 1*, 1–15.

Nuckolls, K.B., Cassel, J., & Kaplan, B.H. (1972). Psychological assets, life crises and the prognosis of pregnancy. *American Journal of Epidemiology, 95*, 431–441.

Parke, R.D. (1979). Perspectives on father–infant interaction. In J. Osofsky (Ed.), *Handbook of infant development*. New York: Wiley.

Rapoport, R., Rapoport, R.N., & Streilitz, A., with Kew, S. (1977). *Fathers, mothers and society: Towards new alliances*. New York: Basic Books.

Raush, H.L., Barry, W.A., Hertel, R.K., & Swain, M.A. (1974). *Communication, conflict and marriage*. San Francisco: Jossey-Bass.

Rossi, A. (1968). Transition to parenthood. *Journal of Marriage and the Family, 30*, 26–39.

Russell, C. (1974). Transition to parenthood: Problems and gratifications. *Journal of Marriage and the Family, 36*, 294–302.

Shereshefsky, P.M., & Yarrow, L. (1973). *Psychological aspects of a first pregnancy and early postnatal adaptation*. New York: Raven.

Spanier, G., & Lewis, R. (1980). Marital quality: A review of the seventies. *Journal of Marriage and the Family, 42*, 825–839.

Tinsley, B.R., & Parke, R.D. (1984). Grandparents as support and socialization agents. In M. Lewis (Ed.), *Beyond the dyad*. New York: Plenum.

Wandersman, L.P. (1983). An analysis of the effectiveness of parent-infant support groups. *Journal of Prevention*.

Weissman, M., & Klerman, G. (1977). Sex differences and the epidemiology of depression. *Archives of General Psychiatry, 34*, 98–112.

Wenner, N.K., Cohen, M.B., Weigert, E.V., Kvarnes, R.G., Ohaneson, E.M., & Fearing, J.M. (1969). Emotional problems in pregnancy. *Psychiatry, 32*, 389–410.

Werner, H. (1948). *The comparative psychology of mental development*. New York: Follett.

Wile, D.B. (1981). *Couples therapy: A nontraditional approach*. New York: Wiley.

Zaslow, M., Pedersen, F., Kramer, E., Cain, R., Suwalsky, J., & Fivel, M. (1981, April). *Depressed mood in new fathers: Interview and behavioral correlates*. Paper presented at the biennial meeting of the Society for Research in Child Development, Boston.

Author Index

254 Author Index

Broman, S.H., 207, *223*
Bromwich, R., 148, *157*, 212, *223*
Bronfenbrenner, U., 4, *23*, 26, 27, 32, 38, 39, 63, 82, 84, 94, 108, 109, 197, 223
Brown, G.W., 41, 47, 59, 131, 133, 227, 244, 249
Brown, J.V., 92, 109
Bryant, D.M., 155, 159
Bryant, J., 62, 82
Buckley, D.E., 42, 58
Bumpass, L., 228, 249
Burchinal, M., 62, 82
Burke, R.J., 41, 59
Burns, D., 151, 157, 199, 202, 203, 206, 210–212, 223, 224
Butterfield, P.M., 162, 194
Byrne, D.G., 40, 41, 59

C

Cahill, J., 120, 121, 134
Cain, R., 90, 111, 128, 134, 227, 228, 251
Cairns, R.B., 106, 109
Caldwell, B.M., 100, 109, 143, 145, 157
Callahan, B., 147, 157
Callon, M., 91, 109
Campbell, M., 77, 82
Caplan, G., 121, 133, 229, 249
Caputo, D.V., 162, 195
Carlson, N.A., 7, 24
Carnhan, S., 98, 104, 109
Carveth, W., 62, 82
Casey, P.H., 104, 113
Cassel, J., 228, 250
Cassill, K., 43, 59
Celhoffer, L., 61, 78, 83, 92, 110, 212, 224
Chamberlin, R.W., 104, 109
Chandler, M., 63, 83
Cherniss, D.S., 79, 164, 195, 229
Chess, S., 162, 196
Chinsky, J.M., 109
Clapp, 121
Clark, B., 144, 157
Clarke-Stewart, K.A., 150, 157
Clulow, C.F., 232, 233, 245, 249
Cobb, S., 26, 39, 152, 157
Cochran, M., 3, 4, 22, 25, 27, 38, 39, 65, 77, 82, 84, 99, 109, 114
Cochrane, R., 11, 23
Cogan, R., 85, 109
Cohen, J., 13, 23
Cohen, L., 162, 195

Cohen, M.B., 229, 251
Cohen, P., 13, 23
Cohen, S.E., 131, 133, 162, 196
Cohler, B.J., 41, 42, 59
Coie, J.D., 232, 233, 238, 240, 249
Coie, L., 232, 233, 238, 240, 249
Cole, S., 226, 250
Colletta, N., 8, 15, 17, 22, 62, 82, 116, 133, 147, 152, 157
Collier, H.L., 43, 59
Conway, E., 86, 109
Cook, S.J., 151, 158
Coppel, D., 77, 82
Corter, C., 61, 78, 83, 91, 110, 224
Covi, L., 45, 59
Cowan, C.P., 35, 36, 39, 79, 139, 149, 157, 227, 232, 233, 238, 240, 249
Cowan, P.A., 35, 36, 39, 79, 139, 149, 157, 227, 232, 233, 238, 240, 249
Coysh, W.S., 247, 249
Crawford, A., 7, 23
Crnic, K.A., 6, 18, 23, 27–29, 37, 39, 62, 63, 82, 94, 112, 114, 116, 129, 131, 133, 152, 157
Crockenberg, S., 6, 8, 10, 20, 23, 27, 34, 36, 39, 62, 67, 71, 78, 82, 83, 114, 128, 133, 228, 229, 249
Cronenwett, L.R., 17, 157
Cross, A., 77, 82
Cross, T.N., 42, 58
Crouter, A., 94, 109
Curtis-Boles, H., 239, 249

D

Daniels, P., 93, 109
David, J., 105, 113
Dawson, P., 139, 149, 157
Dean, A., 4, 23
Dean, S., 147, 157
Deboer, M., 210–212, 223
Delongis, A., 35, 40
Depner, L., 244, 249
Derogatis, L.R., 45, 59
Desmond, M.M., 162, 195
Deutsch, C.P., 211, 223
Dickerscheid, J.D., 86, 112
Dickie, J.R., 88, 98, 104, 109, 139, 149, 157, 231, 249
Diskin, S.D., 37, 39
Divitto, B., 78, 80, 83
Doering, S.G., 85, 87, 89, 90, 109, 230, 249

Subject Index